CULTURE
TECHNOLOGY
& CREATIVITY

IN T

D1144389

For my sister Julia

CULTURE
TECHNOLOGY
& CREATIVITY

IN THE LATE TWENTIETH CENTURY

edited by philip hayward

John Libbey
LONDON · PARIS · ROME

British Library Cataloguing in Publication Data
Hayward, Philip
    Culture, technology and creativity
    1. Technology. Cultural aspects
    I. Title   II. Arts Council of Great Britain
    303.483

    ISBN 0-86196-266-4

Published by

John Libbey & Company Ltd,
13 Smiths Yard, Summerley Street, London SW18 4HR, UK.
Tel: +44 (0)81 947 2777
Fax: +44 (0)81 947 2664

John Libbey Eurotext Ltd,
6 rue Blanche, 92120 Montrouge, France.

John Libbey-CIC s.r.l.,
via L. Spallanzani 11, 00161 Rome, Italy.

Printed in Great Britain by Whitstable Litho Ltd.,
Whitstable, Kent

Contents

Acknowledgements

Thanks to David Curtis, Rodney Wilson and Willem Velthoven for their useful early suggestions about the direction this project should take; to Tony Langford and Paul Mcdonald for their research assistance; to Philip Bell, Howard Felperin, Tony Fry, Peter Goodall, Jill Scott and Theo van Leeuwen for their illuminating comments on earlier drafts of my chapters; to Manuel Alvarado, Steven Bode and Dee Varney for their various help and assistance; to Teresa Groom for secretarial assistance; to Rebecca Coyle for advice and assistance at all stages of the editing process; and a special thanks to Will Bell for his commitment to bringing this project to fruition.

Preface

This is the second volume in a series of books on the way the media has transformed our understanding of art. The first volume, *Picture This: Media Representations of Visual Art and Artists*, dealt with a wide range of topics: the history of arts coverage on British TV; the representation of visual art in popular cinema; and how broadcast television has revolutionised our relationship to culture and cultural practices. Today, more people receive their information about culture and the arts through television than from visits to live events. It is the Arts Council's belief that one way of understanding the social importance of the arts is to study the major means by which they are mediated.

Like *Picture This*, this book concentrates principally on the visual arts. The next publication in the series will change the emphasis by looking at Dance and Television. Further volumes will deal with how culturally diverse arts practices are represented by Film and Television and Opera on Film and Television.

We would like to take this opportunity to thank Philip Hayward for editing this anthology and the publisher John Libbey who joined us in its production. We are grateful to them for the untiring and thoughtful way in which they have approached the task.

Finally, the views expressed herein are those of the authors and should not be taken as a statement of Arts Council policy.

Rodney Wilson
Director (Film, Video and Broadcasting)

Summer 1990

Foreword

Culture, Technology and Creativity has been a challenging project. Video, computers and the emerging interactive systems have created inestimable creative possibilities that could not have been conceived of as little as a decade ago. The spectacular developments in the technologies that reproduce and *create* images and sounds challenge us to re-examine our relationship to our cultures and the way we represent them. Playfully we could have called this volume 'After Benjamin' or 'Forget Bazin', as the epistemology of the former and the 'realist' aesthetic of the latter are fundamentally challenged by recent technological developments.

These developments raise important questions about the traditional role of artist and audience but, perhaps more importantly, they question our very understanding of what artistic creativity is. New technologies have already revolutionised the way we receive and make information, now new creative possibilities are potentially as *fantastic* as the futuristic machines that are already with us. As we move towards the beginning of a new millennium and a new milieu it is appropriate that we begin to look at these issues.

Here we present a collection of essays that chart a history of creativity and technologies; while interrogating the conceptual shifts in the way we explain that relationship. However, this book was never intended to be a comprehensive guide, rather, it is an *instantané* or *snapshot* of possible ways to understand that complex set of issues.

This book is aimed at teachers of art, media educators and students. It is our intention that the book should provide a conceptual and thematic framework that can be easily adapted into teaching programmes or read for private study and research. It is meant to inform, confront and provoke.

Will Bell
Education Officer (Film, Video and Broadcasting)

1 Introduction

TECHNOLOGY AND THE (*TRANS*)FORMATION OF CULTURE

PHILIP HAYWARD

In one sense the project of this anthology primarily involves a return to an earlier definition of the term 'Technology' itself. While its current usage refers to various aspects of machinery (mechanical or electronic) and/or its industrial application, its origins are, as a number of previous commentators have pointed out,[1] broader and more philosophical. The term, derived from the Greek *technologia* ('systematic treatment'), was introduced into the English language in the early Seventeenth Century, a time of political and institutional upheavals and cultural and mechanical innovations. As befits this context, its original definition was both broad and dualistic, as both 'a discourse or treatise on an art or arts and the scientific study of the practical or industrial arts'.[2] By the height of the Industrial Revolution in the mid-Nineteenth Century, this usage had however contracted to a less prosaic collective term for the range of practical 'arts' employed in both science and industry.[3] If the earlier sense of the term were still prevalent it would have been pertinent to simply name this anthology *Technology*; since it is the duality of these original definitions which this book addresses.

Given the contemporary cultural focus of this anthology, *New Technology* might have appeared an even better title. But while this term signifies the recent development of specific technologies and their application to commercial-industrial contexts, it has an additional associative meaning too. The term also connotes these new technologies as innately 'progressive', as beneficial to both industry, communications and the general advancement of a society increasingly dependent on a technological base. Indeed, the most zealous proponents of this view have seen new technologies and new approaches to these technologies as *necessarily inaugurative* of an utopian era where all facets of technology and culture are combined and reconciled. Significantly, such perceptions have been shared by dominant interest groups in both the industrial capitalist West and the communist Eastern Bloc. Soviet industrial designer Yuri Soloviev, for example, provided a

particularly striking expression of this in his address to a UNESCO symposium held in Tbilisi in 1968. Reflecting on his own sphere of activity he stated that:

> *With industrial design and its synthesis of elements belonging to the engineer, the artist and the scientist, a special language will at the same time evolve to enable all three to co-operate, and new ways will be found to explain their purposes; perhaps also a new and higher creative activity will come into being; designing new material and spiritual values, a kind of synthesis of all the tasks and methods involved in pursuing all the aims of science, technology and art.*[4]

Such views continue to characterise the thinking of many of those involved in advanced technological research and development. As Nicholas Negroponte, director of the Massachusetts Institute of Technology (MIT) Media Lab has, more recently, asserted: 'New theories about signals, symbols and systems will evolve from the merging of engineering, social science and the arts.'[5] The 'progressive' model evident in these statements perceives science, industry and technological development as necessarily beneficial – enabling all manner of new social, cultural and commercial uses which necessarily offer improvements on previous practices.

Such utopian views have not, of course, gone unchallenged. Even prior to current debates about the impact and implications of the latest wave of new technologies, critics such as Lewis Mumford[6] and Jacques Ellul[7] cautioned against technological determinism and emphasised the necessity for society to reconsider the existing bases of technological design, diffusion and consequent use. More recently still, Paul Virilio has advanced a radical thesis which perceives contemporary information technology as being produced to serve the needs of a profoundly militarised global system which has developed its own logistics of perception into the dominant mode of the Twentieth Century.[8]

Although less radical in his analysis than Virilio, Stephen Hill has taken up themes from the earlier work of Mumford and Ellul and synthesised them with more recent critical developments. In his recent book *The Tragedy of Technology*,[9] Hill produces a general model of how technologies and technological systems affect deep levels of society and social behaviour. Drawing upon a series of analyses of particular effects, he goes on to assert the need for a re-insertion of 'human values' into specific technologies and broad

Charlie Chaplin's Modern Times (1935) – An early representation of the individual in the machine age of the Twentieth Century

technological developments affecting contemporary society. As he states, the project of his book is to explore 'the culture defining power of technology through an analysis of technology as a "cultural text" – that is, imbued with cultural meanings that communicate much more than just the use value of the artefacts themselves'.[10]

This is an important emphasis which opens up a valuable debate about the relation between culture and technology which is also central to this anthology. But whereas Hill goes on to argue that 'the dominant mode of the culture of modern industrial society is *dependent*, passively constituted within the culture-technology alignment that has been erected historically',[11] this anthology attempts a less prescriptive analysis of the *active* production of culture. Similarly, it takes a more positive view of the whole cultural field than that which Hill elaborates in a metaphoric style reminiscent of Jean Baudrillard:

> *It is the culture of mirrors to an evolving 'tragedy of technology'. As in the Echo/Narcissus legend, the culture-technology alignment projects cultural atrophy in the face of self-absorption within a cultural world view that is seemingly commanded by the values of technological systems, rather than by participation and engagement within everyday life.*[12]

In part then, this anthology serves as a response to Hill's general project, sketched on the narrower terrain of contemporary cultural production – specifically, aspects of electronic media practice, industrial design and the inter-relation of these.

In his subtitle to *The Tragedy of Technology*, Hill establishes a binary opposition which he returns to as both a characterisation and implicit paradigm – that of *Human Liberation versus Domination (in the Late Twentieth Century)*. Though unstated in any subtitle, a binary opposition also informs the broad project of *Culture, Technology and Creativity*. The opposition here, one which all contributors were asked to address, is that of 'determination versus enablement'. This opposition was intended to prompt discussion of the extent to which new technologies and specific hardware and software *determine* the precise nature of their human use and therefore cultural 'creativity' and the texts produced by them; as opposed to the extent to which various new technologies *enable* their users to produce distinctive new cultural forms. As should be apparent however, and as is explicitly detailed in individual chapters, the crude opposition between determination and enablement can *only* serve as an initial analytic paradigm whose usefulness is superceded by more complex formulations.

Before going on to outline the nature of the analyses offered in this volume, it is important to site its project in a historical context. Though this anthology is exclusively concerned with contemporary issues of technology and cultural production, there is nothing specifically contemporary about the *general* interrelation of these. Historical study has served to emphasise how developments in various technologies have both directly contributed to specific cultural forms or otherwise provided a range of influential precedents for cultural developments. In no real sense can there be said to have been any model 'organic' past where the expressive impulse or productive craft was untrammeled by various enabling and prescriptive uses of tools or technologies. Even the most traditionally *artistic* forms of cultural production have been profoundly influenced by various mechanical and scientific innovations.

The critically privileged form of Western oil painting is, for example, a form where the human authorship and physical contribution of the *auteur* has usually been seen as both paramount and relatively 'autonomous' of technological influences. However, even a brief examination reveals that, in addition to the important contribution of continuing developments of chemical processes and combinations to the development of painting, varnishing, stucco etc, painting has been affected by technology in a complex variety of ways. Both specific technologies and the contribution of science and technology in general have played a significant part in the development of painting and the range of cultural and scientific discourses which have influenced it (processes which can be seen to converge in the person of Leonardo da Vinci – the Renaissance figure whose name has been adopted as an emblematic title by the contemporary American Art and Science journal *Leonardo*).

With regard to the development of particular visual technologies, the invention of the *camera obscura*, was for instance, an important factor in the development of monocular perspective painting as a dominant representational mode after its initial theorisation and introduction through the work of the fifteenth century Italian painter Filippo Brunelleschi.[13] Just as Brunelleschi's perspective system and the technology of the camera obscura affected a significant change in both styles of visual representation and theories of visual perception, so the rapid serial photography of Etienne-Jules Marey and Eadweard Muybridge similarly affected a change in how we both perceive elements of visual motion and their representation. Indeed, as Aaron Scharf comprehensively documents,[14] the invention and popularisation of photography produced a whole range of effects in nineteenth century European painting.

The influence of photography on visual art also continued further, both as a general social and cultural influence and through specific paths. These involved both the increasingly conscious use and designation of photography as an 'Art' practice in its own right and the ongoing influence of forms of photography on schools of painters as diverse as the Italian Futurists or American Hyper-Realists. Significantly though, neither the camera obscura, nor photography can be understood to have functioned as crudely *determining* technologies. Rather, they were devices and processes which both resulted from, and thereby operated within, broader discourses (scientific and aesthetic) whose development both affected and was affected by the development of schools of European painting themselves.

Such emphases are particularly necessary for the consideration of contemporary cultural technologies such as those discussed in this volume. The various combinations of hardware and software involved in these are, after all, designed, manufactured and marketed as processes and devices capable of producing cultural texts themselves. In this sense they may be seen as *determining*, but as the analyses in this volume confirm, the range of potential applications of advanced cultural technologies is necessarily beyond the precise intentionality of its designers and manufacturers. In the case of individually customised, adapted or combined systems, their operations often deviate considerably from the functions and potential uses originally conceived for them. In this way, advanced cultural technologies can be seen to set up a system of enablements within two polarities: 'preferred' or conventional uses (designated or indicated by the technology and its accompanying packaging, instructions or contexts of use); or more original applications (arising from both the manner and method of their employment of technologies and also the design and contextual application of the texts so produced).

Though various ideas about the function and purpose of art inform Rebecca Coyle's account of the development of holography; Jeremy Welsh's discussion of contemporary visual technologies; Tony Fry's discussion of the implications of Postmodernity on contemporary culture; and Paul Brown's heady speculations on the future of art and culture in the age of advanced computers; the contributions and general project of *Culture, Technology and Creativity* largely avoid dwelling on contemporary inflections of the debate as to whether technological forms can be 'Art' (those questions which for instance dogged the early days of cinema criticism[14]). Nor, with the exception of Andrew Murphie's discussion of the body and technology in contemporary performance work, do its contributions engage with those critical perspectives which view contemporary Postmodern culture as radically *de-aurated* and thereby differentiated from previous cultural paradigms.[15] The designation of the book as about contemporary culture and creativity and their relation to technology, represents an attempt to sidestep inherited critical positions and focus on what is currently *happening* in the cultural field. In this manner, it approaches contemporary practices as as inherently 'valid' as any others.

The anthology attempts to develop a series of critical perspectives on the relation of cultural practice to technology across a range of media.[16] This involves a threefold project:

(a) An analysis of the manner in which new technologies, computer programmes and applications can be said to be *determining* styles and developments in cultural practice in any qualitatively different manner from those of preceding generations of new technologies (ie photography, phonographic recording, film, television etc).

(b) An investigation of the ways in which the creative use of new technologies in various cultural contexts has effectively determined the design, development and application of these and subsequent technologies.

(c) A discussion of the implications of technological innovations to particular forms of artistic and cultural practice and the broader spheres of culture and creativity in general.

In addition to this introduction, which serves to characterise the anthology's field of inquiry, the analyses in this volume fall into three categories. These, of necessity, interrelate and to an appreciable degree, cross over each other. They can however be characterised as follows: the collaboration and intervention of the artist in technological development (Chapters Two to Four); the development of specific styles of cultural production resulting from the introduction of new models or combinations of technologies (Chapters Five to Eight); and the potentially transformative effects of new technologies on the fundamental bases of particular cultural media (Chapters Nine to Thirteen). There is therefore a clear – and approximately chronological – shift from the early discussions of Art and Technology in the Sixties and Seventies, individual instances of significant technological application in the Seventies and Eighties and the closing section on the transformations affecting cultural media in the final decade of the Twentieth Century.

Chapters Two to Four address three areas in which scientific and technological trajectories have, to a greater or lesser extent, been informed and influenced by the contributions of artists – the early American 'Experiments in Art and Technology' (E.A.T.) of the Sixties and the development of holographic and computer image technologies. These chapters offer accounts of the manner in which artists have both engaged with advanced technological developments and the general *fields* of science and technology. Their analyses describe the manner in which the various aesthetic and social concerns of artists relate to industrial research and development practices and have been affected by these. As the 'qualified failure' of the broad E.A.T. group signifies, many of these collaborations and exchanges were marked by tension, misunderstanding and the failure to synthesise both the fields of Science, Technology and Art and the sensibilities and projects of scientists, engineers and artists. Much of this impasse can be seen to derive from the highly traditional nature of the concepts of Art and the artist involved in such projects. Many of these still primarily involved the *entry* of the 'elevated' artist into the 'mundane' world of technology, rather than any *union* of the two purposes and sensibilities – the creation of new Renaissance figures such as the emblematic Leonardo himself or the sort of new practitioner variously advocated in this volume by Marga Bijvoet, Andrew Murphie, Jeremy Welsh and the holographer Paula Dawson.[17]

Chapters Five to Eight provide a series of case studies of how the development of successive generations of audio-visual technology have precipitated significant developments in cultural production. In doing this, they also detail how such developments have arisen through a combination of creative experimentation and various commercial imperatives. Philip Brophy's analysis of the combined significance of spectral sound mixing techniques and systems of speaker alignments shows, for example, how the combination and application of relatively modest developments in technology can offer radical new possibilities for even such an established practice as cinema-sound composition (now after all in its seventh decade). This serves to emphasise that it is not always *revolutionary* developments in technologies which lead to distinctive forms of use. George Barber's account similarly emphasises how the introduction of a new model of video edit suite technology, the Sony Series V, *physically* enabled the user to combine edit functions in a way which allowed a

more advanced approach to video collage than that previously available – a facility which resulted in both the specific form known as Scratch Video and a whole host of other applications in audio-visual media.

Chapters Seven and Eight discuss the manner in which two different audio-visual production sectors – music video and video art – have engaged with new image technologies over the last decade and how their engagements have been determined by economic factors and imperatives. Chapter Seven details how commercial pressures for constant stylistic innovation have lead to the rapid adoption of new forms of video collage, matting and digital editing technology in music video production and, in the process, created a distinct aesthetic basis for the form. Addressing these issues from another standpoint, Jeremy Welsh's discussion of new computer and video graphic technologies emphasises how questions of availability, access and appropriate use are key considerations for contemporary visual artists – those who are actually involved in the production of new cultural forms and artefacts rather than the marketing and promotion of their productive technologies.

Chapters Nine to Thirteen analyse aspects of the various realignments of cultural production and (individual and collective) creativity currently manifest in the advanced technological society of the Nineties. Prefaced by Tony Fry's essay on time, economy and the cultural practices of Postmodernism, this section looks at the impact of digital technologies on photography and (popular) music production; the effect of a range of technologies on performance and theatre; and the use of advanced computer technologies by artists involved in radical new forms of media and communication practices.

These analyses describe a variety of levels of cultural realignment, from the modest to the radically disjunctive. Alan Durant's study indicates, for example, how the introduction of a new technology, in this case digital audio-recording, has had a profound effect on contemporary music production with regard to issues of technological availability, skills competence, copyright and, not least, the nature of creativity. Similarly, Anne Marie Willis's discussion illustrates how the utilisation of digital recording, and particularly storage, necessitates a reconsideration of the nature of photographs as documentary artefacts, and further; how the potential of manipulating digital data inevitably diminishes the 'veracity status' of photography as a representational system. Andrew Murphie's discussion of performance and theatre offers an even more precise characterisation of the implications of technology on the *essence* of an established area of cultural practice – the effective withdrawal of the body-as-truth in performance in favour of an effective discourse about the relationship *between* the body and technology.

Each of these, and the other pieces in Section III, engage in various ways with the nature of creativity in contemporary media. As Tony Fry emphasises in his chapter 'Art Byting the Dust', despite massive changes in culture and theoretical understandings of language and ideology, creativity 'stands alone almost unscathed', 'taken for granted' and thereby necessitates investigation.[18] As individual chapters emphasise, the determinations and enablements of both the creative imagination and impulse, and indeed, the constitution of creative subjectivity, must be understood in terms of their engagement with technological systems and the new conceptual and aesthetic spaces of computer and other advanced electronic technologies. Taking this one (giant) step further, Paul Brown's closing chapter discusses a range of possibilities for 21st Century cultural media. As described, these range from extensions of various existing kinds of computer arts practice, through interactive human-computer processes of various kinds and, eventually, the production of sophisticated cultural forms and artefacts by super-intelligent computers operating relatively autonomously. With the latter scenario we are close to witnessing the ceding of the human creative impulse from its supposedly human wellspring to that not only designed in its likeness, but ultimately, designed to be its superior.

Given the different considerations and emphases advanced in this anthology, the question arises as to whether there is any *grand recit* capable of accounting for the plurality of cultural phenomena in the late Twentieth Century and their myriad engagements with technology. In common with the broader philosophical speculations of contemporary theorists, such as Jean Francois Lyotard in *The Postmodern Condition*,[19] the contributions to this collection would suggest that there is not. Or at least, if there *is*, that it is so complex, diffuse and contingent that it is ineffective as a model against which developments in contemporary culture be read off. In that this anthology can be said to identify a common tendency in the number of cultural practices it analyses, it is one which derives from, and partially transcends a familiar theme of Postmodern criticism over the last decade – the erosion and collapse of differences between forms of 'high' and 'popular' culture. Along with charting the tendency for once separate cultural media to become increasingly integrated into (technological) 'metamedia'; the individual accounts in this anthology observe the often awkward emergence of new creative engagements with contemporary technologies in contexts outside those usually seen to constitute a privileged cultural terrain.

This is then the project of the anthology, *the charting of points of cultural emergence* which represent, if not a *coupure*, then a pronounced shift from previous cultural practices in terms of the complexity of their profound interrelations with (advanced) technology. Its cultural practices therefore take place in an environment marked by the complexities of the *aura* of 'virtual space' and the multiple reproductive fidelities of digital culture. Speculations on the nature of art and culture in the world of advanced technologies need therefore to approach the mapping of this virgin terrain with new models developed for the task, rather than attempt to fit their analyses with paradigms developed for the analyses of previous generations of new technologies and characterisations of 'Modernity'. While this volume cannot supply a comprehensive range of such models, its case studies can at least indicate the ways in which they might be further elaborated. In this manner, its analytic project is, like the contemporary cultural production it analyses, also in the process of emergence.

PHILIP HAYWARD

1 See for instance, Stephen Hill *The Tragedy of Technology: Human Liberation Versus Domination in the Late Twentieth Century* London, Pluto 1988 pp37-39

2 *Shorter Oxford English Dictionary* Oxford, Oxford University Press (1978 Edition), p2,253

3 *ibid*

4 Yuri Soloviev, quoted by d'Arcy Hayman in his 'Unesco Symposium on Technology and Artistic Creation in the Contemporary World' *Leonardo* v1 n4 October 1968 p442

5 Nicholas Negroponte, cited in Stuart Brand *The Media Lab: inventing the future at M I T* Harmonsworth, Penguin 1988 p11

6 See for instance, Lewis Mumford *Technics and Civilization* New York, Harcourt Brace 1934

7 See for instance, Jacques Ellul *The Technological Society* New York, Vintage Books 1964

8 Paul Virilio *War and Cinema: the Logistics of Perception* London, Verso 1989

9 Stephen Hill *op cit*

10 *ibid* p4

11 *ibid* p18

12 *ibid*

13 For a summary of this interrelation see Steven Neale *Cinema and Technology: Image, Sound, Colour* London, BFI 1985 pp11-19

14 See Aaron Scharf *Art and Photography* Harmonsworth, Penguin 1974

15 For discussion of this see Victor Perkins *Film as Film* London, Penguin 1973

16 It should be emphasised however, that this volume does not attempt to give any kind of comprehensive survey of contemporary developments of cultural technologies across the complete range of electronic and/or mechanical media – such an attempt would require a whole series of volumes in itself. Nor does it attempt to capture the immediate *cutting edge* of 'state of the art' cultural technologies since the characterisation of these in such a technologically accelerated environment as the 1990s would be rendered obsolete in the delay between knowledge acquisition and this volume's appearance in print (and thereby more properly belongs to the domain of the data base).

17 For further discussion of this see both Walter Benjamin, 'The Work of Art in the Age of Mechanical Reproduction' in his *Illuminations* London, Jonathan Cape 1970 and Fredric Jameson 'Postmodernism, or the cultural logic of Late Capitalism' in *New Left Review* n146 July-August 1984.

18 See the general discussions cited by Rebecca Coyle in her 'Holography – Art in the Space of Technology', this volume.

19 Tony Fry 'Art Byting the Dust' this volume.

20 Jean Francois Lyotard *The Postmodern Condition: A Report on Knowledge* Manchester, Manchester University Press 1984

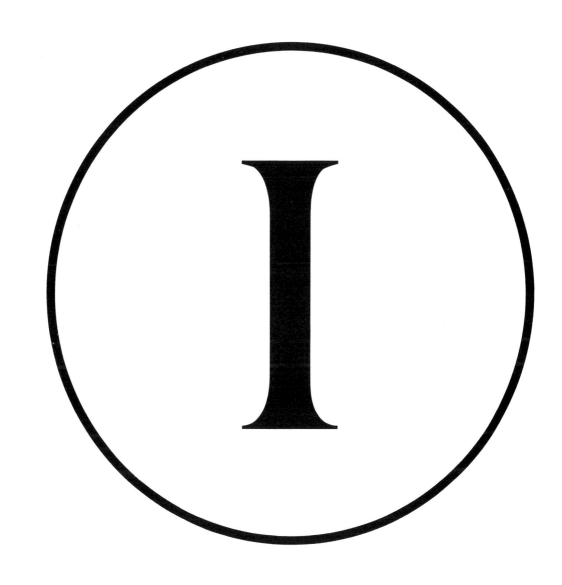

ART AND TECHNOLOGY –
COLLABORATIONS
AND DIVERGENCIES

2
HOW INTIMATE CAN ART AND TECHNOLOGY REALLY BE?
A Survey of The Art and Technology Movement of the Sixties

MARGA BIJVOET

Introduction

The Twentieth Century has been marked by several waves of scientific discovery and technological innovation. One such wave occurred in the late Sixties and early Seventies when electronic media and computer technologies – media which were to have a profound effect on our perception of the world – became widely available for the first time. During this period the relationship between art, technology and science was a much debated issue. The concerns shown in these debates also had a concrete manifestation in the form of the Art and Technology movement which sprang up in the USA. The movement attracted the energies of artists, scientists and technicians and resulted in a series of innovative projects which established new frameworks for collaboration. In short, the period constituted one of those rare occasions when art and technology have entered into a relationship deeper than mere 'dialogue' – the word 'marriage' was even used.

Yet, some two decades later, both these practical initiatives and the debates which informed them have been largely forgotten or relegated to the realm of history. This chapter will focus on those aspects which distinguished the art and technology initiatives of the period from previous ones and attempt to establish how they provide a significant precedent for much contemporary work. Although the Art and Technology movement has been called 'a panacea that failed', it would seem that certain of its ideas had a permanent effect on the arts of the incipient communications era while others ultimately proved dysfunctional.

Setting the stage – a preface

Although the relationships between major twentieth century art movements and various aspects of science and technology have been amply documented elsewhere, a brief survey is probably useful here. The Futurists were fascinated with the machine and the notion of speed. As we know from paintings and sculptures by Giacomo Balla or Umberto Boccioni, they emphasised the poetic qualities of such phenomena. The Surrealists, on the other hand, revealed the disquieting, frightening and unconscious aspects of the machine. The Cubists were mainly interested in mechanical qualities and the man-machine relationship – see, for example, the collages of Marcel Duchamp and Francis Picabia or the work of Fernand Léger (who painted a world of valves, conduits and steel structures which posited the rhythm of the machine as analogous to everyday human activity). With the Constructivists however, the attention shifted to new materials (such as steel, glass and plastics) but also, more importantly, to a consideration of the broader implications of industrial technologies for society and the future role and function of art.

Along with industrial developments, the beginning of the Twentieth Century was marked by a 180° change in scientific thinking – classical physics was replaced by atomic theory. In 1899 Max Planck published his first paper on quantum theory and this was followed by Einstein's Theory of Relativity six years later. It would lead us too far astray to give a detailed account of all subsequent discoveries in quantum physics, biophysics, biochemistry etc, but suffice it to say that science had to re-define its concept of the 'natural world'.[1]

A number of artists connected with the Constructivist movement were familiar with these novel concepts, Theo van Doesburg, Georges VanTongerloo, Naum Gabo, Antoine Pevsner, to mention but a few. One may speculate to what extent new scientific analyses or modes of thinking were applied to art and sculpture, but as early as 1930 Georges VanTongerloo said

> . . . already we see art disengaging itself from a quasi-philosophical artiness to become more and more a science and form at one with a new society. (Do not confuse this with utilitarian art.) But the field of action for the artist is not open yet. The artist is still condemned to exhibit art as an object: art is still part of the old organisation. But since this organisation cannot persist forever, it must one day

cede its place to an organisation better adapted to the present.[2]

Sculptor Alexander Archipenko also emphasised that contemporary art and science 'both tend toward abstract forces. Art becomes preoccupied with the expression of transcendency; science with the materialisation of abstract energy, such as radio, electrical and atomic'.[3]

The new engineering technology and its underlying scientific models soon entered the vocabulary of the modern sculptor. The mathematical geometric constructions made of steel, plexiglass or nylon by Antoine Pevsner and his brother Naum Gabo were therefore the expression of a new visual aesthetic which suggested parallel modes of enquiry between art and science. Yet while the Constructivists and members of De Stijl investigated and applied new techniques and had a great interest in scientific analysis, they generally held the firm opinion that the ultimate goals of art and science were fundamentally different.

Naum Gabo, who had a training in engineering, mathematics, physics and medicine, has expressed his views about the relation of art and science extensively. In an essay of 1937, he wrote that the

> *Constructivist idea does not see that the function of Art is to represent the World. It does not impose on Art the function of Science. Art and Science are two different streams which rise from the same creative force and flow into the same ocean of the common culture, but the currents of these two streams flow in different directions.*[4]

Twenty years later he elaborated on this, arguing that

> *The new scientific vision of the world may affect and enhance the vision of the artist as a human being but from there on the artist goes his own way and his art remains independent of sciences; from there on he carries his own vision bringing forth visual images which react on the common human psychology and transfer his feelings to the feelings of men in general, including the scientists.*[5]

With the introduction of electrical engineering and its multiple applications (such as electric lighting and electronic means of controlling movement), society accepted a range of new systems. These could not *but* create artistic interest and saw the rise of a direction in art which focused primarily on the investigation of energy controlled movement, a tendency called 'Kineticism'. The Kinetic Art movement was, to a large extent, premised on 'scientific' research into the dynamics of motion and how motion affects visual perception. Consequently, the widespread use of plastics, perspex, reflecting materials and resin was augmented with electronic technology to create an art which investigated optical effects and controlled movement – an approach which would not have been possible with traditional mechanics.

Theorist-artist László Moholy-Nagy strongly advocated the development of motion and kinetic art, seeing it as offering sculpture a way in which it could exchange static values for dynamic ones. He published these views in *The New Vision: From Material to Architecture* (1930), a work which was later expanded into *Vision in Motion*, published in 1947.[6] Moholy-Nagy, best known for his experimental photograms, only created one kinetic sculpture however, his famous *Light-Space Modulator* (1922-31).

During the Fifties and Sixties, the Kinetic movement developed in various directions. Frank Popper identified three principal strands, some of which overlapped: *Op(tical) Art* (which included the work of European groups such as the Groupe Recherché d'Art Visuel and ZERO), the *Machines and Mobiles* school (as exemplified by artists such as Jean Tinguely and Alexander Calder), and the *Lightcinetics* school (including both Moholy-Nagy and members of the Groupe Recherché d'Art Visuel and ZERO).[7] Although the project of these groups represented a progression from the mechanical into the electronic age, most kinetic works, with the exception of light programming, did not rely on the most advanced of contemporary technologies. And here too, the scientific concept of field dynamics, on which the repetitive field structures of many optical works were based, had already been superceded. This tends to confirm Marshall McLuhan's dictum that a particular technology only becomes a subject for the artist when it has been superceded by the next one.

Towards a 'systems-aesthetic'

The Sixties were a turbulent era. Speculations about the possible social, political and economic effects of the new electronic and computer technologies quickly found their way into print and were widely read. The theories of Marshall McLuhan and Buckminster Fuller were, for example, common knowledge and Norton Wiener's theory of cybernetics gained wide recognition. As for the art world, new materials were introduced, all relating to technics. But that was not all, a number of artists argued for a whole new structure for the arts and made a general critique of the traditional role and position of galleries and museums. This in turn was instrumental in inspiring a large group of artists to discard 'precious object' art and turn to so-called *dematerialised* works. The new materials (plastics, video, acrylics) and technologies (synthesizers, electronics and computers etc) appeared to have just the immaterial, experimental qualities the artists were striving for. They also represented something deeply ingrained in the American soul – progress.

The late Sixties and early Seventies saw a flurry of publications reflecting different opinions about the role of the arts in science and technology; with writers such as Charles Snow, Frank Marina and Pierre Restany keen to stress the differences between art and science.[8] In his book *Science and Technology in Art Today*, Jonathan Benthall also drew on his analysis of the relationship between contemporary art and media to reach a similar conclusion, namely that the activities of the scientist and the artist can only be closely identified if we view both as modes of enquiry.[9] More significant however, was the publication in 1968 of Jack Burnham's book *Beyond Modern Sculpture – The Effects of Science and Technology on the Sculpture of this Century*.[10]

Although Burnham's methodology and approach were criticised by a number of art scholars, the book became a 'must' for those interested in how the relationship between art, science and technology had affected the development of twentieth century sculpture. Burnham held the opinion that the traditional tools of art history and criticism – stylistics, iconographical analysis, historical context and formal analysis – were insufficient to explain what had happened in sculpture during the last sixty years. So instead of presenting the reader with a traditional chronological description of twentieth century sculptural movements, which would include discussion of new materials as part of a stylistic analysis, Burnham took a more *functional* approach. According to his account, the most important development in twentieth century sculpture was its change from *objet d'art* into *système d'art*. As Frank Popper noted, Burnham's analyses lead him to the conclusion that sculpture was 'not simply adopting new materials and new standards of fabrication, but on a more important level, evolving a new aesthetic which is synchronised with scientific and technical goals.'[11]

For Burnham, there was a direct relationship between new theories in the sciences (starting with Einstein's theory of relativity, and going on through quantum physics, developments in biochemistry and microphysiology etc), the introduction of new technologies (such as new means of production made possible through the development of electro-mechanical, electronic and computer systems) and the gradual shift towards the use of 'immaterial' and 'ephemeral' qualities in sculpture. Moreover, as Burnham argues, the technological world has become a systems-orientated one, a 'systematised environment' in which 'to a marked extent the object has lost its independent status in technological society; the object becomes one of the many means by which a systems-oriented culture functions at increasing levels of complexity tempered by efficiency'.[12] As he also went on to say, the 'system, as expressed through Kinetic Art, Light Sculpture, some Environmental Art and Cybernetic Art, has become a viable, if evanescent, aesthetic preoccupation'.[13]

I have dwelt upon Burnham's *Beyond Modern Sculpture* to set a theoretical context for the activities of the Art and Technology Movement as it developed in the United States during the second half of the Sixties. Burnham's systems point of view is important since his methodology, whether ultimately valid or not, is the art theoretical equivalent of the 'new model' which was used to analyse the patterns of organisation which developed from the advance of technological culture – *systems analysis*. Ludwig von Bertalanffy, systems biologist and father of the theory, defined the 'system' as 'a complex of components in interaction . . . comprised of material, energy and information in various degrees of organisation'.[14] Burnham signalled its implications for the development of a new art aesthetic as follows:

> The scope of a systems esthetic presumes that problems cannot be solved by a single technical solution, but must be attacked on a multi-leveled interdisciplinary basis. Consequently some of the more aware sculptors no longer think like sculptors, but they assume a span of problems more natural to architects, urban planners, civil engineers, electronic technicians and cultural anthropologists. This is not as pretentious as some critics have insisted. It is a legitimate extension of McLuhan's remark about Pop Art when he said that it was an announcement that the entire environment was ready to become a work of art.[15]

Together with an increasing application of systems analysis in a broad spectrum of both sciences and industries, the popularisation of cybernetics theory was also significant. This achieved a degree of acceptance as a scientific discipline through the publication of Norbert Weiner's *Cybernetics: Or Control and Communication in the Animal and the Machine*.[16] Cybernetics theory originated during World War Two, when Weiner and other scientists at the Massachusetts Institute of Technology and Harvard University envisioned the need for cross-disciplinary scientific projects. They began to search for a system of logic which would allow different scientific disciplines to make comparative analyses of parallel phenomena, a system that would be capable of fusing aspects of, for example, pure mathematics, electrical engineering and neurophysiology – an 'intelligent' systems analysis which would show some degree of environmental adaptability. Cybernetics is therefore, put simply, the science of the organisation of information, based on mathematical formulae.

The Art and Technology Movement

In retrospect, it is clear that the growth of the Art and Technology Movement depended substantially upon the enthusiasm and energy of one person, Billy Klüver. The radical development in technologies which took place in the Sixties would undoubtedly have affected the arts anyway but Klüver's involvement ensured this took place within an identifiable project. Born in Sweden, Klüver moved to the United States in 1954 where he studied at the University of California at Berkeley obtaining a PhD in Electrical Engineering. From 1959 he was employed at Bell Telephone Laboratories in New Jersey, working as a research engineer specialising in laser technology. His interests went beyond the research laboratory however and throughout this period he maintained a friendship with the Swiss born artist Jean Tinguely, assisting the artist with his motorised devices. Klüver and Tinguely were also friends of Pontus Hultén, who became the director of the Modern Musset in Stockholm in 1955 and later went on to the Pompidou Centre in Paris. Hultén was himself particularly interested in the use of movement in art and organised an exhibition of 'Art in Motion' in 1961. Klüver put together an American contribution to the show and in the following year assisted with another exhibition of four American artists including Jasper Johns and Robert Rauschenberg.

After helping Tinguely build his self destroying machine for the famous *Homage to New York* event in 1960, Klüver also began working with other artists. During the following six years he worked with Jasper Johns on his paintings with neon lights, with Andy Warhol on his helium filled 'clouds' project and with other artists such as Merce Cunningham, Claes Oldenburg and Rauschenberg. Best known of these projects was Rauschenberg's *Soundings*, for which the artist worked with Klüver and a team of engineers. The piece consisted of nine 8-foot high panels with silvered imagery (silk screened on plexiglass) in which the viewer at first only saw their reflection. When the viewer spoke however, the piece came to life and responded to the varying resonances of the speaker's voice. For different speakers, and for different combinations of words and sounds, different combinations of chair images appeared and disappeared – with the panel wired up for 200 different combinations of response.

Nine Evenings

In 1966 Klüver and Rauschenberg became involved in the organisation of the (in)famous *Nine Evenings: Theater and Engineering* which took place at the Armory Building in New York from October 13-23. The event grew out of the cancellation of a festival of 'art and technology' originally scheduled for Stockholm in Autumn 1966 in which Klüver had been invited to participate, providing technical support. This fell through for a number of reasons but the original American version turned into the *Nine Evenings*. The idea behind the *Nine Evenings* was that engineers should *collaborate* with artists on their projects – not simply furnishing technical assistance but being equal partners in the creative process. In his introduction to the catalogue, Klüver stated that,

> *Today it seems incredible that only 50 years ago there existed a 'right' and a 'wrong' science. Battles were fought and lost that now seem inconsequential . . . Contemporary art is somewhat in the same position as science was during the explosive years between 1900 and 1910. Millions of people have become aware of contemporary art. For some art is an argument, an insult, a joke, a toy, a pastime or a sacred object. Art has become something to practically everybody. With the result that the artist must spend hours justifying himself and what he is doing . . . 9 Evenings is a truly cooperative venture. All participants had an equal voice in the direction and all responsibility was shared jointly . . .*

He then went on to sketch a blueprint for the future with his declaration that:

The objectives of the 9 Evenings will be continued by 'Experiments in Art and Technology, Inc'. This foundation will further the creative interaction between industry, engineers and artists. 9 Evenings is an experiment in the true sense of the word: its results are open for the future.[17]

Despite the positive tone of Klüver's assertions, it is clear, from reading comments written after the event, that the relationship between the artists and engineers was not necessarily the 'easy' one Klüver suggests. However, after commenting that 'Klüver was available, and the artists used him, no more', Douglas Davis, for example, went on to emphasise that the 'radical alteration in this alliance lies in the growing willingness of the contemporary artist to cede technology – either the engineer or the machine – a full partnership in the creative process'.[18] Davis' remark is important in this context since it illustrates how the event not only changed the attitudes of the participating engineers and scientists towards the arts, but required the artist to develop a new attitude towards both the work process itself and the final product as 'art object'. This aspect marks the essence of Klüver's ideal, one which, if consistently pursued, might have lead to a re-definition of traditional role models.

The organisation of the *Nine Evenings* required enormous effort and patience from all participants and it was clear from the start that it was going to be both a spectacular event in its own right and a landmark in the history of performance/theatre/multimedia art. Douglas Davis reported that it was estimated 'that over 859 engineering hours went into the preparation of *Nine Evenings*, worth on paper at least $150,000 . . . Nineteen engineers contributed more than 2,500 hours. The real cost of the extravaganza was more than $100,000 . . . The total audience for the nine days was 10,000 . . .'[19] To give some idea of the efforts expended, a complex electronic environmental system was specially built for the event by engineer Larry Robinson. This system, called THEME (Theater Environmental Modular Electronic) was described by John Gruen as the most ambitious of the technical projects to be put in use by artists and as a small masterpiece of electronic invention.[20] The system was a 'patchboard' to which each artist's equipment was connected and included amplifiers, relays, decoders, tone control units, transmitters and receivers.

The final programme consisted of a series of nine performances all of which took place twice. These comprised: Steve Paxton's *Physical Things*, Alex Hay's *Grass Field*, Robert Rauschenberg's *Open Score*, David Tudor's *Bandoneon*, Yvonne

Rainer's *Carriage Discreteness*, John Cage's *Variations VI*,
Lucinda Child's *Vehicle*, Öyvind Fahlström's *Kisses Sweeter than
Wine* and Robert Whitman's *Two Holes of Water*.

Rauschenberg's contribution to the event seems to have
been one of the most spectacular. Nilo Lindgren, a staff
reporter from *IEEE Spectrum* reported that the performance
took place in an

> . . . *enormous half-barreled space. The Armory floor becomes
> a tennis court, and as the two players hit the ball back and
> forth, its sound against the racket is transmitted from the
> radios inside the racket handles and amplified through
> speakers. As the play proceeds, the lights illuminating the
> court are extinguished one by one each time the ball is struck,
> until the stage is dark, at which the game ends. At that
> point, hundreds of people move onto the Armory floor where
> they are illuminated with infra-red lights; the crowd scene
> in the darkness is picked up with infra-red sensitive television
> cameras, then projected on three large screens, so that the
> audience feels the presence of a large crowd without being
> able to see it except on the reproduced screen images. When
> the lights go finally on, the huge crowd of 'actors' bows to
> the audience seated on the bleachers.*[21]

Rauschenberg emphasised that by using these devices, he
wanted 'the audience to **sense** the live presence of the cast'
and emphasised that he wished the audience 'to **see** the
performance in *reproduction* only, via TV screens' and wanted
'to destroy the audience's habitual response to live
performances', concluding that he wished 'to present them
with a set of **sensory illusions**'.[22]

A number of other performances combined the use of
carefully programmed and designed systems with various
'found' signals and images, used as either compositional
elements or instructional 'triggers'. According to John Cage
for example, his performance of *Variations VII* only used sound
sources which were 'in the air at the moment of performance,
picked up via communication bands, telephone lines and
microphones, together with, instead of musical instruments,
a variety of household appliances and frequency generators'.[23]
David Tudor's *Bandoneon* took another approach,
incorporating audio-circuits, loud-speakers, TV images and
lights to both produce sounds and visual images and 'for the
activation of programming devices controlling the audio-
visual environment'.[24] Similarly, in Lucinda Child's *Vehicle*,

the 'dance' was lit, in part, 'by incoming sound waves from radio station WQXR; depending on their frequency, the waves turned the lights on and off, thus participating in the creation of the visual structure'.[25]

Rauschenberg in particular was positive about the collaboration between artists and engineers and clear in his view of the use of new technologies by artists, stating that working with engineers 'is inspiring. I could not do what I want to do without them. It is no longer possible to by-pass the whole area of technology . . . We can't afford to wait. We must force a relationship on technology in order to continue and we must move quickly. The most positive thing I can say is that technology does not lead us back into history – but advances us into the unknown'.[26] But despite Rauschenberg's assessment, and the positive accounts of critics such as Gruen, Perrault and Davis,[27] the *Nine Evenings* proved to be highly controversial with the event itself receiving highly critical reviews.

This negative response was mainly due to technical failures which made spectators wait unduly long times for performances to proceed. As Brian O'Doherty wrote later, 'the evenings received, on the whole, an appalling press – based mainly on the justifiable irritation of interminable delays, technical failures of the most basic sort, and long, dead spaces between, and sometimes in the middle of pieces'. But, as he went on to say, 'as such irritation faded away, one is left with startlingly persistent residual images, and strong hints of an alternative theater that has been lagging in its post-Happenings penumbra between art and theatre'.[28]

Lucy Lippard provided one of the most thorough critiques, discussing the *Nine Evenings* mainly within the context of the visual arts. For Lippard, the *result* is the basis upon which to judge a work of art, not the processes behind it, nor an appraisal which takes account of any technical failures which might occur:

> *A professional performance is a professional performance . . . The best of experimental arts are not experiment for experiment's sake but the essence distilled . . . Given the high quality of the previous work by the same people, the departures in* Nine Evenings *were superficial rather than fundamental . . . In most of the* Nine Evenings, *the various arts were less assimilated into theatre than sidetracked by technology. The result was too often a collage effect even where one was not intended: and an uncontrolled collage is a pastiche.*[29]

But as Jack Burnham has since commented

> *Few if any had the prescience to appreciate the events for what they were:* man-made systems *with a completely different set of values from those found in structured dramatics or the one night kinetic spectacular . . . This suggests that systems-oriented art – dropping the term 'sculpture' will deal less with artifacts contrived from their formal value, and increasingly* **men** *enmeshed with and within purposeful responsive systems. Such a shift should gradually diminish the distinction between biological and non-biological systems, ie man and the system as functioning but organisationally separate entities. The outcome will neither be the fragile cybernetic organisms now built nor the cumbersome electronic 'environments' just coming into being. Rather, the system itself will be made intelligent and sensitive to the human invading its territorial and sensorial domain.*[30]

Interestingly the engineers' contributions to the performances were seldom mentioned in art critiques. Their contributions to the *Nine Evenings* were however remarkable and were not just limited to technical performance. The engineering crew, the majority of whom came from Bell Laboratories where Klüver worked, designed a wide variety of systems and equipment. Peter Hirsch for example, designed an 80-kHz Doppler sonar for Lucinda Child's *Vehicle* performance; Harold Hodges built an 'anti-missile system' and 'floating snowflakes' for Öyvind Fahlström's *Kisses Sweeter Than Wine*; Dick Wolff developed a radio loop system for Steve Paxton's *Physical Things*; and Herb Schneider took over performance planning for all the artists. Incidentally, the artists and engineers working collaboratively on the *Nine Evenings* even made a few discoveries which turned out to be useful for further scientific research and commercial applications.[31]

Experiments in Art and Technology

Despite mixed critical and public responses to the *Nine Evenings*, Klüver and Rauschenberg continued to address themselves to the task of developing the artist's role in contemporary society and investigating how technology might best serve this. The next phase of their collaborative project was the establishment of 'Experiments in Art and Technology', whose birth was proclaimed in *The New York Times* on Wednesday 11th October 1967 under the headline

> *modest and uncertain merger seeks to bridge the gap between the two worlds. It is intended to bring modern technological tools to the artist for creating new art forms and fresh insights and viewpoints to the engineer for creating a 'people-oriented' technology.*[32]

The press conference held at Rauschenberg's loft included films, an exhibition of works incorporating technology and a formal presentation that explained the wide range of E.A.T.'s programme. E.A.T. had set up during the preceding year in a loft on East 16th Street New York which served as an office space, storage area for equipment and a meeting place for artists and engineers. Their first newsletter was published in January 1967, followed by a second in June which included a statement of the organisation's objectives as follows:

> ★ *The purpose of Experiments in Art and Technology, Inc. is to catalyze the inevitable active involvement of industry, technology and the arts. E.A.T. has assumed the responsibility of developing an effective relationship between artists and engineers.*

> ★ *E.A.T. will guide the artist in achieving new art through new technology and work for the professional recognition of the engineer's technical contribution within the engineering community . . .*

> ★ *To ensure a continued fruitful interaction between a rapidly advancing technology and the arts, E.A.T. will work for a high standard technical innovation in collaborative projects.*

> ★ *E.A.T. is founded on the strong belief that an industrially sponsored, effective working relationship between the artists and engineers will lead to new possibilities which will benefit society as a whole.*[33]

In its early phase the organisation concentrated on improving communications between interested parties. During its first year, it published an E.A.T. newsletter to keep its membership informed of its activities, before changing this format to an informational bulletin entitled *E.A.T. Operations and Information* from March 1968 onwards. In the following year it also attempted to launch a newspaper entitled *TECHNE*, which was intended to present 'projects, processes and physical problems and opportunities presented by the relationship between rapidly expanding technology and the individual'[34] – but despite these ambitious intentions, it only actually appeared a few times before folding.

The organisation kept a detailed record of all the projects and lectures it was involved in and detailed lists of collaborators. These records, known as the *Proceedings*, document the initial fast growth of the organisation between 1967 and 1969. At first the number of artists outnumbered the engineers but their numbers grew equal and by the early Seventies the 6,000 members were equally divided between artists and engineers. During the organisation's first two years of operation nearly 500 works were created through successful matches between artists and engineers. Through contacts with the Institute of Electrical and Electronic Engineers (IEEE), news about E.A.T. soon circulated in the technical press. By 1968 the organisation had already managed to obtain considerable support from the industrial and public sector, in addition to public grants from the Rockefeller Brothers Fund ($25,000) and the National Endowment for the Arts ($50,000). This trend continued over the next two years and the enthusiasm and pertinacity with which staff at the E.A.T. pursued its goals contributed greatly to the success of its first phase.

Despite the broad base of its initial projects, it became clear at an early stage that E.A.T.'s objectives were not so much premised on extensive theorisations but rather, of necessity, reflected a pragmatic attitude that believed in acting upon opportunities or possibilities as they arose. Nevertheless, during the first year of its existence it was possible to perceive a slight shift in the formulation of E.A.T.'s objectives. Rhetorical statements such as 'contemporary artists want to use technology as a material . . . And today technology needs the artist just as much as the artist wants technology'[35] were soon toned down and an awareness of the implication of the artist's responsibility towards the new technological developments began to prevail. By 1970 E.A.T. was expressing its objectives as follows:

> *We can no longer claim innocence for the human and social consequences resulting from technological change. We are, in all respects, responsible for the technology that will form our environment tomorrow. This responsibility implies the search for a technology directed towards pleasure and enjoyment. It implies a distinction between functional and ecological aspects of technology.*[36]

Despite excellent documentation, it is very difficult to get clear picture of many of the individual projects that were supported by E.A.T. The organisation did however participate in a number of exhibitions which were highly publicised. Apart from the previously discussed *Nine Evenings*, outstanding early collaborations included *Some More Beginnings: Experiments in Art and Technology* (held in between July 1968 and January 1969) and the *Pavilion* designed for the *Expo '70* international world fair in Osaka.

Some More Beginnings originated from a proposal put to E.A.T. by Pontus Hultén requesting them to provide works for his exhibition *The Machine as seen at the End of the Mechanical Age*. The organisation responded by offering to sponsor a competition for the most inventive technical contribution by an engineer to a work of art produced in collaboration with an artist. The competition was announced on 12 November, 1967 in *The New York Times*, *Scientific American* and fifteen technical journals. Publicity for the competition was aimed at the technical community in an attempt to get engineers interested in working with artists. Hultén chose ten works for his exhibition at New York's Museum of Modern Art (MOMA), but it was subsequently decided to exhibit all of the works submitted to the competition when the director of the Brooklyn Museum offered space for the show. *Some More Beginnings* opened there in November 1968 and received remarkable coverage from newspapers, television and magazines. A catalogue with photographs and some technical information about the works was published at the last minute and 18,000 visitors attended the show.[37]

The Pavilion project got underway in the same year, when E.A.T. agreed to supervise the development of an art project for the *Expo '70* world fair in Osaka, Japan. The Pepsi-Cola Corporation offered sponsorship for the undertaking and a team of artists and engineers began to develop ideas. This collaboration resulted in a programmed environment of sound and reflected imagery being designed for the inside of a pavilion. As Klüver emphasised, the whole project attempted to fulfil the ideals of the E.A.T. project,

> *The organization and process of doing the project was in fact a 'mirror image' of the results we wanted to achieve, and was based on collaboration, personal responsibility, and experimenting. Most of the work on specific elements was*

done through collaborations which involved over 75 engineers and artists, and industries in Japan and different parts of the United States . . . As a work of art. The Pavilion *and its operation would be an open-ended situation, an experiment in the scientific sense of the word.*[38]

Though, as discussed further below, the construction and organisation ran into a number of problems, the descriptions of the pavilion in its short programme booklet indicate that it must have been a spectacular experience:

The white dome of the Pavilion is surrounded by a changing cloud bank generated by an atomizer system. At night, high intensity multicolored beams of light . . . frame the site, creating patterns in the cloud bank and reflections on the Pavilion . . . The entrance to the Pavilion is a shiny tunnel, which leads to distribution booths where silver suited hostesses will give earphone headsets and instructions to visitors.[39]

An area called the 'Clam Room' provided a central feature for the pavilion. The entrance to this space was fitted with a 'soft floor' from which the first 'sound experience', comprising the 'reverberation of any comment or sound' made by the visitor was transmitted to their headsets. The room itself featured a floor which illuminated footprints and a laser light scanning the ceiling. From the Clam Room, stairs lead to a spherical dome above. As the programme booklet described it, the 'floor at the entrance of the dome is made of grass and the sounds are those of nature – birds, frogs, rustling trees. The inside of the dome is a spherical mirror, 90 feet in diameter, where images appear in many different perspectives'.[40]

In addition to the general environmental installations and individual listening 'experiences' of visitors, there was a programme of performances, music and dance. Participating performers included now well-known artists: dancer Remy Charlip, performance artist Alan Kaprow, composer-musicians Alvin Lucier, Terry Riley, Pauline Oliveros, David Tudor, La Monte Young and Marion Zazeela.

Though the technical complexities of the event had been greatly under-estimated, they lead to a number of interesting new designs. The 'cloud' surrounding the pavilion was developed by Fukiko Nakaya and generated by an atomiser system which was, at the time, the largest pure water vapour system ever constructed. The complicated sound system was constructed for automated control, which could also be overridden by live manipulation, and the 'Mirror Dome' – a spherical mirror, 9 feet in diameter 'had the unique optical property of reproducing an object or a person as a real image in suspended space'.[41] But despite its ambitious conception and technological ingenuity, the whole project did not evolve as fluently as it appears from the E.A.T. files and was subject to many delays and failures in the development of the technical facilities. As a result of factors such as the book it published to accompany the exhibition, it also significantly overdrew its budget and Pepsi-Cola eventually withdrew its support when E.A.T. presented it with a maintenance contract for some $220,000 more than the sum originally proposed – $185,000.

The Gradual Demise

It appears that from 1972 onwards E.A.T. became more directed toward the science and engineering world than artistic society. Although their original policies were not abandoned immediately, new projects initiated by E.A.T. took a different turn. Jack Burnham has suggested that E.A.T. gradually lost its image as a corporate mediator due to the unfortunate experience with Pepsi-Cola over *The Pavilion* and because it was perceived that it had become an 'elitist' organisation, mainly catering for the needs of its own staff and a few favoured big-time artists in the New York area. By 1975 Frank Popper observed that

> . . . the E.A.T. organisation, and their director Billy Klüver, seems to have finally shifted its emphasis to the engineer, to the detriment of artist and public . . . From matching artists and engineers they have reached a point where they are encouraging them to go their separate ways and the bulk of their publicity is now devoted to engineers. This may be the reason why artists have become estranged from the E.A.T. organisation.[42]

The final change in E.A.T.'s direction was made explicit in a paper Klüver prepared for the International Institute of Communications (IIC) Annual Conference 1977 in Washington. The paper comprised a re-evaluation of the Art and Technology programme in view of the new technologies generating new communications systems and suggested that 'an effective way to develop a well-designed interface between the individual and the new systems and structures is for artists to participate in the international and governmental decision-making, planning and regulatory activities associated with systems design, deployment and regulations'. Klüver also emphasised that many 'of the projects E.A.T. initiated and administered took place in non-art areas as well as situations where technology was used to create works of art or was integrated into theater performances. Many of these collaborative projects involved television and other modes of communication'.[43]

A number of the ambitious international schemes that were developed in the Seventies indicate the degree of E.A.T.'s departure from the traditional arts arena. In the United States for instance, E.A.T. submitted a proposal to RCA Laboratories to establish a research laboratory in entertainment programming. This was intended as a location where artists could collaborate with television research engineers, sociologists etc to explore new forms of entertainment programming which could give television a more effective social role. Other E.A.T. projects involved work with the Nehru Institute for Development in India working on the development of instructional TV programmes for eventual broadcast by the SITE satellite and a collaboration with the El Salvador Department of Culture on a scheme to develop regional video production for educational and community development purposes.

We can conclude then, that the direction of Experiments in Art and Technology was very much one of *practice*, of aiming to bring artists in contact with engineers and scientists in order to solve specific problems, ideally on an equal creative basis. It was this aspect which made the movement different from previous attempts to link art and technology. One important result of its activities was that it allowed artists to gain access to advanced technology which would otherwise have been near-impossible to secure. For some artists at least, it reduced the time-lag that existed before a new technology 'trickled down' and was available for use. Though collaborations with artists occasionally led the engineer or scientist to make new discoveries or technical breakthroughs, the most important aspect of this joint activity seems to have been the process of mutual learning and the exploration of each other's area of expertise.

This is particularly clear when one looks at the works originating from another prestigious project organised by the Los Angeles County Museum of Art from 1967-71, the 'Art and Technology Program'. Initiated by Maurice Tuchman, the programme set out to 'bring together the incredible resources and advanced technology of industry together with the equally incredible imagination and talent of the best artists at work today'.[44] Those artists invited to submit a proposal to the programme were connected with a company to develop a project during a ten to twelve week long artist-in-residency programme at the company plant. Again, the idea was to bring artists in touch with new technologies and industry in order to induce future collaborations. In his report on the scheme, Tuchman describes one of the initial problems as bringing the artists together with the 'right' companies, and particularly, the right department or person within that company.

The organisers approached a large number of artists, of whom only a minority had been actively involved with 'technology' before and initially, almost everybody was interested in participating. A significant number of female artists also sent in unsolicited proposals for the scheme, though none were eventually chosen . . . In the event, thirty seven corporations in Southern California, most of them involved with aeronautics and space technology, contributed to the programme. Twenty seven artists worked directly with individual companies and about twenty collaborations resulted in 'tangible' artwork. A number of these were exhibited in the US Pavilion at *Expo '70* and all projects were subsequently exhibited at the Los Angeles County Museum in September 1971.

Two of the more spectacular of these were Newton Harrison's collaboration with the Jet Propulsion Laboratory in Pasadena and Rockne Kreb's collaboration with Hewlett Packard. Harrison's piece was based on a 'forest' of plexiglass cylinders that were filled with glowing gas plasmas. As Harrison described it, it was set up

> . . . so that the gas was injected in such a way that it started out as lightning, stayed lightning for about two minutes; became an arc; stayed an arc for about three minutes, became a glow – a total glow in the tube . . . the glow started to break down into placelets and I shot more gas in so it would be an arc again.[45]

Krebs' piece was a complicated laser environment, which as he subsequently emphasised, he could not have made without the assistance of programming specialists. As he describes it, the 'configurations of light were programmed to run through a repetitive cycle; they would pop back and forth, or seem to swing . . . just as the spectator began to apprehend the pattern from one point of view, it would suddenly enter a 'dialogue' phase, popping back and forth across the space'.[46]

The Art and Technology Program was unique in that it provided an opportunity for artists and engineers and scientists to familiarise themselves with each other's working methods (and also allowed artists to produce works which they could not have otherwise attempted). But even at the time, doubts were cast about the actual potential for more long term collaborations. Jane Livingston argued for instance, that the

> . . . development of the various experimental interchanges in Art and Technology was on the whole a polymorphous, discursive and nonorganic process. Indeed it now appears simply that the relationship between artists and technological corporations is an intrinsically non-organic one – at least on an a priori basis.[47]

Interestingly, Tuchman also remarked, in 1971, that 'if Art and Technology were beginning now instead of in 1967, in a climate of increased polarisation and organised determination to protest against the policies supported by so many American business interests and so violently opposed by the art community, many of the same artists would not have participated'.[48]

Few artists had shown any resistance or 'moral opposition' to collaborating with the 'temples of Capitalism' at the time, but by the early Seventies the social and political situation had changed dramatically in the United States. When Douglas Davis published his Art and the Future in 1973, he wrote in the introduction,

> I am more than normally aware that the heady euphoria of the mid-1960s, when artist and engineers came together in significant numbers for the first time, has passed . . . the (Vietnam) war has sickened us all and we hear little at this hour about the creative potential of technology and much about its destructive capacity . . . This position cannot long endure, of course. Art can no more reject either technology or science than it can reject the world itself.[49]

Of course Davis turned out to be right. The complicated social and political situation in the United States saw a lot of artists turning to different directions. There was a renewed interest in traditional artforms such as painting, sculpture and photography and public and environmental related sculptural works flourished. But the demise of the Art and Technology movement did not mean that artists were no longer using technological expertise and facilities. Artists have *always* used new technologies when it suited their artistic purpose. From then on though, collaborations such as those envisioned by E.A.T. were rare. Artists would subsequently rather *commission* the expertise of specialists to solve a specific project related problem.

Thus, Klüver's *ideal* of a network of artists collaborating with science and industry, mutually exchanging ideas, with engineers developing projects together with artists and, ultimately, artists influencing certain technological or scientific developments, remained just that – an ideal. As indicated above, the ultimate consequences of Klüver's ideas would have been the creation of a network – a system – of inter-relations between the arts (or rather certain *types* of art) and industry. Not in a *commercial* sense, but as an exchange of creativity where artists could partake directly in the industrial process and influence subsequent developments of their collaborative initiatives. For Klüver I think that this meant not so much that art was given up, but that art would change societal structures.

For the majority of the artists this was obviously too radical a step, since it meant a re-defining of their role and that of the function of 'Art'. The same is true for the scientific and corporate-industrial communities, whose members are still very wary of artists in general. But whatever the failure of Art and Technology's 'grand design', there were some positive developments. There are now, for example, quite a few companies with artist-in-residency schemes which give the artist an opportunity to become acquainted with a field of research within the company. This arrangement is mutually beneficial, since, as companies have learnt, they can benefit from the artistic and creative insights the artist brings to bear. It is still practically the only way for artists to gain direct access to the latest technology or scientific research. But in all significant respects, nothing much has changed. As many of the chapters in this anthology emphasise, in the relationship between art, science and industry, art is still running behind much as it used to.

MARGA BIJVOET

1 There is an incredible amount of literature on the subject. E J Dijksterhuis *The Mechanization of the World Picture* New York University Press 1963 is a good classic survey.

2 Georges VanTongerloo, cited in Jack Burnham *Beyond Modern Sculpture – The Effects of Science and Technology on the Sculpture of this Century* New York, George Baziller Inc 1968 p115.

3 Alexander Archipenko, cited in Jack Burnham *ibid* p117.

4 Naum Gabo *Gabo: Construction, Sculpture, Paintings, Drawings, Engravings* Cambridge (USA), Harvard University Press 1957 p164.

5 *ibid* p180.

6 László Moholy-Nagy *Vision in Motion* Chicago, Theobald 1947.

7 See Frank Popper *Art-action and Participation* New York, New York University Press 1975

8 See for instance Charles Percy Snow *The Two Cultures* New York, New York Library 1964

9 Jonathan Benthall *Science and Technology in Art Today* London, Thames and Hudson 1972.

10 Jack Burnham *op cit*.

11 Frank Popper *op cit* p204.

12 Jack Burnham *op cit* p10.

13 *ibid*.

14 Ludwig von Bertalanffy *Robots, Men and Minds* New York, George Baziller Inc 1967 p69.

15 Jack Burnham 'Systems Esthetic' *Artforum* September 1968 p34.

16 Norbert Weiner *Cybernetics: Or Control and Communication in the Animal and Machine* Cambridge (USA), MIT Press 1948; also see his *Use of Human Beings* Boston, Mifflin 1950.

17 Billy Klüver, in his introduction to Klüver (ed) *Nine Evenings: Theater and Engineering* (catalogue), New York, Foundation for the Performing Arts 1966 p3.

18 Douglas Davis *Art and The Future* New York, Praeger 1973 p68.

19 *ibid* p72.

20 John Gruen, 'Art Meets Technology' *World Journal Tribune* (magazine section), New York – cited in *E.A.T. Clippings* v1 n1 (July 1969) p4.

21 Nilo Lindgren, 'Art and Technology II – A Call for Collaboration' *IEEE Spectrum* May 1969 p50; also see his 'Art and Technology I – Steps toward a new synergism' *IEEE Spectrum* April 1969 p59-68.

22 Robert Rauschenberg interviewed by Nilo Lindgen in Nilo Lindgren (May 1969) *op cit*.

23 John Cage, cited by Douglas Davis *op cit* p69.

24 David Tudor, cited by Douglas Davis *op cit* p70.

25 Lucinda Childs, cited by Douglas Davis *op cit* p71.

26 Robert Rauschenberg, in Nilo Lindgren (May 1969) *op cit*.

27 See for instance, John Gruen *op cit*; John Perrault 'Art to make it new' *The Village Voice* 5 December, 1968 p16; and Douglas Davis 'Art and Technology – The New Combine' *Art in America* January-February 1968.

28 Brian O'Doherty, cited by Nilo Lindgren (May 1969) *op cit* p47.

29 Lucy Lippard 'Total Theatre' *Art International* 20 January 1967 p39.

30 Jack Burnham *op cit* p363.

31 Such as discovering a phosphor that could be used in infra-red laser research and designing a small power amplifier and a

proportional control system which varied sound and light on stage simply by passing a small flashlight over a glass covering sixteen photocells.

32 Cited in *E.A.T. News* v1 n1 (no original page reference given).
33 From the E.A.T. *Manifesto* signed by Billy Klüver and Robert Rauschenberg, October 1967.
34 *TECHNE* v1 n1 April 1969 (unattributed) front page statement.
35 *E.A.T. News*, v1 n4 (unattributed) front page statement.
36 *TECHNE* v1 n2 November 1970, unattributed statement (actually by Billy Klüver) on front page.
37 (Unattributed) *Description of the Pepsi-Cola Pavilion for the Japan World Exhibition* Osaka 1970.
38 Billy Klüver, statement on front page of *TECHNE* v1 n1 April 1969.
39 Description from *E.A.T. Proceedings* n8 25 March 1969.
40 *ibid*.
41 *ibid*.
42 Frank Popper *op cit* pp210-211.
43 Billy Klüver in his address to the IIIC Annual Conference 1977 (Washington DC), Group Session V: Art and Technology – a paper entitled 'the Artists' Expertise for Communication Planning'.
44 Maurice Tuchman in his introduction to Tuchman (ed) *A Report on the Art and Technology Program of the Los Angeles County Museum of Art* Los Angeles, LACMA 1971 p9.
45 Newton Harrison, cited in Gail Scott 'Newton Harrison' in Tuchman (ed) *ibid* p122.
46 Rockne Krebs, cited in Jane Livingston 'Rockne Krebs' in Tuchman (ed) *op cit* p174.
47 Jane Livingston 'Thoughts on Art and Technology' in Tuchman (ed) *op cit*.
48 Maurice Tuchman *op cit*.
49 Douglas Davis (1973) *op cit* unpaginated introduction.

3

FROM ABSTRACTION
TO SIMULATION:
Notes on the History
of Computer Imaging

ANDY DARLEY

I

The production and manipulation of images by computer has a short history. Dating from the 1950's such imaging has grown and developed from simple sine/cosine-type display graphics on the monitors of projects such as military defence systems, to highly complex and sophisticated visual representations which are today playing an increasingly significant part in a whole range of practices and disciplines. These involve areas as diverse as scientific and medical research, architectural and commodity design, the production of television titles, advertisements, films (both commercial and independent), the traditional arts such as painting and sculpture, as well as games and video.

Indeed it would not be too far fetched to say that the majority of the images we now see in contemporary everyday life have at some stage in their production involved a computer. This may mean nothing more – as in the case of newspaper or magazine images for example – than their having been digitally composited or arranged together with text on a page. More and more of the standard recording equipment (both audio and visual) in everyday use in the production of film, television and video, is coming to utilise digital technology as microprocessing systems become embedded within traditional technologies, taking over and enhancing old functions and adding new ones.

One of the problems however, certainly with much of the dominant thinking about computers and culture to date, is that it remains characterised by what I would describe as an extreme form of 'technicism': it is almost wholly understood and assessed in relation to technical terms and criteria.[1] For those who are sceptical about this claim I would suggest a visit or glance through the programmes and/or proceedings to date of some of the most prestigious events in the computer graphics calender: the American ACM-SIGGRAPH

(Association for Computer Machinery, Special Interest Group in Computer Graphics and Interactive Technologies) Convention for example, or the annual Monte Carlo International Forum on New Images (IMAGINA). The majority of events and papers at these are both highly technical in their titles and themes and predominantly preoccupied with 'naive realist' imaging concerns.

Moreover, if the above characterises the dominant view associated with the mass media industries, then the predominant perspective within the alternative, so-called 'independent' sphere – those in the visual arts who are attempting to work with computers – tends towards the adoption of an optimistic neo-McLuhanist position. This perspective is characterised by an unquestioning and celebratory acceptance of the potential of the computer as both medium and metaphor. This tendency has its roots still firmly grounded in a late (High) Modernist aesthetic which involves, as an underlying tenet, the effective *autonomy* of art from other aspects of the social world. All too often it appears easily contented with both theoretical and aesthetic formalism (something, curiously enough, which the now readily available techniques of computer image manipulation mentioned below seem to promote and encourage in the artist). Moreover, modernist aesthetic concern with pure formal visual play also frequently gets grafted onto partially grasped or fashionable interpretations of poststructuralist/ modernist theories. These themselves conveniently appear to uncouple representation from other important aspects of the social world – the economic and the historical for example. There is indeed much to be excited about when considering the potential of these new techniques. Nevertheless, the sense of *déjà vu* which the uncritical attitude (or 'happy technophilia') underlying dominant attitudes in each of the two camps mentioned provokes, seems to me a cause for some reflection. I hope that the brief look at history which follows will begin to show why this should be so.

II

The beginnings of computer imaging in the Sixties occurred at a moment in history when students of culture believed they could locate the onset of important shifts and radical departures – a kind of watershed – in areas of both cultural and aesthetic practice and theory. Sixties America was an extremely interesting and important historical moment both politically and culturally speaking. The Cold War, vigorously waged by the United States after World War II, was one of the major motive forces for the intense pace and growth of new technological development which had taken place since the mid-Forties. The vast sums of money given over to the military for 'defence' purposes – and later as part of the 'space race' – was (arguably) the most important factor in ensuring rapid developments in the field of electronics, and particularly in the area of information and computer technology, and it wasn't long before it had opened the way for commercial development. Research and development (R&D) in the area of computers grew exponentially during the Fifties, and has continued almost unabated to the present. Moreover, computers are by this time *already* viewed as the central technological (and metaphorical) element in this new post-war context – frequently referred to at the time as the 'cybernetic era' – in which new levels of integration were occurring between science and technology. This was premised upon the birth of such new interrelated disciplines as cybernetics, game and systems theory, and information and communication theory. American social theorist, Daniel Bell, calls this new development 'intellectual technology'.[2] Such methods, in continual development and refinement ever since, have come to constitute the new steering systems of post-industrial society.

Firstly, it is important to note the complex of differing interests and motivations of those directly involved in this early period of computer image development, a development which took place largely within the United States. Two somewhat different types of research and development appear to constitute and characterise work on computer imaging in the initial period. In the first place there is the applied research of computer scientists and engineers; in the second, there is the experimental work undertaken in the area by artists. Things were never quite as simple as this however, for almost without exception, the artists involved worked in close collaboration with computer scientists and programme researchers. At the same time, many of the engineers who had come into contact with artists became producers of 'computer art' (as opposed to computer graphics) in their own right. Other engineers however carried on research into graphics potentialities which were of a much more functional and applied kind and showed little or no interest or involvement with art.[3]

From the start there had been military and commercial involvements. The former was responsible for encouraging the rapid advances in computing which took place during World War II. This was largely in connection with the development of various weapons systems, including the development of the atomic bomb. The important ties which were developing between the military and the corporate sector, and between both of these and the scientific research departments of universities like MIT and Iowa State, continued into the Sixties and were further developed and strengthened. As the technology developed and the commercial possibilities attached to computer imaging were perceived, in relation, for example, to the interactive computer graphics being utilised in flight simulators or air defence tracking systems, increasing amounts of financial and other resources were given over to researching computer graphics as an area in its own right. Computer scientists became interested in producing images via computer and to this end strove to develop and improve both hardware and software.

The advances were not long in coming. For example, in 1963, Ivan Sutherland, then a post-graduate student at MIT developed a method of real-time interactive computer graphics called *Sketchpad*, which involved drawing directly on to a cathode ray tube display screen with a 'light-pen' and then modifying the geometrical image possibilities so obtained with a keyboard. *Sketchpad* is considered by many today as a crucial breakthrough, from which have sprung most of the other technical developments to date, up to and including the various 'paintbox' systems which are so prevalent today (such as the *Quantel Paintbox* and its moving image adjunct *Harry*). By the mid-Sixties, General Motors were utilising a system similar to Sutherland's which involved computer image modification in the design of car bodies – a precursor of current CAD/CAM systems. And by 1963, computer generated line animation films were being produced at Bell Laboratories utilising the primitive vector display ('wire frame') technique. These were initially used as visual simulations of scientific and technical ideas. [See for example, E E Zajec's *Simulation of a Two Giro Gravity-gradient Attitude Control System.*]

The other important element in this complex of initial research and experimentation comprises those artists – all of whom were already part of the discursive practices which constituted Modernist visual art (eg painting, sculpture and experimental film making) – who wanted to explore the possibilities of this new means of image production. John Whitney is today the best known of these early computer-artist experimenters. Other important contributors include James Whitney, Stan Vanderbeek, Lillian Schwartz, Charles Csuri and John Stehura. The interest such artists took in this still novel area led, in almost every case, to close collaboration with computer scientists and technicians. This usually implied as well, industrial sponsorship of one kind or another, primarily because both the expensive machinery and the technical expertise were in the hands of large affluent institutions.

To this day, John Whitney's computer film work has been guided by what has come to constitute one of the central aesthetic concerns of those in the visual arts working within mainstream Modernism – an engagement with considerations which involve visual abstraction (in this instance, of motion structured through time). This has largely determined his work to date and has involved him in attempts to draw a working analogy between such visual experimentation and music (with its power to 'evoke the most explicit emotions directly by its simple patterned configurations of tones in time and motion'[4]). After working with his brother James on a series of experimental films entitled *Abstract Film Exercises 1-5* (1943-44), Whitney first got involved in computer imaging in the late Fifties. Utilising outdated surplus computing equipment, junked by the military after the war, he began to construct computerised drawing machines. This eventually led to the development of a fully automated system which involved high precision integrated coordination and control of the entire production process (including drawing, motions, lighting and exposures) – a mechanical analogue computer, specifically designed to produce complex abstract film animations.

Though a film entitled *Catalog* (1961), comprising a collection of short abstract exercises, is the only existing example of the experimental film work that Whitney himself produced using this system, two of his sons, John Junior and Michael, worked extensively with it. The former, experimenting with the device's 'slit-scan' potential, produced the successful film *Byjina Flores* (1964). Between 1963 and 1966 Whitney's brother James also made extensive use of the system to create the acclaimed film *Lapis* (1966). In the meantime Whitney had set up a company based on this novel technology which he called Motion Graphics Inc, and undertook numerous commercial assignments utilising the analogue computer. In this regard the example of his work most often cited is the short title sequences produced for Hitchcock's film *Vertigo* (1958).

In 1966, by which time John Whitney's reputation in the world of 'avant-garde' film-art was already considerable due in large part to his pioneering work in computer film techniques, he was offered a position as 'artist in residence' by IBM. At the time of accepting this bursary, Whitney had already been informally collaborating with Jack Citron, an IBM computer engineer who had taken an interest in the artist's mechanical computer imaging techniques. The new position at IBM carried the brief of exploring the aesthetic possibilities of computer imaging, initially in relation to their new IBM 360 *digital* computers, which had been introduced the previous year and which were among the first to utilise micro-chip technology, along with the software programs and Graphic Display Consoles then being developed for them. Whitney's collaboration with Citron continued and resulted in the latter writing an imaging program (GRAF) in the Fortran computer language to fit Whitney's non-representational imaging needs. Whitney has described using this program as being something like playing a piano.[5] The first and perhaps most famous film to emerge from this collaboration was *Permutations* (1968). A typical Whitney film, *Permutations* was inimitably described by one contemporary reviewer, Gene Youngblood, as

> *a dazzling display of serial imagery that seems to express specific ideas or chains of ideas through hypersensitive manipulation of kinetic empathy. The patterns, colours, and motions dancing before us seem to be addressing the inarticulate conscious with a new kind of language.*[6]

The association between Whitney and IBM continues into the present. Today he is producing integrated music and graphic works – through a process he has dubbed, 'digital harmonisation' – on software designed by computer programming expert Jerry Reed. This enables simultaneous real-time computation of both visual and audio elements. Significantly, Whitney views the work of developing a computer instrument of the aural and visual as falling directly within the American High Modernist tradition of Abstract Expressionist painting. Though it is hard to gauge the extent to which IBM has directly benefitted from this sponsorship, Whitney's pioneering work in motion-control techniques, linked to his early experimentation and development of the analogue computer film, has certainly connected with important aesthetic aspects of post-Sixties mainstream cinema; particularly in relation to the production of spectacular visual effects. The first of these was the so-called 'stargate-corridor' sequence in the film *2001: A Space Odyssey* (1968). This involved a slit-scan device similar to the one originally invented by Whitney, and in a major part seems inspired by Whitney's early efforts in the direction of abstract visual effects.[7]

Whitney was only one of many fine artists at this time to receive assistance from corporate sources. Two other names of note are those of Stan Vanderbeek and Lillian Schwartz both of whom worked with technicians from Bell Laboratories, notably Kenneth Knowlton. Working with imaging systems which were already under development at Bell, such as the graphics programming software *Beflix* (one of the earliest languages designed for imaging purposes), experimental film maker Vanderbeek and the research engineer Knowlton were working together on digitally produced computer films as early as 1964, two years ahead of John Whitney. This early work resulted in the *Poem Fields* series of computer animated abstract films, which display constantly transforming mosaic-like patterns. Lillian Schwartz, like John Whitney, is one of those artists who took an early interest in the computer as medium, and has managed to sustain and develop her interest through to the present. She also – again like John Whitney – currently maintains her association with the company that initially sponsored her work, Bell Labs. A look at her computer film work from the late Sixties, when she began working with Knowlton, through to today, shows how she has attempted to work with a variety of techniques. These range from the programmed generation of abstract images such as those in *Pixillation* (1969); the manipulation of already existing images through quantising and digitising techniques evident in her film *Pictures From a Gallery* (1976); to, in her 1986 film *Beyond Picasso*, where she programmed the computer to simulate the styles of an artist in order to produce 'original' works.

The painter Charles Csuri, who in 1967 was a Professor of Art at Ohio State University, is interesting precisely because he was *not* one of those artists originally drawn to computer applications who either lost interest in the area or continued – as did Whitney and Schwartz – to develop fine art orientated work. In the late sixties, Csuri began to develop an interest in computer imaging through collaborating with computer programmer James Schaffer in the university's computing department. They produced both graphics and computer animated films, among them what is now frequently seen as the path-breaking computer animation film *Hummingbird* (1967) – a line animation showing the slow, computer randomised disintegration and eventual restitution of a Hummingbird image. This initial interest in researching computer imaging for artistic purposes eventually led to the establishment of a commercial company Cranston-Csuri Productions. Today the company is one of the top US commercial computer graphics studios, producing TV logos, medical and scientific simulations, commercials and so forth and continues research into computer image applications driven largely by considerations of the requirements of these client domains. Csuri, in other words, has tended to redirect his creative curiosity into areas which lie somewhat outside notions of art conceived through High Modernist categories.

III

What is interesting about the rapidity of scientific and technological advances and their proliferating commercial utilisation in the US after the war, is the ideas, attitudes and debates that accompanied them. In this sense, the Sixties can be viewed as a period where questions about this new technological expansion came to a head for the first time. The Sixties is an era not only of intense practical development of the new electronically based technologies, but one also of increased ideological debate as to the nature of such technology and the promise it held for the future of society. Speculation was rife within the academic, political, cultural and business communities. The area was thought about in terms of the new cultural forms which would spring from it; the new aesthetics it was bringing about; the new disciplines it was thought to be spawning; the profound effects it would have on society. The dominant tone of this thinking was one of extreme optimism with regard to technology, particularly the new computer based technology and the promise it held for the future. There was general agreement that such technology was largely responsible for bringing society to the threshold of a radically new age, and for the first time ideas of *post*mechanical, *post*industrial and *post*modern society were generally espoused and discussed.

At the time, the dominant attitude among artists towards the burgeoning new electronic technology and the cybernetic discourse surrounding it was also one of high optimism. For many, the older mechanical technology had negative connotations and associations. The new stuff on the other hand seemed to promise new forms – less elitist than those of the previous period – which were in keeping with the dawning of a new postindustrial age, the 'global village' as McLuhan called it. Needless to say, the computer art experimentation which took place during this period was an important aspect of the 'investment' in new technology then being pursued by artists. Unlike that other highly significant new movement Pop Art however, much of this artistic fascination with technology did not have the dubious alibi of refocussing attention on questions of representation, for it was still very much concerned with the extension of the High Modernist visual aesthetic.[8] The majority of technological applications were caught up in a discourse centred around the utilisation of technology for the production of purely formal novelty. Reading some of the papers and books produced by artists and theorists at the time reveals just how deeply entrenched this conception was. It is particularly revealing in this respect to read some of the papers produced by the engineers and technicians who had begun to collaborate with artists at this time, for they had arrived at understandings of what constitutes art, largely through those artists with whom they had come to form close working associations.

To take one example, which appears to stem specifically from the collaboration of artists and computer engineers, there arose a peculiar notion which tied creativity directly and unilaterally to the emotional mental states of the artist. On this view, those special individuals who are artists come to be defined as such because of the peculiar and exceptional nature of their emotions. This premise lead computer research engineer Michael Noll to speculate about the rich possibilities of art produced by direct 'communication of the actual subconscious emotional state of the artist'[9] to the computer, for translation (feedback) into art-works – literally plugging-in to the artist to record a new piece! Though quite clearly a cybernetic metaphor underlies such views of human-machine interaction, the then prevalent High Modernist concept of art in its highly individualistic, formalist, 'expressionist' focus on the moment of creation, seeing itself as completely autonomous from other aspects of the world in which it exists – makes it a perfect foil for such (today) whacky technicist conceptions.

One exemplary expression of these optimistic attempts to reunite art and technology can be found in the writings of the critic Gene Youngblood. His book *Expanded Cinema* (1970), though in many respects a perfect example of some of the more uncritical excesses of Sixties' new consciousness, nevertheless expresses and underscores what was seen as essential to the new art. Sharing the same euphoric, futurist tone as the work of McLuhan – which it in large part fed on – in its invocation of the 'Paleocybernetic Age'; the book traces the evolution of a new cinematic language, premised on the proliferating communication and computer technology, which entails the end of fiction, drama and realism: the collapse of art into life. Familiar conceptual fascinations permeate his discourse, a similar questioning of traditional notions of reality and representation, content and meaning, and an emphasis on the ways in which the emerging new forms involve the recapturing of the senses from the mind or intellect.

The nascent 'synaesthetic cinema' for example '. . . pure drama of confrontation. It has no "meaning" in the conventional sense. Its meaning is the relationship between film and viewer. We are interested more in what it *does* than in what it *is* as an icon. The confrontation of art and spectator, and the spectator's resultant self-perception, is an *experience* rather than a meaning.'[10] As for the trend in computer imaging he says:

If the visual subsystems exist today, it's folly to assume that the computing hardware won't exist tomorrow. The notion of 'reality' will be utterly and finally obscured when we reach that point . . . [of generating] totally convincing reality within the information processing system . . . We're entering a mythic age of electronic realities that exist only on a metaphysical plane.[11]

Further expression of such notions are found in the pronouncements of video artist, Nam June Paik, who began to talk, in the late-'60s, of future art forms in terms which anticipate completely new levels of *interaction* and *interfacing* between the artist and/or participant and the work itself, calling such art 'Direct-Contact Art'.[12]

Thus the experimentation by artists with computers in the Sixties was very much part and parcel of an emerging 'new sensibility' described at the time by such influential (proto-postmodernist) cultural theorists as Marshall McLuhan and Susan Sontag. This may be described as an euphoric technological determinism coupled to the celebration of the senses over the intellect.[13] As such it seems to have been all but exhausted as a movement by the turn of the Seventies. Work undertaken by artists in the Sixties with the new electronic technology, didn't produce the kind of results expected. The initial stir caused by the eruption of Pop Art had been negotiated and recuperated to finally hang respectably on museum walls. The more directly technological art on the other hand never really seemed to get off the ground. Not only computer films, but other works produced at that time under the broad banner of new technological or cybernetic art – light shows, kinetic works, systems art, intermedia theatre, expanded cinema, and so forth – seemed to disappear in the early Seventies, exhausted. This movement never really began to prove itself as the panacea for the malaise modern art found itself in as it entered the Sixties. One of the main reasons given for this fall was that of a growing disenchantment with technology by the end of the Sixties. By the early Seventies the extremely damaging effects which many technologies were having on the environment had quickly led to a strong and growing ecological movement in the United States. Similarly, critical connections were beginning to be made between the 'state of the art' technologies being deployed at the time in the 'automated battlefield' that was Vietnam and the precise nature of the costs they entailed. Finally, the new media, especially television, came in for revised critical scrutiny: no longer, pace McLuhan, the means whereby 'community' is returned to the whole of humankind, rather, a means for maintaining mass docility through the promotion of ignorance.[14]

A casualty of this general disillusionment with technology, it seems that computer art had gone as far as it could within the then current technological state of the art, and that this hadn't in fact been very far at all. Again, Michael Noll, who'd been involved in computer graphics research at Bell Labs since the early Sixties encapsulates the emerging reservations. In a paper published in 1970 – which was significantly less sanguine than the one he wrote in 1967 – he wrote that

> *The computer has only been used to copy aesthetic effects easily obtained with the use of conventional media, although the computer does its work with phenomenal speed and eliminates considerable drudgery. The use of computers in the arts has yet to produce anything approaching entirely new aesthetic experiences.*[15]

Although artists do not drop completely out of the developmental picture at this stage, it is other currents with different motivations and ideas which take on the project and continue to explore the imaging potential of computers. Before long the unsystematic experimentation of the Sixties disappears and is replaced by research and development programmes geared much more to commercial utilisation.

Pausing momentarily to take another look at the specific use to which the computer was being put in the visual arts at this time, it is I believe significant that a great deal of energy, in certain quarters at any rate, went into attempting to utilise the formidable *copying* or *simulational* power of computers. This was already being looked upon as one of the computer's most interesting and promising features. At the end of the Sixties, according to art theorist Jack Burnham, who at that time was involved in putting together an exhibition called 'Software' for the Jewish Museum in New York: 'At least two-thirds of extant "computer art" consisted of computer programmes designed to simulate existing styles.'[16] A good example of the latter are the series of original computer-generated simulations of Piet Mondrian's abstract painting style from the period around 1917 which were produced by Noll at Bell Laboratories and exhibited in the *Cybernetic Serendipity* show held at the ICA in London in 1968.

As to the 'entirely new aesthetic experiences', mentioned by Noll, though not yet technically feasible, they were already being anticipated and moreover actively sought by workers in the field. Cybernetics, with its ideas of artificial intelligence,

human/machine symbiosis and the like, helped greatly with the location and definition of the key elements around which it was felt future forms based on computer technology would revolve. The most important thing to note in all of this though is that it was *not* those artists interested in computers who were the ones working towards the realisation of these perceived possibilities. It was rather those tied to the R&D sections of the military, large corporations, universities and so forth. Significantly, by the early Seventies the computer scientist Ivan Sutherland (inventor of 'Sketchpad' and later, founder of the giant computer corporation Evans & Sutherland), having extended his initial research in computer graphics into the realms of colour and the simulated experience of three-dimensional space, claimed that through his computer displays he had, 'landed an airplane on the deck of a moving carrier, observed a nuclear particle hit a potential wall and flown in a rocket at the speed of light'.[17]

This statement is illuminating. It signifies at once not only the fascinations and preoccupations of the technician, as well as the kinds of uses and applications to which computer imaging research has subsequently been put, but is also interesting insofar as it coincides with much of the later, present day, mass cultural developments of both form and

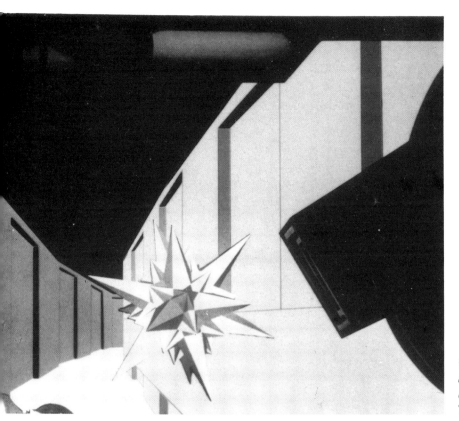

*Computer and live
action image
combination (from
Tron)*

content. We need only think, for examples, of the arcade 'wargames' or 'shoot-em-ups' and the spaceship or aeroplane pilot positioning or point of view of the player in such games; or of the (hard) science fiction content of both computer games and recent computer-assisted feature films, *The Last Starfighter* (1984) for example.

In a certain sense, Nam June Paik, Jack Burnham, Gene Youngblood and the other artists and critics of the Sixties who, somewhat prefiguratively, saw a future for the new computer-based technology in terms of *interaction* and *simulation*, were quite right. Simulation, the representational copying or modelling of phenomenal reality on a two dimensional screen (as well as in three dimensional, *occupiable* space) has increasingly engaged the attention of computer graphics research since the turn of the Seventies. The difference however is that the applications to which this has been put, and the different forms which have developed out of it, especially within the cultural sphere, do not coincide with the ones anticipated by those involved in Sixties art. Computer technology and especially its imaging potential has developed and flourished within a context which dearly holds onto and promotes – as perhaps its most fundamental tenet – a still dominant ethos of optimistic technophilia. What distinguishes the Eighties from the Sixties however, is that in the meantime this ethos has been in a sense *domesticated* within the discourses, forms and institutions of a mass mediated or so-called popular cultural sphere which is largely controlled and determined by multi-national entertainment corporations.

Thus the second period of computer imaging development, stretching from the late Seventies to the present, and involving massive commercial expansion based upon the huge reduction in costs which followed the intense development of microelectronic circuits, is today largely determined by a new set of discourses which revolve around a certain notion of aesthetic realism. In part this rested on developments in technical means which significantly improved image quality and definition ('raster graphics') and opened up new vistas in the mid-'70s for those attempting to generate (or simulate) more 'realistic' looking imagery. It also coincides with the so-called 'return to representation' seen as one of the characterising features of the 'postmodern era'. The three major strands of research, development and utilisation to have emerged in the area in the Eighties are commonly referred to as 'image-manipulation', 'image generation', and 'virtual reality research'. Each of them (though in somewhat different ways) is caught up in this simulational or realist thrust.

Computer image manipulation, or image processing as it is also referred to, is different from the other two strands insofar as the computer is used in such a process to affect changes in images which it has not itself been involved in producing. Thus already existing images (for example, photographs, photographic reproductions, films and videos) are digitally stored in the computer, to be worked on in a multitude of possible ways – from the addition or enhancement of colour to the 'undetectable' addition, rearrangement, replacement or removal of certain features within the image. In 1981 such techniques were only available to those who could afford large and powerful computers. Since then further developments in microelectronics have reduced costs even further while at the same time increasing capacity so that they are now widely used within television, advertising, publishing, video and cinema production. Moreover they are now almost within the reach of personal computer users. With the addition of a digitiser, a monitor and the appropriate software, it is for example, perfectly possible to process or manipulate images on Apple Macintosh's 'Mac II'.

Some indication of the way in which those developing and selling this kind of computer imaging capability understand it can be gleaned from various product reviews. Thus in 1985 when such techniques were really beginning to make an impact in the cultural domain, one review of the TARGA image processing system (similar to the 'Harry' and designed with graphics studios in mind) is entitled 'Captive Video – Editing Reality'.[18] In answer to the question of what one can do with a video image 'captured' by the computer the reviewer says, '. . . paint on it, move pieces of it around, add characters . . . You can alter reality as easily as you can generate a spreadsheet or type a letter.'[19] Though the notion that one is somehow able to alter or transform reality with such techniques is, on the face of it, dubious such ideas are important since they feed directly into crucial, and already well established, debates around questions of realism and photography – on the status of the photograph as (documentary) evidence for example. It is precisely such concern about these proliferating techniques in terms of the weight they begin to add to *relativist* arguments about photography and representation, which is prompting renewed debates in the area of photographic theory.[20]

The progenitor and paradigm for work in the area of what is dubbed (oxymoronically) 'artificial realities' is undoubtedly the flight simulator, which the corporation established by computer imaging pioneer Ivan Sutherland – Evans and Sutherland – has been so instrumental in developing. 'Artificial realities', 'virtual realities', and 'responsive environments' – though not exactly referring to the same thing – stand for an area of research into computer simulation which involves computer imaging as one of its central components. The other major component is the aspect of 'interfacing' or 'interacting' with the programmed simulation. The goal of such research, simply stated, is the construction of computer systems (hardware and software) which construct an 'artificial reality' with which the user may interact as *if* in everyday phenomenal space and time. There are various research projects presently underway in this area of computer simulation, again, primarily it would seem in the United States.[21] These provide a grounding for those who speculate (more or less soberly) on future art and entertainment forms in which they quite literally envisage us as physically 'taking part' in 'films'.

It is perhaps in the area of computer image generation that the realistic aesthetic goal has been most tenacious and influential. The key defining feature of image generation is that the images so produced are created *within* the computer. Basically, there are three stages to this. The first involves the input of data to the computer's memory, which effectively describes or *models*, and then stores, whatever is to be imaged. Once this is done the model can be manipulated, that is, altered or refined in some way. Next the model is converted into a picture; a particular view of the model is chosen and various techniques are then employed to complete or *render* the final image. A variety of techniques have been developed both for the initial introduction of the abstract model into the computer's memory and for the completion process – the viewing and rendering – of the final image. Most of the concentration in recent years has been on the generation of *three-dimensional* imagery, so-called because of the initial model described and stored in the computer. An underlying model which is three-dimensional – even though it is eventually to be seen as a flat image, perhaps printed on paper or displayed on a video monitor or film screen – produces solid looking and hence potentially more 'realistic' imagery.

Since the late 1970s, and thinking here specifically of the mass cultural sphere (television, commercials, feature films, games), billions of dollars have been given over to perfecting both hardware and software systems which will deliver computer generated moving images which appear photographically realistic. Such research has developed and improved all of the stages involved in 3-D image generation mentioned above, including new or improved techniques of modelling, rendering and shading, texture mapping, animation, and so-called 'ray tracing' (a technique which is used to produce photographically realistic effects of transparency, reflection, and refraction).

Speculations in popular writing on the area have turned into or fed the goals of those directly involved in perfecting such techniques. Thus, to take one example, in an early article in *Popular Photography* written in 1976 – ostensibly a review of a small sequence of the film *Futureworld* (1976) which utilises computer image generation – Don Sutherland introduces a range of considerations, among which is the question as to how soon it will be before ('live-action') films will be made without the present technical apparatus. By which he means without actors, sets, cameras and the like, all of which will be replaced by the computer.[22] Somewhat ironically perhaps, one researcher in the field today in dogged pursuit of just this possibility is John Whitney Jnr, son of the earlier computer imaging pioneer. The work Whitney Jnr describes and the ideas he puts forward make him one of the most consistent practical and ideological champions of the kind of realism which dominates current computer imaging. Whitney's term for this visual aesthetic is 'digital scene simulation'. For him the key to simulating live action is 'level of detail and level of detail translates into high resolution pictures containing hundreds of thousands of polygons.'[23] An extraordinarily narrow view of visual aesthetic production emerges from this and similar pronouncements: one which appears to reduce it to the technical manipulation of digital information.[24]

It was the computer graphics company Digital Productions – established jointly by Whitney Jnr and Gary Demos (as teenagers they had worked together on experimental films using Whitney Snr's analogue device) – which developed and produced the (technically speaking) highly sophisticated 'photo-realistic' computer imagery for the feature film *The Last Starfighter* (1985). In order to get the 'hundreds of thousands of polygons' necessary for such high resolution images, plus speed of computation, the company used its Cray X-MP supercomputer, which at that time was the most powerful (and presumably expensive) computer in the world. Teams of designers, engineers and programmers were employed on the project for over two years. The 25 minutes of computer generated film which eventually found its way into *The Last Starfighter* was seen by many reviewers at the time, not only as a milestone in 'realistic' computer graphics, but as the beginning of the gradual, yet eventual, take over of Hollywood by computers'.[25]

Even if by 1988, one can detect a certain disenchantment or wariness on the part of feature film producers with respect to computer graphics and special effects, the reasons for this are not, as one might perhaps be forgiven for assuming, due to any perceived aesthetic shortcomings, not in any straightforward sense anyway. In effect they appear to be twofold and interrelated. Simply, although computer graphics can be less expensive than other ways (eg motion control) of producing special 'realistic' effects, still, the 'level of reality' so produced does not yet justify the savings. This was the verdict of the film production companies when the question of the current state of computer imaging was discussed at the 1988 SIGGRAPH conference. The message then was that, 'the technology hadn't gone far enough'. Nevertheless, Peter Sörenson, reporting on the debate, summed up the feelings which emerged from the meeting with the conclusion that '. . . as the computer graphics cost/realism ratio steadily improves and the expense of building traditional physical sets climbs ever higher (a problem that is already driving a lot of productions south of the border), the outcome will inevitably be resolved in favor (sic) of the digital solution.'[26] Work currently underway on the generation of 'realistic' computer imagery is exemplified by productions coming out of the Lucasfilm spin-off company Pixar (*Luxo Jnr* (1986), *Red's Dream* (1987), and *Tin Toy* (1988)). In addition there are research teams working at the MIT Media Lab, attempting to utilise artificial intelligence to produce 'intelligent' computer generated characters, whilst others are working hard attempting to overcome the problems involved in simulating 'realistic' human action, speech and expression.[27] All of these testify to the continued drive for the kind of images the film producers are looking for.

Of course, there is a huge (and increasing) amount of work involving computer imaging underway in sectors not directly connected to the mass cultural domain. Such realist imaging goals are for example being pursued in military and civil aviation projects, in scientific and medical fields, and in architectural design. However, the reasons given for pursuing research into and/or for computer generated realist images appears to vary somewhat between those who are concerned with broadly cultural (art and entertainment) uses, and those who are looking to more functional uses. In the case of scientists, doctors, architects, designers and so forth, the visual aspect is perhaps less likely to be valued for itself, more likely as a means to some other end. Thus it is important to point out that not all computer imaging researchers operate with the 'photo-realism' conception alluded to above. In such areas as astrophysics and scientific and medical visualisation for example, it has been argued that it is the realistic accuracy of the underlying model or simulation, together with the facility of being able to *interact* with it, which is valued above precise photo-realist representations.[28] And even where such realism is being striven for, in industrial and architectural design for example, the benefits of the high degree of computer produced photorealism in these areas is usually argued along lines such as the following: '. . . if you have ever tried to imagine what a new office would look like from a 2-D layout, compared to actually walking through the facility, you will get the picture. It is now possible to virtually walk through a factory or office on the computer screen, viewing all objects as they would appear in reality, *before anything has been built.*' [my emphasis][29] Similarly, the reason most often given for improved image realism in flight simulation techniques are the benefits involved in such *virtual* rehearsal or testing: 'realism without risk' as one commentator puts it. Though it is important to point out that – just as with the entertainment sphere – high on the scale of underlying motives pressing for developments of this nature are considerations of (eventually) greatly reduced costs. 'Crashing' a simulation of a Moonshuttle or a Jumbo Jet, to take generous examples, saves both money and lives.

On the face of it the two phases of computer imaging development introduced above are somewhat dissimilar, at least when looked at from the point of view of cultural concerns. In the first place, a high modernist aesthetic ethos dominates the initial period in the Sixties, whereas by the beginning of the Eighties a mass cultural ethos dominates. In the former it is abstraction and formal considerations which are crucial, in the latter, photo-realist representation. In the second place, unsystematic experimentation by artists and artist/engineer collaborations gives way to a systematised, applied and commercially oriented development in all spheres, including and especially the cultural. Thirdly, it is crucial to note some of the very different conjunctural features that bear on each phase. On the one hand, the Sixties in the West was a generally euphoric period, economically prosperous, a period of political liberalisation; a time of an initial and generous (both popular and critical) reception of the new electronic technologies. The Seventies on the other hand, sees the emergence of more sober reflections, a deepening economic recession, a political retrenchment, which by the Eighties is constituted by a vicious new conservatism. Eventually, the rhetoric around new technology gets attached to discourses of 'efficiency' and 'consumerism' (functionalism), as it begins finally to 'deliver the goods': things such as, office computerisation, fully-automated manufacture, home computers, and digital systems such as video recorders, cameras, calculators, watches, music systems and computer games.

However, in at least two respects there are important latent connections between the two otherwise different phases of computer imaging history. The first has to do with the initiation and growth of interdependencies between the cultural and the (broadly) scientific domain, the second with questions of postmodernism.

Though little is made of it in the writing on this area to date, one interesting feature which is frequently mentioned or alluded to is the way in which research and development of computer imaging has, from the first, straddled several very different domains. In addition, as I have already noted, apart from the applied research that went on in areas such as flight simulation, scientific visualisation, and computer aided design; there was also, from the beginning, a novel artist/technician collaboration. This last aspect was one of the factors which led several commentators of the late Sixties to herald the dawn of a new art based on a rapprochement between art, technology and science.[30] With the exception of certain isolated instances of artistic sponsorship – William Latham's current Research Fellowship at IBM (UK) for example or the work in 'scientific visualisation' conducted in the United States by teams of engineers, scientists, programmers and artists – such collaborations between visual artists and technicians have patently failed to develop, of if they have, it has not been in a way that was anticipated in the Sixties. What does seem to be happening is a growing interpenetration of techniques and ideas between the mass cultural and the scientific/technological domains.

The instances of computer image researchers presently working in the entertainment sphere who have scientific, military or space development backgrounds appears to be very high. Thus in one review we discover that '. . . the makers of *Star Trek II* . . . needed to show a dead world blossoming with life. [So] they called upon Edwin Catmull, now of Lucasfilm, who sharpened his computerised pencil by simulating spaceflights for the Jet Propulsion Laboratory . . .'[31] Similarly, Gary Demos of Digital Productions and *Last Starfighter* fame, had previously worked on the development of 3-D imaging software for NASA's Space Shuttle simulator. By comparing references to the same person in different articles, a picture begins to emerge of a fairly transient community of researchers moving between domains, though predominantly perhaps the move is away from strictly scientific-functional applications into entertainment related spheres (where, or so one imagines, the financial rewards are much greater). Again, it is possible to discern developments whereby 'realistic' imaging techniques developed in one domain, cross-over and are applied in the other. The cross-over of personnel and techniques are of course part and parcel of the same process of technical diffusion. Developments in the techniques of flight simulation are the example most often mentioned in relation to the development of 'realistic' imagery in other domains.[32] Though, to take another more specific example, the work initiated by Mandelbrot at IBM on fractal geometry and developed later by among others, Loren Carpenter (who was later to join the computer research and development team at Lucasfilm) has been exported and further developed in the domains of commercial graphics and entertainment films.[33]

The extent to which this movement of personnel, techniques and *ideas* involves a two way traffic, that is, a concomitant flow in the reverse direction from 'entertainment' to 'science'; and the speed and level of such movement, is not as easy to discern. This aspect of the history of computer imaging does however raise further questions for those ongoing debates around the ways in which the relatively recent *systematisation* of science-driven research and development has penetrated and determined the increasingly technologically based cultural/aesthetic aspect of modern societies. Or the extent to which, *interdependencies* may be growing between the aesthetic and the (broadly) scientific domains.[34] (As one writer says, commenting on the *subject matter* of much computer imagery: 'No technology previous to computer animation has given such visible identity to our society's worship of technology.')[35]

The current drive towards 'photographic' realism in computer imaging relates to questions of postmodernism in that it is part of the 'return to representation' and the collapsing of distinctions between high and 'popular' culture which has been characteristic of cultural aesthetic developments of the past two decades.[36] Thus from one view, it might be taken as a new (somewhat regressive) expression of the perspectivalist tradition which has dominated Western representation and vision since the Renaissance, and which, despite being challenged by various currents within modernism, is reasserting itself once more in this newly emerging area of image production. However things are, I believe, more paradoxical than this. Simulation appears to be the computer's forte, and its capacity for both manipulating already existing images and for generating *non-indexical* ones seems to mark it as a technology crucial to the increasing autonomisation of the sphere of representation, what Baudrillard sees as the end point of our history of disengagement with the real.[37]

A technology specifically designed for simulation – one moreover that appears to be very much at home manipulating from *within* (so to speak) the already reproduced image ('Paintbox', 'Harry' etc.) – arises thereby at the very moment that culture *becomes* simulation. We only have to think of the computer's utilisation to date in military and civil simulation projects, its increasing role in feature films, advertising, television, arcade and home computer games and so forth; and the kinds of projections which commercial development has in mind once they have perfected the technique. We may cite, for example, the work already underway on the production of simulated, photo-realist stars who will act in feature films alongside live actors; and ideas for the simulated faces of dead rock and film stars to be superimposed over those of live actors in order to produce new rock videos and feature films. Or, beyond this, the work being carried out on the development of 'interactive' or 'virtual realities'. Will such work eventually produce the mass entertainment forms of the future – already anticipated in the narratives of feature films like *TRON* and *The Last Starfighter* – where the participatory adventurer actually comes to physically interact with the simulated characters, objects and events within the game?

Despite the (often) highly exaggerated claims and descriptions of the current state of things which emanate from much of the new cultural theory, the thesis that our proliferating technological media are somehow (and in a profound way) confounding distinctions between the real and representation does seem to be highly persuasive. In this sense present day efforts to further perfect and develop the kind of computer image manipulation and simulation already mentioned seem set to further deepen this confusion. On the face of it there appears to be a much more integrated, systematic and totalising character to the evolution of cultural forms and the practices (of both production and consumption) associated with them than there was; certainly before the Second World War (but also in the Fifties and Sixties). The space for independent developments appears to have progressively shrunk in proportion to the development and proliferation of technical forms – thinking here of the integrative incorporation of the idea of the 'spin off' – as the ties between the various sectors of research and development (military, scientific, corporate) grow ever closer in the post-industrial world. Has the possibility of utilising computers, or indeed any new technological medium, as part of an independent and/or oppositional practice been effectively negated in light of such corporate control? A control which allows, with the resources involved, a constant fuelling of the means of perfecting the vast specular machine that is the media. Though this aspect of postmodern cultural development, tied as it is to Baudrillard's view, carries with it an aura of intense pessimism, it is hard all the same to deny

Acting with computer graphics (from Tron)

its apparent weight as a description of what is happening.

With regard to both cultural practice and theory, the move today, as it was in the Sixties, is away from the exploration of historical, political and economic determinants – considered as somehow inappropriate, passé and unfashionable – and towards the espousal of formalist and indeterminist approaches. In Baudrillard's seemingly hopeless scenario, computers, with their far from fully realised simulation potential, appear to be the last word in the future refinement of the hyperreal: the ultimate technology of an irreversibly imploding system bringing about the disappearance of the real and meaning, the growth of fascination with surface and hyperconformity. The extent of the inevitability of this state of affairs, and the propriety of such positions, constitute vital and pressing questions for both practitioners and cultural theorists alike as such new media forms evolve and begin to take effect.

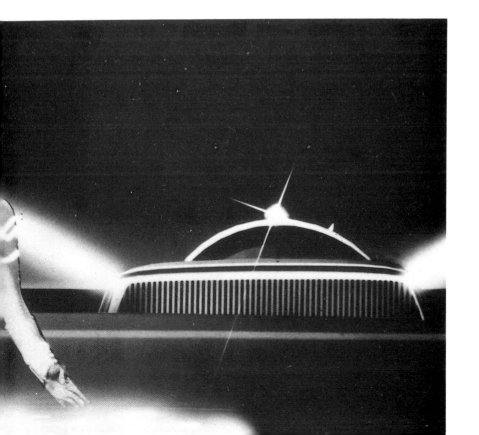

Notes

1 Where 'technical' is understood, in a very narrow sense, as having to do solely with the development of new or improved ways and means to produce images and effects, (usually of a kind that aim for photographic realism).

2 Daniel Bell *The Coming of Post-Industrial Society: A Venture in Social Forecasting* London, Penguin 1976.

3 Ivan Sutherland is, I believe, someone who exemplifies such a position. I introduce the important work he has undertaken in the main body of the text.

4 John Whitney Senior 'Animation Mechanisms' *American Cinematographer* January 1971 p26.

5 See the interview with John Whitney Senior in Gene Youngblood *Expanded Cinema* New York, Dutton, 1970 pp213-217.

6 Gene Youngblood *ibid* p215.

7 John Whitney Senior 'Motion Control: An Overview' *American Cinematographer* December 1981 pp1220-1262.

8 Though much interesting previous commentary on Pop Art has been concerned with attempting an assessment and understanding of it in terms of its significance (or lack of it) as either critical or affirmative art, it is rather the aspect of Pop Art's return to representation, and particularly its turn to *representation itself* for its content or subject matter which I would like to signal for the purposes of this essay.

9 Michael Noll 'The Digital Computer as a Creative Medium' *IEEE Spectrum* October 1967 pp89-94.

10 Gene Youngblood *op cit* p126.

11 *ibid* p206.

12 Nam June Paik, cited in David Douglas *Art and the Future: A History, Prophecy of the Collaboration between Science, Technology and Art* New York, Praeger 1973 p106.

13 See Marshall McLuhan *Understanding Media: The Extension of Man* London, Routledge and Keegan Paul 1968; and Susan Sontag *Against Interpretation* New York, Delta, 1978.

14 This last point is I believe significant. For as the 1970's progress, both the dominant tone as well as the emphasis of the discourse on art or culture and technology appears to change somewhat markedly. This undoubtedly has a great deal to do with the increasing reception and absorption of – rediscovered and reinflected – structuralist, semiological and formalist approaches to understanding culture and society. Two important upshots of this were that in the first place, it brought about a revised emphasis on the exploration of language and meaning and in the second, it encouraged a broader approach to the study of culture; cultural theorists and critics began to treat mass culture with the kind of seriousness they had previously only really reserved for high art. Thus for example in the highly influential theories of Roland Barthes, literary criticism initially discovers a way of reinvigorating and legitimating the concern with meaning and messages while at the same time strengthening commitments to Marxist ideology critique. Similarly, with Louis Althusser's structuralist ideas about ideology and representation, where meaning is not demoted as in the work already alluded to in the Sixties, but is rather recast as an effect of the complex system of structural relations which play the central determining role in the construction of the world. Ultimately however what lurks – certainly behind the

poststructuralist emanations of such explorations of structure and language – with their radical questioning of the idea of the subject, the critique of enlightenment rationality, of dominant ideas of history, and the idea of language as convention, is the question of the legitimacy of the distinction between the real and our way of representing it.

15 Cited in Douglas Davis *op cit* p111.

16 Jack Burnham. 'Art and Technology: The Panacea that Failed', in Kathleen Woodward (ed) *The Myths of Information: Technology and Post-Industrial Culture*, Bloomington (USA) Indiana University Press 1980 p205.

17 Cited in Douglas Davis *op cit* p103.

18 Barbara Robertson. 'Captive Video – Editing Reality' *Computer Graphics World* v8 n12 1985 pp59-62.

19 *ibid* p60.

20 See Martha Rosler 'Image Simulations, Computer Manipulations: Some Ethical Considerations' *Women artists Slide Library Journal* n29 pp18-22.

21 See for example, James D Foley 'Interfaces for Advanced Computing' *Scientific American* v257 n4 1987, pp82-90; and Myron Krueger *Artificial Reality* Addison Wesley p240.

22 Don Sutherland, 'Electric Clones are Coming; Will the Real Peter Fonda please stand up?' *Popular Photography* December 1976.

23 L P Robley, 'Digital Simulations for *The Last Starfighter*', *American Cinematographer* December 1984 p86.

24 This is a conception that bears a striking resemblance to the Shannon and Weaver model of communication as the mathematical transmission of information. See Claude Shannon and Warren Weaver *The Mathematical Theory of Communication* Urbana (USA), the University of Illinois Press 1949.

25 See Peter Sorenson 'Simulating Reality with Computer Graphics' *BYTE* March 1984 pp106-134.

26 Peter Sorenson, 'When Will Computer Graphics Get its Star on Hollywood Boulevard' *Computer Graphics World* 1986 v11 p56.

27 Such work is being conducted for example by Daniel and Nadia Thalman of the University of Montreal Business School and formed the basis of recent PhD research undertaken by Keith Waters at Middlesex Polytechnic.

28 See in this regard, Paul Brown 'The Art of Science' *Computer Images International* October 1988 pp36-39.

29 Robert Burgess 'Simulating Reality with Visual Computing' *Canadian Data Systems* v20 p37.

30 See for example Douglas Davis *op cit*, Jack Burnham (1968) *op cit* and Jasia Reichardt (ed) 'Cybernetic Serendipity: The Computer and the Arts' *Studio International* London 1968.

31 D A Fryxell 'Future films' *HORIZON* July-August 1984 p60.

32 See for example, Don Sutherland *op cit*, and Annabel Jankel and Rocky Morton *Creative Computer Graphics* Cambridge, Cambridge University Press 1984.

33 Robert Rivlin 'The Algorithmic Image: The Challenge of Simulating Nature' *Computer Graphics World* v9 n8 pp58-66.

34 For a fascinating discussion of this question see Paul Virilio *War and Cinema: The Logistics of Perception* London, Verso 1989.

35 Neal Weinstock *Computer Animation* Reading (USA), Addison-Wesley 1986 p253.

36 It is important to note that much of what passes for postmodernist work and theory today is closely associated with that which was characteristic of the crisis of modern art at the

end of the Sixties. The radical shifts of perspective that Pop Art and cultural thinkers of the time such as Susan Sontag and Marshall McLuhan initiated, seem to directly prefigure much of what has resurged as postmodernism in the Eighties. The Sixties, which saw computers used for the very first time for imaging purposes, is an important cultural period. It is the moment when the initial practical utilisation and theoretical reception of media based on the rapid developments which had been taking place since the Second World War in information and systems theory and electronic and computer technologies comes to a head. New forms and conceptions arise in response to these new conditions and there is a strong case to be made for understanding some of them at least, as prototypical ideas of a discourse which though pretty much in abeyance for much of the Seventies has resurfaced again in certain strands of influential Eighties postmodernist practice and thinking.

37   Jean Baudrillard 'The Orders of Simulacra' *Simulations* New York Semiotext(e) 1983.

4

HOLOGRAPHY – ART IN THE SPACE OF TECHNOLOGY
Margaret Benyon, Paula Dawson and the development of Holographic Arts Practice

REBECCA COYLE

A series of experiments with electron microscopy and light led the Hungarian scientist, Dennis Gabor, to first propound the theory of holography in a paper published in 1948.[1] The discovery aroused some interest in scientific circles, but problems with obtaining a light source sufficiently powerful (or 'coherent') enough to produce adequate images meant that holographic technology advanced little during the Fifties. It was not until the introduction of laser technology in the Sixties[2] that a suitable light source was developed to enable effective holographic work.

Holography is a technique of using light waves to record an image of a three-dimensional (3D) object on a two-dimensional photosensitive plate. A laser beam is split into two and, via carefully placed lenses and mirrors, one beam is directed onto the object while the other is sent directly to the plate. The 3D effect of the hologram is created by the 'interference pattern' caused by the scattered light beam reflected from the object meeting the coherent light and being recorded in the photosensitive emulsion. The plate is then processed in a similar fashion to other photographic film. To reconstruct the image, holograms can be viewed by laser light (laser transmission holograms) or by white light, including candlelight or sunlight (white light still transmission or reflection holograms). As a result of different methods of holographic recording, the object seen by the viewer can appear to be behind the holographic surface (a 'virtual' image), in front of it (a 'real' image), apparently inside out (a 'pseudoscopic' image), like the original object (an 'orthoscopic' image) or even on both sides of the holographic plate (an 'image plane').[3]

The technology of a basic hologram is simple and the derivation of the term clear enough (originating from the Green, *holos* – 'whole' and *gramma* – 'message'[4]), yet the cultural form of holography has been characterised in various ways. As Margaret Benyon noted in 1973, the dominant perception of a hologram continues to be as a '3D photograph'.[5] But more recent views have shifted this emphasis, with practitioners in commercial holography such as Paul Newman arguing that 'the greatest thing about holograms is the intensity of spectral colours and movement you can achieve, not the 3D-ness'.[6]

Early holographic work was restricted to the scientific laboratory because of the reliance on laser light and the vibration free environment necessary for a steady image. At this stage, public perception of holographic and laser technology was principally derived from the fantastic applications dreamt up for them in comics such as *Flash Gordon* and *Wonder Woman*.[7] Meanwhile, scientists were developing holography for other purposes, for example, exploring the theory of 'interferometry', or the reaction of seemingly immobile objects to heat, cold and vibration. Later applications led to the use of holography in technological monitoring and other medical, aerodynamic, data storage and optical areas of work.

It was not until the mid to late Sixties that there was any substantial discussion of holography's potential as a medium for art. Prior to this, discussions of artistic merit or implications were generally limited to assertions about the beauty of interferometric movement. In 1968, for example, the Swedish physicist Hans Wilhelmsson, in an article entitled 'Holography: A New Scientific Technique of Possible Use to Artists', enthused that, 'Extremely beautiful results have been obtained with holographic recordings of the distribution of density of gases and in shock waves, which are produced in a gas when a bullet is fired through it.[8] Such associations inevitably led to a pessimistic view of this technology by those less enamoured by the pseudo-Futurist pleasures it appeared to offer. But as the pioneer holographic artist Margaret Benyon emphasised in 1973, 'An artist working with aspects of new technology should share the concern for the social misuse of it . . . instead of sitting back and 'doom-watching'. I see holography as being part of a future world in which the grass would also grow.'[9]

The growing use of computers and video by artists, prompted in part by the activities of the Art and Technology Movement, led a number of artists to explore the potential of the holographic medium. In 1968, a new form of white light transmission hologram (also known as a 'rainbow' or 'Benton' hologram) was introduced. This form, developed by Stephen Benton of the Polaroid Corporation, had full prismatic colouring. It dispensed with the need for laser to illuminate holographic images, instead using a simple white light source. Both the vivid colouring and the clarity of these holograms had a considerable impact on artists interested in the medium. During this period Lloyd Cross and Gerry Pethick also made holography much more accessible to the layperson by inventing the relatively inexpensive and easily constructed sandbox vibration isolation system. As a result of these innovations and the foreshadowed broadening of the holographic sector, the first holographic gallery, Editions Inc, opened in Ann Arbor in 1968, exhibiting both technical and 'creative' holograms.

Around this time, artists such as Margaret Benyon (in Britain) and Bruce Nauman (in the USA) began to produce a significant body of holographic work. Benyon's optical paintings and work with scientists at the National Physical Laboratories led to an art fellowship studying holography at Nottingham University. In 1969, the University art gallery hosted an exhibition of her holographic work, now acknowledged as the first solo art holography show. Bruce Nauman developed pulsed laser portrait holograms with the Conductron Corporation and, in 1969, exhibited at the Knoedler Gallery in New York. As with other late Sixties media such as video, these public displays of new technology artworks attracted the attention of certain of the more fashionable art institutions and entrepreneurs. With this, holography moved out of the laboratory and into the public cultural arena.

In the early Seventies, holographic research focused primarily on data storage rather than on new recording systems.[10] One result of this was the introduction of new fine resolution emulsions developed specifically for holography by Kodak and Agfa Gevaert. These facilitated sharper and brighter holographic images and thereby heightened commercial and art market interest in the medium. One notable early instance of the improvement in visual definition and quality was demonstrated in a hologram of a hand holding a diamond bracelet which appeared to protrude from Cartier's New York showroom. This attracted huge crowds, caused traffic disruptions and drew mixed reactions from critics and commentators.[11]

By the mid Seventies, gradual development of the medium resulted in a variety of holographic phenomena, such as early animated portraits using pulsed laser, the development of motion picture ('multiplex') holograms, refined acoustical holography, and, perhaps most significantly for its commercial contexts, the establishment of means and facilities to mass produce embossed holograms.[12] As the Seventies progressed, holograms were gradually introduced into a variety of public contexts such as shop window displays, commercial exhibitions and portraiture. These uses have now expanded to include routine applications on everyday items such as credit cards, souvenir trinkets, home video packaging and the covers of magazines and blockbuster novels.

The Seventies was also a significant period for the development of holography production training in Britain and the United States, with innovative courses offered at centres such as Lake Forest College in Illinois and Goldsmiths' College of Art in London. A number of artist-in-residency programmes were also developed during this period, such as that mounted by the Arts Council of Great Britain to encourage artists from other disciplines to use holography. The first regular holographic publication also emerged in New York, *Holosphere*, a monthly newsletter featuring contributions from both scientists and artists.[13]

Along with these expansions in commercial use and education came the first institutional legitimation of holography as a creative medium: the establishment of the state-funded Museum of Holography in New York in 1975.[14] The museum's collection of early holograms and exhibitions of holographic art have made it an important focus for holographic work over the last fifteen years. After 1975, further holographic galleries and museums opened in several major cities, including 'Laser Light Concepts' in New York, 'Third Eye' in Paris, 'The Hologram Place' in London and Yuri Denisyuk's museum in Leningrad. A number of significant shows exhibiting holographic work in traditional fine art contexts also took place in this period: the two 'Light Fantastic' shows at the Royal Academy of Arts in London, 'Sculptures de Lumière' in Strasbourg, and the American 'N-Dimensional Space' show – which attracted additional attention through the (minimal) participation of ageing Surrealist artist Salvador Dali. The interest that such exhibitions developed in the late Seventies became apparent when Eve Ritscher staged the 'Light Years Ahead' holographic show at the Photographer's Gallery in London in 1980 and broke all previous attendance records.

Although these holographic exhibitions attracted critical interest and were fairly extensively reviewed, critics seemed hampered by the lack of a vocabulary with which to describe and critique the form. Even artists themselves seemed at a loss to adequately describe their work. In 1978, for instance, the best description which American holographer Anait Arutunoff Stephens could come up with was that 'hanging "space" on a wall' and 'sculpting with light waves' made her feel that she was 'in real "space-time"'.[15] Although a little more circumspect, S Baher reviewed the New York Museum of Holography's travelling show, 'Through The Looking Glass', with a mixture of reservation and wonder, rather than critical analysis, stating that

> . . . there is something of the conjurer's art here, and a great deal of technical proficiency. I know it is still in its infancy, I know that holographic techniques haven't worked out the problems of color and the limitations of size, but holography is still one of the most exciting, visionary, promising art forms around.[16]

The *God-Given* Art of Technology

> Holography is going to develop as soon as it gets the money. It certainly won't go away; it's based on the fundamental principles of light. It's so fundamental it seems almost God-given.[17]

Rob Munday, Royal College of Art, London, 1988.

Institutional and critical responses to holography were somewhat tentative in the Seventies, with critics only engaging with holography in the most superficial and/or speculative of ways. Yet a small group of artists was already beginning to explore the more profound implications and potential of the medium. Prime amongst these was the British holographer Margaret Benyon. Benyon had begun her involvement with holography at an early stage in its development. She describes her early work and attitudes to holography in a seminal article 'Holography as an Art Medium' published in *Leonardo* in 1973.[18] After graduating from the Slade School of Art in 1962, she began working on projects which attempted to question and re-figure a number of contemporary assumptions about the nature of visual art. As early as 1963-64, for instance, she was using the interference pattern on which holography is based, 'in order to question the abstract expressionists' assumption that the criterion of excellence in a painting was that it should be treated as a flat surface.'[19] For her, the purpose of using such technology was that it 'offered a means of altering the picture plane spatially without reverting to Renaissance space, perspective and traditional illusionism.'[20]

Benyon's holographic work went on to challenge other accepted notions of fine art and experimented with pictorial elements such as light, space, colour and form. Cubism provided an important starting point in this area and she responded to Cubist attempts to render three dimensional materiality without recourse to traditional painting techniques of perspectival or colouristic logic. Playing on the familiarity of the early Cubist work by Picasso, *Les Demoiselles d'Avignon*, which Douglas Cooper has described as 'an invaluable lexicon for the early phase of Cubism',[21] she produced a hologram of a three-dimensional model of the painting in 1970. In this, she attempted to 'comment on the way holography automatically achieves the aim of Cubism to show three dimensions on a two-dimensional surface'.[22] Her concern with aspects of spatial and tactile reality relevant to the representation of material objects on a two-dimensional surface and her awareness of the viewer's desire to *take hold of* holographic objects, paralleled the concerns of Cubists such as Georges Braque, who once said, 'It is not enough to make people see what one has painted . . . one must also make them touch it.'[23]

Benyon's art historical trajectory was modified at an early stage by her concern to broaden the potential public for holographic images and work. During 1969-70, she produced a series of holographic still-lifes in which she attempted to familiarise viewers with less 'abstruse subject matter.'[24] However, this approach also had its problems since the veracity of the representational images gave them a 'wonder effect' which arrested viewers' attention:

> *The reaction of most people on their first look at a hologram is one of astonishment and occasionally disbelief. They look through what appears to be an almost clear piece of glass, as if through a window, to see on the other side a three-dimensional image which looks like an actual scene but exists only in the form of light. They have a strong desire to reach round the glass and touch objects that they can see round and behind, and, if they attempt to do this, their fingers pass right through the image.*[25]

Benyon's identification of the 'wonder effect' as an impediment to deeper engagement with the medium developed into an attempt to demystify holography and holographic production. Although she continues to identify herself as 'a worker in the blurred area traditionally known as fine art',[26] she has always been concerned to break down the barriers between fine art, especially painting, and the general public. In her 1973 *Leonardo* article, she argued that holography's relative lack of prescription by complex cultural tradition and codes has meant that it is 'perceptually a more direct medium', by which she meant that 'to experience a hologram one needs no special art education. The illusion is self-evident.' But, as she also emphasised: 'This is not to say that there are no difficulties in viewing the hologram – in our culture a sophisticated awareness of three-dimensions is undeveloped.'[27] In her later work, Benyon overtly attempted to demystify holography and educate the public by creating, for example, hand held pieces on rocks 'that can be handed around' and work 'as part of the furniture' hanging on the wall 'in a way you can live with'.[28] Her perception of holography as 'a powerful way of affecting human sensory response' led her to challenge accepted notions of reality through work with pseudoscopic space, that is, turning objects 'inside out'; holograms of phenomena normally invisible to the eye, such as currents of hot air (see Fig 5: *Hot Air*[29]); doubly exposed holograms in which objects appeared to float in space; and triply exposed holograms in which three separate images can be seen as the holographic plate is turned from side to side.

Benyon collaborated with many scientists, engineers and technicians in order to build up a repertoire of holographic skills. She was a pioneer in creating her own holograms and is interested to develop new techniques of holography. Yet, like many artists, she eschews technical development for its own sake. In 1973, she stated that, 'Increasing the availability and flexibility of the medium is of more interest to me than virtuoso work, such as full-colour holography.'[30] The tension between highly developed technical skills and artistic content was still seen to be a problem in 1988, according to David Trayner of Richmond Holographics in London: 'One of the problems with holography has been that often more creativity is put into the application of a technique than the subject of the hologram'.[31]

As holography moved into the Eighties, certain categories of holographers developed. In 1988, artist Andrew Pepper characterised these as follows:

– The holographer, 'as someone who makes holograms, perhaps on a technical level'.

– The creative holographer, 'someone who uses the process in a creative way, not just as a technical recording process'.

– The holographic artist, 'someone who is an artist working exclusively with holography'.

– The holographic designer, 'someone who applies creative ability and knowledge to solve a particular problem provided by a client'.[32]

Margaret Benyon's
Tiresias
(1981 – white light
hologram)

While these distinctions are to some extent arbitrary and serve to reinforce assumptions about the differences between 'technical facilitation' and creativity, the identification of distinct occupational sectors serves to indicate the development and divergences in holographic practice during the Eighties.

In particular, the spread of relatively low budget commercial work and the privileging of the scientist in the holographic arena caused concern amongst many holographic artists in the mid to late Eighties. In 1985, Harriet Casdin-Silver argued that commercial-industrial holography was creating a proliferation of cheap low standard work[33] which was likely to adversely affect public perceptions of holographic art. She then declared 'another concern' to be 'the second class citizenship in this supposed union of scientists and artists' and went on to assert that the "step-child" syndrome of the holographic artist must be dealt with'.[34] Debates around the relative status of artist and scientist in holographic practice continue today, focusing on the argument that artists have relied too heavily on the research and development by scientists mainly in commercial companies. But as Benyon has emphasised, 'usually it's the artists who develop the forms of holographic technique – the scientists have had a big influence on quality but most of the techniques involved in display holography have been developed by artists'.[35]

In that holography, particularly in the early days, required either a collaboration between a scientist and artist, or the combined skills of artist/scientist, holography called for a new attitude to the production and final outcome of the creative holographic process. These factors concern not only the artist but how 'art objects' are received by public, curators and critics. Furthermore, they beg the question of recognition of those scientists contributing to the creative process. As Benyon points out: 'The credit for exhibitions arranged by artists of laser beams as purely physical phenomena, for instance, should go to the inventor and manufacturers of the laser, rather than to the 'artist'.[36] In 1985, A P Hariharan, a scientist contributing to developments in display holography, summed up the confused role of holography in his query:

A number of people with little or no scientific training are making holograms. It is only too easy to reach the conclusion that display holography has moved out of the realm of science.

The question then is, if display holography cannot be considered a branch of science, and if many of the people involved with it are artists, can it be classified as a branch of art?[37]

The arguments were not, and are still not, unique to holography. Debates around these issues were significant in the Art and Technology Movement in the Sixties. In addition, as the German video and art curator, Friedemann Malsch, points out, 'under the specific terms of so-called Modern Art, holography seems to us more a technique to SERVE art than to BE art. The only value to be art is seen in its 'innovative' character . . . holography is able to produce images never physically seen before.'[38] Furthermore, the arguments do not stop at the medium's association with 'hi-tech'. Critics are still reluctant to accept holography as an art medium due to the vexed issue of the artist's role in the holographic production process. Art critic Peter Fuller, in 1980, questioned where the artist and artistry fitted into holographic art objects, arguing that, 'the very *process* of making a hologram does not allow for the admission of a human imaginative or physical expressive element at any point. The representation is not worked; it is posed and processed . . . hence the hologram remains a particularly dead phenomenon compared with painting.'[39]

But, as Margaret Benyon argued in her 1973 article, the 'requirement of direct intervention of the artist's hand would rule out a large amount of established work in this century . . . In any case, it is becoming widely acknowledged that art does not reside in material entities. The choice of medium is not in itself significant'.[40] Interestingly, in a letter to Benyon in 1988, Simon Wilson from The Tate Gallery's Education Department used a very similar argument to elaborate his previous view that 'these things (computer drawings, holograms, micro-photographs) are not art as understood by the Tate'.[41] He stated that, 'Modern art is notoriously not medium specific and this question therefore is not one of medium but of the thing's . . . quality as art', before raising the possibility that 'the Tate might be in ignorance of the existence of high quality art being made in the medium of holography'.[42]

The progress of holography's claims to be taken seriously as an art practice have not always been aided by those involved in holographic practice. Some practitioners have aspired to traditional artistic status without being sufficiently familiar with the complexities of the nature and function of art in (Western) culture. As recently as 1988, holographer Nancy

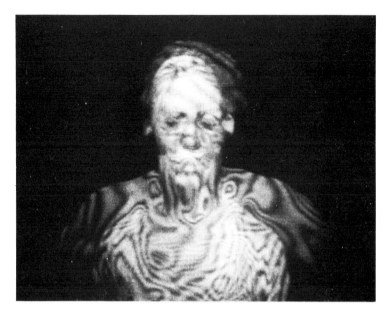

Margaret Benyon's Hot Air (1970 – laser transmission hologram)

Gorglione of the Cherry Optical Company in California could still assert that:

> *Holography offers new, unexplored opportunities for the creation of beauty.* **The function of art is the creation of beauty.** *The study of three-dimensions: depth, projection, parallax, space, space within space, volume, planes, kinetics and color shifts join the artist's traditional challenges of the arrangement of color, line, composition and form in search of beauty.*[43] (my emphases)

Such a description may describe decorative visual practice but effectively reinforces and colludes with the opinions of traditional critics such as Fuller. These critics have been keen to dismiss the medium for its new technological basis rather than acknowledge its potential for communicating powerful human and aesthetic values – a potential which holographers have finally begun to address in the Eighties.

Reinscribing the Human Dimension

> *Technology was something which was over, which was completely unfashionable. It wasn't yet the wave of the new conservatism and Post Modernism wasn't really thought*

of. We were studying people like John Cage, Robert Smithson, EAT and MIT with nostalgia. We looked back at the way technology was seen as a humanising influence, of amplifying small human things in order to make them obvious. That whole aesthetic was the wonder and beauty of technology. But I'm part of a new generation of technology artists who have really changed the paradigm completely.[44]

Paula Dawson, 1989

By the Eighties, as Dawson emphasises, the euphoria over technology and the Art and Technology Movement had faded at the same time as artists' use of various cheaply available forms of new technology had become relatively commonplace. Holography had also established itself and, to an appreciable degree, stabilised. The Museum of Holography in New York continued to attract a modest flow of visitors, exhibitions came and went in other Western cities and basic holographic work began to manifest itself in commercial contexts, on credit cards, magazines like *The National Geographic*, 'special' promotional packaging and the like. The 'realist' aesthetic, typified by Benyon's 1973 description of the hologram as '3D photograph'[45] became the dominant style and perception of holography and indeed the purpose, function and aesthetic of holography in general.

   Whereas the majority of holographic artists working in the Sixties and Seventies had been mainly involved in establishing and consolidating this realist aesthetic, a new wave of Eighties practitioners began working *against* this. This follows the classic pattern of avant garde (modernist) rejections of the dominant realist aesthetics of other forms such as painting, sculpture, literature, cinema and so on. A significant strand of recent holographic work has therefore seen a conscious rejection of realist aesthetic conventions in favour of formal experiments which have attempted to critique and deconstruct just what the previous generation of practitioners had seen as *essential* and *implicit* in holography. In the mid Eighties, artist Al Razutis summed up this tendency, stating that:

> *. . . in the last few years, and especially at the level of formal development, all hell has broken loose in holography . . . we have an abundance of strangeness and 'shaking loose' of the syntax. We also have, which is more important, constructivism, expressionism, etc that must be read as a departure from its painterly equivalents.*[46]

Such approaches were important for the medium to demonstrate its potential to develop beyond the parameters it had adopted for itself – though whether they will ever develop sufficiently to constitute more than mere formal experimentation is, of course, open to question. More interesting as an exploration and extension of holographic work has been the address in some artists' work to issues of human values and subjectivity, and the manner in which they can be addressed in holography.

Otto Piene, head of the M I T Centre for Advanced Visual Studies, has identified three elements in the environment which have been traditionally viewed as hostile to new technology – dirt and dust, anything sexual, and anything wet or liquidised.[47] It is, however, just these aspects that new holographic artists wishing to re-inscribe the human dimension in holography have turned to. As Dawson notes, high-technology work such as holography has customarily been situated 'in a sort of asexual environment' where 'bodily functions and such things are subverted in favour of keeping the support system and the machine going'. But she states that these elements are 'entirely the subject matter of my work – places which are dirty, and watery and emotional and sexual or sensual . . . that's why my work just doesn't cut with that tradition . . . my work typifies what I think the newer generation of technology artists have to say'.

Dawson is one of the most prominent of the new generation of holographic artists. After completing studies in art education at the State College of Victoria at Melbourne in 1975, she won artist-in-residence positions with several holographic establishments and research centres.[48] Like Benyon, Dawson has worked alongside scientists and technicians but is not motivated by the technology of holography per se. Unlike many other contemporary technology-artists, her entry into holography was not through an early fascination with the medium itself but rather because she 'was doing dance and performance which had to do with time. I was finding that that wasn't exactly the best way of doing it. I didn't really want to make myself the object. I wanted to be abstracted from my work, yet present an object – and found that very problematic. It was the concept that came first and holography next'. She sees herself and her generation as moving beyond the concerns and tradition of Sixties practice and groups such as E A T. Yet her attraction to holography was the result of the convergence of a conceptual approach and previous holographic work:

'For me, an important influence was the idea of neo-Platonism and notions of the object having layers of meaning. So I wanted to engage viewers on various levels and the way of doing that came from reading about Margaret Benyon's work.'

The fact that holography can be appreciated by viewers with different levels of art education and critical awareness continues to interest Dawson. Like Benyon's work, Dawson's holograms work on different levels of understanding. A grasp of art history reveals links between some of Benyon's work and elements of Cubist painting. Dawson also claims to be influenced by notions explored in Cubism but defines her orientation as 'post-Cubist'. Yet while Benyon's early work in particular is concerned with its place within the art establishment, as well as in the eye of the public, Dawson sees herself as being free to operate as a subset of both, readily accepting disassociation from the established art world and yet recognising the easy appeal of holograms in everyday use:

Your appreciation of any art work is of course dependent on your education. I think it goes without saying that people can appreciate a hologram in any form because of its 'ooh aah value'. So I've felt that I can be as esoteric as I like in the medium. It has given me the freedom to add the depth that I want, yet it's so weighted with trash and kitsch that it's absolutely liberating. It's not taken seriously by the established art world anyway so I have no axe to grind. There's no barrier to break down because there's no barrier there in the first place.

Where some artists have worked solely with white light transmission of 'rainbow' holograms, Dawson's holographic work to date, with one exception, requires reproduction by laser and must be viewed in low interior light. This has placed some limitations on the possibilities open to her but also created advantages for how the work is viewed. It removes her work from the standard gallery interactive exhibit, with all the associated rituals, expectations and forms of behaviour; as she emphasises:

One of the things that I don't like is the feeling that people are on display when they're viewing art in an art gallery. Any interactive work . . . becomes more or less a performance

on the part of the person who's interacting . . . Up to now, my holographic work you have to look at in the dark, so the performance aspect is removed. It's more like going to the cinema . . . You as a person aren't being challenged; you're almost invisible. I try to make my work as cosy as possible so that you're not feeling threatened.[49]

'Notions of time' and the 'degeneration of orderliness' in Paula Dawson's To Absent Friends (1989)

This element of 'cosiness' is fostered to the extent that the viewer reacts to the work with familiarity:

People come up so close to the picture plane that they actually touch it . . . It's very unlike a painting which forces you to stand at a particular distance – it beckons you, it calls you to come up . . . I like that kind of interaction between people who are viewing the work and the work itself.

Dawson refers back to certain elements of the Sixties techno-art tradition, such as combined light and sound works, by incorporating ironic references to them in her work. Her 1989 work, *To Absent Friends* is based on an hotel bar room and includes a jukebox synchronising music and lights in what she describes as 'the general public assimilation of Sixties high technology art; that is, an item which one can purchase which has become part of every bar'. The new generation of artists departs from the predominant drive of the Art and Technology movement and from former technology artists and theorists in two main ways: first, in their treatment of the medium as more a tool than an awe-inspiring phenomenon. Many holographers by the Eighties had backgrounds in technology arts rather than in painting and more traditional fine art skills. Second, the new generation of artists is breaking down old stereotypes of holography and creating a new holographic paradigm in the subjects chosen for their work. Dawson's declared preoccupation over the last nine years has been with what she terms 'domestic architecture'. This work has caused misunderstanding and misrepresentation not only because of its making art of everyday objects in a manner eschewed by other recent holographic artists, but also because of its conceptual and material connection of high technology with commonplace elements considered, by some, to be inappropriate in the lab or studio of the technology artist.

Dawson's *There's No Place Like Home* (henceforth *Home*) was made in 1980 and uses holographic images to represent a lounge room within the installation of a suburban home exterior: 'The space depicted in the image matched exactly with the space of the construction of the house. Viewers could enter the house and view the empty space which the image had occupied when they were on the exterior of the house.'[50] The manner in which viewers can see one side of the picture plane and then 'enter the realm of the image' by walking around the 'room' is not only an exciting concept in relation to art but also a challenge to notions of holographic art. Added to this, *Home* explores the role of objects and images in holographic work, and concepts of time and memory. Positions of items and furniture in *Home*, for example, signify past or present uses and emotional bonds with them. The inclusion of unfocused family photographs in the lounge room plays more specifically with time and memory.

At the time of its completion in 1980, *Home* was unusual in its size – being the largest hologram ever made – its use of light sources and its definition of space. For the viewer, the light sources used to create the image appeared to be 'authentic' in that they originated from objects within it. The light from the television set held the reference beam that formed the basis for the hologram of all the items in the room, yet appeared to be a 'logical' light source within the context of an average lounge room. The space prescribed by the holographic image was identifiable and defined by the walls of the living room, unlike many holograms that seemingly float in space, without boundary, or on black backgrounds.

All the items in *Home* were selected for suitability in the vibration-free laboratory – where the hologram was made from a model – and also to consciously represent and fabricate an archetypal living room and the function of objects within it. On one level, the room reflects 'complete normality and banality' and on that level challenges perceptions of reality as the viewer walks into the room, only to discover that the appearance of something familiar, when viewed from another angle, has deceived them. But this very normality and object familiarity in the hologram also provoked superficial interpretations of the work by certain viewers. Several men, for example, concluded that *Home* was about Dawson's love of her own home and therefore served as a holographic snapshot of it.[51]

For all that *Home* uses the precise mathematics and technology of holography, it also represents Dawson's attitude to developing and using high technology for its own sake. She remains convinced that the technique should be subservient to the concept. *Home* was constructed from a model built in the lab and using the most fundamental holographic principles and can be seen therefore as ironically 'home-made'. In that her 1989 work, *To Absent Friends*, also deals with an internal environment, time in relation to stages of life, familiar objects and an emotional context; it represents an addition to her defined body of work spanning a nine year period.[52] Yet *To Absent Friends* moves out of the immediate home and into a place in (Australian) culture where many people (particularly men) go to escape domesticity – the bar. The work incorporates holographic images of bottles, glasses and all the paraphernalia of a working bar in mirrors behind the bar, on the bar counter and table tops, in Christmas decorations and the juke box dome. The time setting is New Year's Eve and, as viewers, we see the degeneration of orderliness in the bar as the evening progresses. Notions of time are once again incorporated into the concept as, with the new year celebrations, we recall the past, enjoy the present and consider the future.

Dawson's latest work-in-progress represents something of a departure from her previous work both in terms of its apparent subject matter and the technology employed. Instead of being based on interior locations, her latest work situates itself in the (natural) landscape. Yet while it moves outside the immediate location of the home, it maintains a commitment to the reality of the everyday. As she emphasises 'the new work is about "nature" or the environment which we, in our new "green" world, have a sentimental view of as "home", that is, as a repository of "true" values, and so on'. In common with her earlier work, she intends her latest piece to explore elements of time, memory and space. The piece is intended to both depict the degeneration of a landscape through careless use by people or changes wrought by natural elements – engaging with the current sentimentality for the environment and the obsession with its preservation – and contrast such changes with the concept of 'enhancement'.

While her work to date has used the most basic of holographic techniques, her new project will use both rainbow holograms, which only require natural light for their reconstruction, and advanced computer technology. She has eschewed computer generated images in the past due to a reluctance to work with material that appeared to be two-dimensional and a dislike of the low resolution of available images but this has now become less of a problem as computer technology has developed. For her new work, she intends to use computer programs to calculate light positions, map landscape contours for the model construction, manipulate information about the surrounding landscape and generate new images for the holograms.

The finished work will be situated at specific sites in the landscape frequented by tourists and will represent a fictitious document about landscape changes in the past and projected onto the future. Its images will be illuminated by moonlight or sunlight at specific times in the night or day and will be a direct comment upon and contrast to the existing landscape. In its subject matter and utilisation of computer, this work intends to experiment with our ability to compact information in an age of high technology. Current facilities available to us via computer and international networking can act as early warning systems to protect our environment from destructive elements. Yet this high technology sits uneasily in the landscape. In this way, the work is consciously an ironic reflection of the 'earthworks' of Sixties techno-art – in which attempts to 'humanise' technology resulted in a glorification of natural phenomena – and recalls earlier uses of it for safety controls in nuclear power plants.[53]

Situating the work outside the gallery context and ensuring its 'user friendly' approach further consolidates Dawson's orientation to the human values in technology. As she emphasises:

There are very exciting and challenging things which need to be addressed in an age which involves the compacting of information due to high technology. There are certain spots on the planet where the impact of this age eludes us and, in general, that's the landscape and our place in the landscape. And that's why it's my site.

Human Values in the Space of Technology

The development of a technology is largely dependent on how much time, money and research is put into it. Hence, technologies linked to defence and commercial applications rapidly advance with assistance from major funders. Dawson argues that this has, to some extent, hampered the growth of holographic art: '. . . things like holography have been really little "ugly sisters" in the information technology world because they don't seem to offer big solutions to problems that fit into those types of parameters. Companies like Polaroid are interested to develop holography for purposes of the home market and domestic usage – miniaturised portraiture for instance – so a tremendous amount of time, money and effort is being spent trying to get colours more real looking.'[54]

In addition, holographic artists, like others working with developing technology, are often tied to 'state-of-the-art' processes and scientists or techno-whizzkids with appropriate knowledge and expertise to assist them realise their ideas. This in itself challenges the notion of the *single* artist and the extent to which the parameters set by the creator of the system or technology limit or contribute to the artistic enterprise. As Dawson has explained, 'particularly if you are working at the leading edge, there's such an enormous amount of information in the process itself to deal with. And then, on top of that, for some artists it means fighting for what they originally set out to do and just trying to keep their head above water in the face of such a daunting and rigid structure.'[55] Sandor Holly, an artist working with a MIDI system interface, has similarly emphasised that problem solving in technology is not necessarily the same as problem solving in art:

People who are coming from the engineering background are notoriously infatuated by the technological challenge, and that keeps them busy enough that they won't have the energy or time to look at what the artistic content of the

*effort is. They may feel that if . . . they conquer the technical
challenges, that automatically qualifies to be an artistic
success, and it's obviously not that way at all.*[56]

As we have seen, in one important sense holography and
holographic arts practice await the communications and media
industries finding a suitable commercial context in which to
exploit holographic technology. Such a context would produce
both a rapid development of broad technology and
commercially available models *and* an expansion of contexts
within which other non-commercial forms might also find
sponsors and audiences. Though still indistinct, there are
signs that these processes are underway. We can, for instance,
perceive the commercial research and development of forms
of expanded cinema such as IMAX and OMNIMAX as
attempts to move towards the, as yet, barely explored
potential of holographic cinema. Additionally, the area of
electro-optics and data storage using holographic principles
seems to be attracting funds and scientific interest. Similarly,
communication technologies might also envisage, develop
and arrive at a use of holography like that pseudo-holographic
message system represented in George Lucas' film *Star Wars*
(1977),[57] where a robot projects a repeated sequence of
Princess Leia calling for help in her fight against the dark
forces of the Empire.

In this way, perhaps the image of Princess Leia is prophetic.
Her plea for help amidst a universe of high technology and
an inter-galactic military order may once have been pure
science fiction. Now, just over a decade after the film's
completion, the American military-industrial combine's
cherished ambition of a real life 'Star Wars' system seems
likely to bring the science fiction to life. In the light of such
concerns, a plea for the reinscription of human values in
technology is all the more crucial.

Thanks are due to: Paula Dawson for granting interviews and
providing assistance with research material; Margaret Benyon
for agreeing to be interviewed; Katie Price for facilitating the
interview with Margaret Benyon; and Friedemann Malsch for
his advice and comments.

1   In his paper 'A New Microscopic Principle' *Nature* May 1948.

2   Emmett Leith and Juris Upatnieks, working at the University of Michigan, effectively re-launched holography by reproducing Gabor's early experiments using Light Amplification by the Stimulated Emission of Radiation (laser) technology. Meanwhile, Yuri Denisyuk in the USSR published papers on white light reflection holograms as early as 1962 but his theories were not taken up until some time later.

3   Other forms of holograms include white light transmission holograms that appear in all the spectral colours and hence are also known as rainbow (or 'Benton' after the inventor) holograms. Multiplex holograms, or holographic movies, are based on putting a specially constructed 35mm film of a rotating object through a special holographic printer to construct a moving, three-dimensional image. Dichromate reflection holograms can be recorded by a special gelatin applied to many different surfaces such as glass. Embossed holograms can be mass produced by white light transmission holograms being embossed onto plastic film from a pattern of microscopic ripples in a metal surface. Pulsed holograms can record living organisms and moving objects using an intense burst of light from a pulsed (as distinct from continuous) laser. These are now commonly used to record portraits of people in action and cute images of lion cubs and puppies. Acoustic holograms use sound instead of light waves, working on the principle of vibration to create an impression on the photographic plate emulsion.

4   *The Shorter Oxford English Dictionary* (revised edition 1978), defines 'Holography' as 'writing wholly by one's own hand' (p975), the prefix *holo* from the Greek as 'whole, entire' (p975), the suffix *-gram* from the Greek as 'something written, letter (of the alphabet)' (p878) and *-graph* as 'The Greek termination was chiefly used in the sense 'written', whence *autograph, holograph, photograph*, etc; sometimes in the active sense 'that writes'.' (p881).

5   Margaret Benyon 'Holography as an Art Medium' *Leonardo* v6 n1 Winter 1973 p4.

6   Paul Newman quoted in Jim Davies 'Gleam Tickets' *Direction* June 1988 p79.

7   These fictitious applications of holography, for example, Wonder Woman driving what is called an holographic car, represent the way that holography, like many other 'new technologies', became a symbol for something new, fantastic and somewhat inexplicable. The popularity of this myth means that for holographic artists, expectations are raised that their work will be animated and in full colour. As Australian artist, Paula Dawson, in an interview with the author in 1990, says, 'the concept of what a hologram is far outstrips its actuality'.

8   Hans Wilhelmsson 'Holography: A New Scientific Technique of Possible Use to Artists' *Leonardo* v1 n2 April 1968 p167.

9   Margaret Benyon (1973) *op cit* pp5-6.

10 This was due in part to cuts in science funding in the early Seventies and some serious questioning of laser safety, most importantly by the Bureau of Radiological Health in the USA. This attracted sufficient publicity to affect the public attitude to laser beams. The prevailing notion of lasers being dangerous or deadly is reflected in popular culture in the use of lasers as

weapons in James Bond movies and *Star Wars*.

11 One older woman tried to attack the 'hand' claiming that it was 'the work of the devil'. Women viewers are commonly observed expressing fear or dislike of holograms. Margaret Benyon speaks of the 'squeals of horror' some of her work has provoked. In an interview with the author, Abe Stiglec, director of the Australian wholesale company, Holographic Imagery, claimed that many women comment on holograms as being 'spooky' or 'weird', regardless of their content. Some commercial companies exploit this attitude and sell holograms of skulls and skeletons.

12 Also of note were: the vast 1 by 1.5 metre hologram of the *Venus de Milo* produced by Jean Marc Fournier and Gilbert Tribillion at Lobe in Besancon, France, in 1975; the production of a holographic motion picture (stereogram) of a computer-generated image of a haemoglobin molecule (called simply *Hemoglobin Molecule*) produced by The New York Art Alliance including Cyrus Leventhal, Hart Perry and Christos Tountas; and the formation of the Multiplex Company production house in San Francisco by Lloyd Cross and Dave Schmidt. Advances in the use of synthesised colour in white light transmission holograms also resulted in Bill Molteni's 'pseudo-colour' holographic stereograms of outdoor scenes which had startlingly accurate localised colour.

13 *Holosphere* was initiated by Bill Bushor and later taken over by the New York Museum of Holography under the editorship of Edward Bush.

14 The Museum of Holography operated as a business by 1975 but was not granted a charter until July 1976. Following this, it was registered as a non-profit organisation, and sought and won state funds. See Posy Jackson Smith 'Posy Writes . . .' *Holographics International* Winter 1989 pp4-5 for further details.

15 Anait Arutunoff Stephens 'My Art in the Domain of Reflection Holography' *Leonardo* v11 n4 Autumn 1978 p307.

16 S Baher in the *Atlanta Gazette* 1978, cited in *Light Dimensions: The Exhibition of the Evolution of Holography* London, Ardentbrook 1983 p40. By 1989, new ways for critics to review holographic work were described by Ian M Lancaster 'A Critic's Lexicon for Holography' and Graham Saxby 'Holospeak: The Linguistics of Holography' in Tung Hon Jeung (ed) *Proceedings of the International Symposium on Display Holography July 18-22 1988* vIII Lake Forest Illinois 1989 pp197-206 and 193-196 respectively.

17 Rob Munday cited in Jim Davies 'Gleam Tickets' *Direction* June 1988 p79.

18 Margaret Benyon (1973) *op cit* pp1-9.

19 *ibid* p4.

20 *ibid*.

21 Douglas Cooper *The Cubist Epoch* New York, Dutton and Co, 1976 p23.

22 Margaret Benyon (1973) *op cit* p4.

23 Georges Braque cited in Douglas Cooper *op cit* p37.

24 Margaret Benyon (1973) *op cit* p4.

25 *ibid* pp1-2.

26 Margaret Benyon (ed) 'Extracts From Writings Pertaining To Creative Holography' in Tung Hon Jeung (ed) (1988) *op cit* p449.

27 Margaret Benyon (1973) *op cit* p4.

28 Margaret Benyon in an interview conducted at her studio in Dorset by Katie Price, February 1990.

29 Margaret Benyon describes this work as, 'the first hologram in

which the technique of backlighting a subject was used . . . This type of hologram, which I called a non-hologram, was later re-named *shadowgram* by Rick Silberman, and is a technique now widely used by artists' (*ibid*).

30   Margaret Benyon (1973) *op cit* p5.
31   David Trayner cited in Jim Davies *op cit* p82.
32   Andrew Pepper cited in Margaret Benyon (ed) (1988) *op cit*, p452.
33   She says: 'I worry about ticky tacky holography. I am wary of the colours in white light holography that make everyone's work look too much alike . . . ' – Harriet Casdin Silver cited in Margaret Benyon (ed) (1988) *op cit* p450.
34   *ibid*.
35   Margaret Benyon (1990) *op cit*.
36   Margaret Benyon (1973) *op cit* p8.
37   A P Hariharan cited in Margaret Benyon (ed) (1988) *op cit* p449.
38   Friedermann Malsch in a letter to the author, February 1990.
39   Peter Fuller cited in Margaret Benyon (ed) (1988) *op cit* p451.
40   Margaret Benyon (1973) *op cit* p8.
41   Simon Wilson cited in Margaret Benyon (ed) 1988 *op cit* p450.
42   Simon Wilson in a letter to Margaret Benyon 1988, cited by Benyon (ed) (1988) *op cit* p450. Friedermann Malsch has argued that reluctance on the part of curators to accept holography within galleries and museums is based on practical considerations such as lack of technical knowledge by museum and gallery staff, lack of hardware for presentation of permanent exhibits, financial considerations (especially for commercial galleries) and, above all, 'the horror which curators have towards the technology' – Friedermann Malsch *op cit*.
43   Nancy Gorglione 'Art and Technology of Cherry Optical Company – 1988' in Tung Hon Jeung (ed) *op cit* p472.
44   This and subsequent quotations, unless otherwise cited, are extracted from an interview with Dawson conducted by the author in Sydney in December 1989.
45   Since 1986 Benyon has been working extensively with holographic portraiture (using pulse laser technology) and face and holographic image painting in works entitled *Cosmetic Series*. These feature holograms of women around the age of 23 years old through which she explores age and the ageing process.
46   Al Razutis cited in Margaret Benyon (ed) (1988) *op cit* p453.
47   Otto Piene paraphrased by Paula Dawson from a speech given at the 1989 Symposium on Art and Technology in Nagoya, Japan.
48   Dawson has held artist-in-residence positions with the Laboratoire de Physique at Optique in France, the Adelaide Festival of Arts in South Australia, New York's Museum of Holography and the Department of Applied Physics at the Royal Melbourne Institute of Technology (and guest worker positions with several scientific companies).
49   Paula Dawson, in an item entitled 'Techno-Art' in the Australian Broadcasting Corporation (ABC) radio programme *Arts National* (produced by Matthew Leonard) broadcast on 7 October, 1989.
50   Paula Dawson 'Holographic Memory Theatre' in Tung Hon Jeung (ed) *op cit* p429.
51   Dawson paraphrased certain viewers' perceptions of *Home* thus: 'These guys said, "oh we think you're a woman and you love your home so much that you made a hologram of it." Well, initially I wanted to punch their faces . . . I learned a lot from that work and the responses to it.'
52   Dawson's *To Absent Friends* shared the Artec Grandprix awarded

by the First International Biennale in Nagoya 1989.

53 For example, Britain's Central Electricity Generating Board using holography to record safety information about advanced gas-cooled nuclear reactors.

54 Paula Dawson in *Arts National* – 'Techno-Art', *op cit*.

55 *ibid*.

56 Sandor Holly, in *Arts National* – 'Techno-Art', *op cit*.

57 The image of Princess Leia was a video effect rather than an actual hologram. But the representation of holographic technology in a Science Fiction movie such as *Star Wars* served to emphasise its high-tech status. Yet, unlike the vast array of hi-tech weaponry in the film, its use to convey a holographic message – a plea for help – gave it a particularly human(e) aspect.

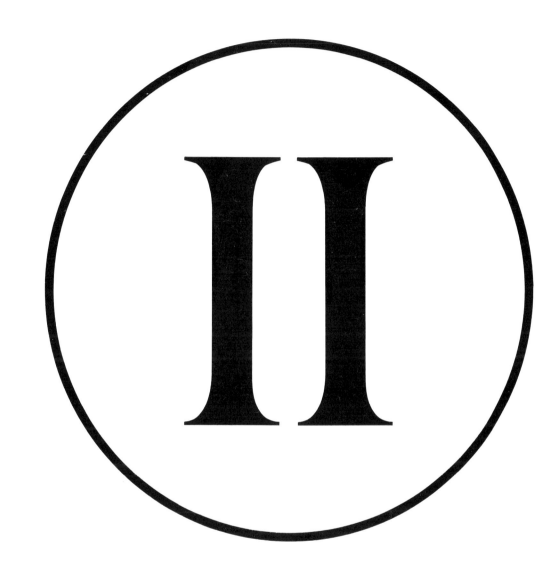

**THE CULTURE INDUSTRIES
AND THE APPLICATION OF
NEW TECHNOLOGIES**

Robert Duvall and
Sean Penn in Colors

THE ARCHITECSONIC OBJECT
Stereo Sound, Cinema & *Colors*

PHILIP BROPHY

Dolby stereo & THX sound

Next to 3-D, stereo soundtrack recording, mixing and presentation are among the most overlooked aspects of film theory and criticism (both modern and postmodern strands). On the one hand, this is understandable. Attempts to describe and articulate the effects of sound in any context – especially one such as film, which is founded on visual discourses and developments – are ultimately disserviced by verbal and literary recourse. On the other hand, it is hard to comprehend this lack of critical inquiry into stereo soundtracks when one considers the *unified* spread of audio-visual technology on the domestic commodity front, as demonstrated by the hand-in-hand proliferation of video formats (VHS, Betacam, Video 8, Video Discs, etc), audio systems (portable hi-fi units, chrome cassette tapes, compact discs, DAT recorders, etc) and the integration of the two. Indeed, the ignorance much film criticism displays with regard to stereo soundtracks finds its reverse image in the familiarity which a large number of consumers have with sophisticated technologies dedicated to fusing hi-fidelity sound with state of the art image reproduction. If hi-fi sound is such an accepted feature in domestic video consumption, why does stereo film sound appear to be so neglected in the critical domain?

This, however, is not to infer that these mass consumers are today's engaged critics, armed with perspectives that afford them instant critical insight, while the learned academics remain stuck in the past with their fading critical methodologies rooted in literature, theatre, painting and photography. Rather, today's mass consumers – *through* their purchase of hi-tech audio visual components for domestic consumption – are possibly more in *material* contact with the contemporary cinematic experience: an experience born from developments in *sound-image fusion* as they have grown over the past fifteen years or so. My point is that while film criticism generally has neglected these developments in sound-image fusion, many people are – without any external critical prompting – totally conscious of the effects, results and plays of these important changes in the cinema. While this observation does not exactly get us anywhere, it is worth noting as a sign of our current technological environment, wherein this is but one of many discursive gaps dotted across the interlocking planes of experience, perception, articulation and consciousness.

Out of such gaps seep the misunderstanding and disinformation which have abounded since the introduction of Dolby soundtracks into cinema chains in the mid Seventies. In fact, the success of the Dolby system may well be responsible for much of the hazy and lazy perception of film sound, accepted as it is despite a widespread unawareness of what it entails. So what is Dolby? Simply, it is a patented noise reduction system employed in the crucial mastering of the final studio mixdown and optical transfer of a film soundtrack[1] which offers a broader frequency range in recording plus minimises surface noise in playback. Combined with high fidelity speakers installed for theatrical playback, the overall sound of a Dolby soundtrack is generally of a higher quality than the forms of optical and magnetic soundtracks film industries had been dealing with over the previous thirty years. In the history of film technology Dolby is a cultural landmark for three reasons:

1   It was the first major advance that brought film sound more in synch with the state of audio recording (for records, hi-fis, etc) which had been developing since the end of WWII.
2   It was a patented system that fairly quickly exerted a monopoly over many film laboratories and theatrical chains, forcing them to go with the market flow and purchase Dolby equipment.
3   It was marketed as a buzz development so that the word 'Dolby' soon became synonymous with 'quality'.

Further to this, the industrial and marketing success of the Dolby system was the prime factor in opening up a broader industrial and artistic context for stereo applications in the construction and presentation of film soundtracks. This is so much so that the phrase 'Dolby Stereo' is perceived as a single technological process, when in fact it is a marriage between a high fidelity recording process (based on encoding and decoding noise reduction) and a 3-channel stereo playback system (left and right surround and/or discrete sound effects with dialogue generally placed centre) – the latter of which had been in existence since the early Fifties.[2]

But even throughout Dolby's first reigning decade, stereo film sound was not entirely without its problems. Apart from the technical problem of projection adaptations, mismatched playback systems and badly designed acoustical set-ups in theatre chains around the world, stereo film sound needed to explore and experiment with its own post-production effects in order to realize what it could contribute to the film narrative without destroying the cinematic text. This means that most stereo mixing in films, right up to the early Eighties, was often as forced and rupturing (or 'artificial' and 'unnatural' if you prefer) as 3-D and all its claims to put you 'into the picture'. Stereo sound generally went for that same, major desire of all postwar technology: to *infuse* you into its environment (aural, visual, tactile, surfacial, sculptural, mobile, etc) through perceptual manipulation – but often with a ridiculously *literal* approach to executing effects, such as:

1 Panning the spoken dialogue across the screen as the characters move across the screen.
2 Alternating the direction of sound occurrences in line with shot/reverse-shot spatial conventions so that when the image cuts to a different perspective the sound simultaneously shifts and suddenly comes from a different point on the screen.
3 Creating ambient or environmental atmosphere sounds in artificial stereo which at times unintentionally make certain scenes appear hollow and cavernous due to the mismatching of on-screen true visual space.
4 Suddenly cutting to a wider stereo mix and often louder surround-sound when musical numbers or manipulative sonic effects overtook the film.

As such, the early stereo soundtrack (which utilised what could be termed a 'planar' approach to spatial mixing, exemplified by the above examples) would often draw attention to itself and break the textual form engineered by the more established production levels of the film. This inevitably went against the grain of many accepted critical modes (most of them unknowingly derived from a Bazanian model of naturalism – yes, Bazin, he who couldn't even handle wide-screen formats!) and thus didn't help push the topic of stereo film sound into the main arena of critical enquiry, dismissed as it generally was as a hi-tech novelty for an audience attracted to fad technologies. (In hindsight, it is amazing that the poststructuralists didn't pick up on the 'rupturing' effect of early stereo film sound mixes, as they sonically blasted you *out* of the movie into the fractured and isolated confines of the theatre.) Whatever the reasons for this dismissal of stereo film sound, the fact remains that it took a decade of experimentation before aural narratology in the cinema could be clearly discerned as having entered a new phase – that of stereo space, sonic detailing across the screen, and contrapuntal movement of sound with mobile camera perspectives (concepts we shall discuss in detail shortly).

Apart from the slow rate at which technological flaws were improved upon in an industry seemingly allergic to change, the narratological ruptures of 'planar' mixing were largely caused by the soundtrack being temporised by the conventional 3-channel set-up. Film sound has had to cope with an inherited logic where spoken dialogue is always placed in the centre (the visual point of conscious focus) with sound effects and music tracks spread into a fairly thin left-right spacing (so as to wrap around the central focus of the dialogue). The point is that sound design here follows the faded yet eternally strained formations of literature and theatre, where 'narrative' is essentially the dramatic housing for character interaction as generated by spoken dialogue.[3] Narrative film is consequently careful to accord a separate and privileged space for spoken dialogue, reinforced by employing stereo spacing in a secondary role, either as (a) an aural background as required by the formalism of an audio-visual reality, or (b) a sensurround 'you-are-there' tactical effect. The transition from mono to stereo film sound has thus been retarded by some overly literal approaches to linking actual acoustic space (by mixing film sound strictly in the left-right-centre framework) with the more complex 'psycho-diegetic' screen space (how one comprehends the conventions of foreground, background, on-screen, off-screen, etc). Even inventive lateral approaches to this problem similarly gambled and lost; such as Sensurround (a cheap but viable carnival-type of trick produced by pumping extra bass frequencies into speakers installed at the rear of the theatre to simulate an intrusion upon the *actual* viewing space, as in *Earthquake* 1974) and Quadrophonic sound (a literal interpretation of sculptural/architectural space which attempted to transform the structural conventions of a four-walled enclosure into a cine-acoustic space, as in *Apocalypse Now*, 1979).

All in all, it had become clear by the early Eighties that the 'planar' approach to the emanation of screen sound was simply too graphic in its spatialisation: film sound needed to be effected and generated in a more *dimensional* way, and that the prime problematic in shaping a dimension was obviously relative to the actual dimensions of the theatre. As the Dolby system was initially linked to a 3-channel technical concept of film sound and thereby linked to speaker configurations which bluntly adhered to the same technical concept, the broadening of the horizons of stereo film sound mixing eventually highlighted the problem with over-simplified and limiting speaker configurations which contributed little to the dimensionality of the acoustic theatre space. Sound mixers were gradually coming to understand how sound could *narrate* within the stereo space of the cinematic text, and their results were making it clear even to producers and directors how important a role speaker placement played in amplifying those effects to an audience. All these factors in one way or another begged a new approach to theatre speaker configuration. Enter THX.

Basically, whereas Dolby is a recording process (or rather, a component incorporated into the recording chain), THX is more specifically a configuration of speaker installment and placement (banks of two-way JBL speakers housed in a specially-built acoustic wall behind the screen, plus attenuated speaker lines around the seating area) designed to enhance and maximise the fidelity of film sound when played back in the acoustic environment of the film theatre. An initial set-back in the Dolby franchise for theatre chains was that – like all audio recording systems – if the speaker installment and placement is not carefully adjusted to its particular environment, the full quality of the recorded sound will not come through in playback.[4] One could say that THX is then more concerned with *playback* while Dolby deals primarily with *recording*, and the THX speaker configuration in many respects *realises* the full sonic potential which the Dolby recording system technically desired. Boasted as 'THX Sound' (and coming complete with its marketing drive as a wonder invention from the Lucas factory) it capitalised on this growing industrial awareness of stereo film sound's greater flexibility and creativity and thus catered to its consequent growing needs by expanding and refining the *acoustic presence* of the stereo soundtrack in playback.

Most importantly, the advent and acceptance of the THX sound system affords us the context to deal with the material production of a 'psycho-diegetics' that is, the means by which one acknowledges the psychological comprehension of dimensionality depicted in film. This involves the reconciliation of perceptual modes with representational codes (which are often at odds with each other) in the projection of a world onto the film's audio-visual screen. (Consider, for example, how images are *on* the screen but sounds come *from* the screen.) 'Psycho-diegetics' are primarily based on a formal relationship between established and accepted time/space factors such as:

1   The physical world as experienced and identified by the viewer.

2 The realistic scenario as translated into a fictional realm.
3 The physical environment of the theatre the viewer sits in.

While it is readily accepted that there are a sophisticated set of visual (photo/cinematographic) and temporal (montage/editing) codes that work in this way and which we read in order to derive a cinematic experience from our cinematic comprehension, it must be highlighted that the same applies to the film soundtrack. This is more marked in stereo soundtrack explorations, mainly because the aural projection of space is difficult to reconcile with the visual framing of space (as mentioned in the early stereo film sound mixing techniques listed above) due to the formal visual logic already established over the past fifty years. Effectively, a total sense of 'psycho-diegetic' space (as opposed to models of either narrative space or on/off-screen space) is needed to fully fuse sound and image under the advanced technological conditions of Dolby and THX. And this is where Spectral Recording comes in.

Spectral Recording

The most recent development to date in this growing field of stereo film sound is a system labelled 'Spectral Recording'. While the spectral process arrived without even the faintest trumpet announcement, its contribution to the technological plane upon which aural narratology grows with continuing strength is major. Credited by its special corporate logo at the end of any film utilising the process, spectral recording is in fact the 4th major development of Dolby noise reduction referred to as 'Dolby SR'. (The other three are Dolby A, B & C.) Like each and every new development in any field of technological invention, Dolby SR 'improves' upon a variety of existing technical processes. In this case the level of sophistication of noise-reduction and consequent signal-to-noise ratio is so great that many recording engineers in the field are comparing the system's capability to digital recording processes. In terms of the system's application in the recording and multi-tracking of a film soundtrack, the increased fidelity also appears to afford greater control in the mixing of film sound.[5] The crucial effects here are to be found not simply in the clarity of sounds, but more so in:

1 *The sonic definition between sounds*, allowing the individual characteristics of multiples of sound to retain their aural identities.
2 *The acoustic definition* between spaces, allowing

interlocking and/or overlapping sounds to be perceived equally in terms of location and movement.

To sum it up, spectral recording thus appears to highlight approaches to *mixing* (as distinct from Dolby's *recording* and THX's *playback*) which fully exploit the broadened audio space offered by wide and multiple speaker placement (such as in THX installations and, to a lesser degree, in some of the better Dolby set-ups in cinemas not carrying the THX system). The finished film sound employing the Spectral process is thereby allowed to inhabit and traverse a variety of spatial dimensions in the theatre, enlivening the film's stereo spacing with a multiplicity of depths, and removing it out of the comparatively flatter, more literal domain of conventional sound mixing as established via the Dolby Stereo 3-channel sound.

Where pre-stereo film sound (since the late Twenties) basically treated the film's audio-visual screen as a static block from which sound emitted as a focussed stream, so that volume was the prime means for articulating spatial difference (low volume = far away; louder volume = nearer; etc), and stereo sound (from the mid Fifties through to the late Seventies) treated the audio-visual screen as a plane divided into channels (devised for a more detailed separation between dialogue, sound effects, atmospheres and music tracks), spectral recording displays the potential to treat the screen effectively as a *spectrum* rather than a *plane*; that is, as a sonic band stretched across to match the peripheral extremes of 70mm screens[6] so that psycho-optical relationships between retinal and corneal fields of vision are matched with the psycho-acoustical sensations of interpreting sophisticated sonic detailing in a full stereo spectrum. In other words, the Spectral process allows the previous *separation* between soundtrack layers (sfx + voice + sfx = left + centre + right) to become fully integrated into a total sonic space.

This fullness of space afforded by the Spectral process allows us to meet the problematics of articulating the effects of stereo film sound head-on because now more than ever, these effects are material and actual. To demonstrate this we will look at a film in detail in order to get a fix on this new phase of aural narratology. It is a new phase because it deals with what I term *'architecsonics'*: the spaces constructed for sounds and musics in the cinematic text, and the consequent ways in which sounds and musics are employed in the construction of narrative. Architecsonics means what it implies: firstly, it is the *sonic* version of 'architectonics' (the systematic arrangement of knowledge as derived from models and principles of architectural structure and practice), dealing for our purposes with acoustic, aural, electronic, harmonic and musical materials and effects which articulate the cinematic text; and secondly, it is the *temporal* reinterpretation of narrative structures as they predominantly exist in the classical architectural manner (ie fixed by frameworks, governed by shape and perceived as an allusion to the logic of 3-dimensional objects).

In looking at *Colors* (1988) we shall see how – due to the film's showcasing of the Spectral process – narrativity is *destructured* and *made temporal*; how it is redefined as a *flow* (not a *shape*) that crosses and creates spaces, contouring and crafting dramatic action so that a 'passage' (in both the spatial and temporal sense) can be presented without recourse to literature's pseudo-architectural scaffolding and ground plans. Plainly, we shall view this film as an *architecsonic* object.

Colors

Before we analyse the soundtrack to *Colors*, it should be pointed out that while this film easily carries the best use to date of the Spectral process, there have been several other major films which have used the same process – explosive films such as *Robocop* (1986), *Innerspace* (1986), *Star Trek IV* (1987), *Action Jackson* (1987), *Moonwalker* (1988), *Batman* (1989). These films, however, feature sound designs based on the creation of a dimensional cacophony into which the viewer/listener is fantastically projected. They do not demonstrate the same sophisticated 'psycho-diegetic' sensibility in their mixing as *Colors*. Herein lies the bluff of technology: any audio or visual recording system by itself never carries an *inherent* capability to realise the extremes of its own potential – let alone transcend them – especially when lateral, multi-disciplinary or creative approaches are required to push a system's effects further than envisaged in its manufacturer's technical design.[7] *Colors*, then, is presented here as an example of the greater cinematic realization of the sonic and textual potential afforded by employing the Spectral process.

So . . . you sit down in a theatre to watch *Colors*. Dolby Stereo, Spectral Recording, THX Sound and 70mm. The works. In total silence, pre-credit information rolls up a black screen, mentioning the gangs in outer LA and the special Flying Crash division of the LAPD assigned to deal with them. Cut to a scene setting up Duval, Penn and other cops at the station. Strictly telemovie stuff. Then cut to inside a police car travelling along a freeway, looking into the car and through the side window to the traffic flashing by. The full stereo sound of some Country and Western music fills the audio-visual screen: crisp, delicate, hi-fi quality. It replaces all other diegetic sound effects except for the occasional distant police siren. The stars' names are superimposed on this travelling shot, so you sit back and relax as you generally do when the credits roll on. Big block letters proclaim ' C O L O R S '.

Suddenly a weird and extremely loud sound – *impossibly* louder than the full sound you're already hearing – comes from . . . somewhere. Not exactly from the screen but . . . everywhere *but* the screen. It's the sound of a spraycan being shaken. Then an incredible slice of hissing white noise sears not just across the screen but throughout the theatre as red paint is spraycanned across the film's title, dripping down like blood. Your first full taste of spectral recording. This first sound of the spraycan is in a sense 'aural graffiti': an intrusion of a defined space (the theatre audience) that leaves its mark *upon* the environment. It functions as a cue for how sound will be worked throughout the film to generate sonic effects which symbolise and simulate the territorial sense of space that governs both the fictional (the gangs-versus-cops plot) and the actual (the listening/viewing experience). In this single, powerful gesture, the textual thrust of the whole film is materially presented, as *Colors* – a story about gangs and cops battling each other and themselves – deals with *territorial sound* and *demarcated space*, where the presence and flow of sound shapes all forms of cinematic space (symbolic, actual, dramatic, cultural, musical) throughout the film.

After the graffiti has sprayed its presence into the acoustics of the theatre – into what effectively is an 'anti-screen' space that taunts our perceptual logic – all screen sounds melt into a wall of stereo reverb as the image dissolves into an overhead helicopter shot of the city at night. The buildings sparkle in the darkness as the sound delicately fades into the depths depicted below. The scene then changes to a street level shot of an outer-suburban block corner at night. No beautiful overhead imagery; no speeding daytime traffic. The scene is empty. Silent. Pregnant. Some hard-core rap appears on the soundtrack but once again comes from an anti-screen space. It replicates the acoustic effect of music played in a wide empty enclosure (say, as in a school quadrangle) where a distinct delayed echo confuses the sound of the music, making a song's rhythm double up on itself to produce an arhythmic effect. But in this instance the effect is even more stylised and apparent because the delay is generated electronically (to simulate the acoustic phenomenon) by mixing the music in extreme stereo separation. The question is begged: *where* is this music coming from? On cue, a van appears on the screen. The music is then assumed to be blaring from the van in the empty streets, but the sonic effect nonetheless remains more impressive than the mimetic presentation of the scene, signalling that this music is *greater* (ie. larger, fuller, stronger) than the confines of the soundtrack: it appears to come from *within* the film as well as from *somewhere* else.

The music in question is laid-back hard-core rap of the LA school – a style distinct from East Coast hip hop permutations. It's the opposite of being wired (tense, frenetic, hyperactive sound collages) – more like the transcendental lows linked to druggy, whacked-out states. The large black van cruises with the same sense of movement: lumbered, but smoothly stealing across its territory. Cut to inside the van: the wide stereo effect of the music track closes up into thin mono. What at first sounds like the vocals to the song are in fact the gang members in the van, toasting and rapping while high on drugs. Their voices sound claustrophobic, rapping on a rhythmic treadmill; trapped in the endlessly cruising van and the territorial confines of their gang life. From outside the van come even stranger noises, this time pushed right back into the spectral anti-screen space: cars passing by, police sirens in the distance. Sounds of possible danger, designed to sonically alienate the audience (via the anti-screen spaces in the film sound mix) so as to generate the sense of unease they give to the gang members.

A new joint is lit: the match flares as the sound burns across the screen, momentarily blocking all other aural details; momentarily sealing off the world outside the van. That 'outside' world is textually split once again into the fictional and the actual: respectively, the threat of the other gang cruising the same zone, and (more importantly) the audience – ie *we* are the world outside, for inside the van is another world we can never experience. And it is the *soundtrack* alone that gives us the experience of being alienated from and by that world. By decisively balancing identification with alienation – each applicable as both our textual mechanisms and the gangs' territorial machinations – *Colors* draws a line on the soundtrack which we cannot cross.[8]

Functioning as a clear outline for much of the film's spacial and sonic self-reflexivity, an early scene where a mother grieves over her dead son as the police arrive to investigate the incident, can be broken down to indicate how the film's textual machinations are mobilised by the material assemblage of the soundtrack, which in turn highlights the territorial demarcations made manifest in this 'dimensional' approach to mixing:

*The Gang as
'community'
(Colors)*

AURAL VOICE –	SONIC SPACE –	LOCATION –
within the narrative	*within the mix*	*within the text*
screaming mother	centrally fixed mono	emotional focal point
dogs barking	'boxed' stereo binaural recording	spatially contained / trapped / trained
police radios	widely spaced stereo spread	pervasive / encompassing / overriding power
orchestral effects	ambient textural sensurround	amorphous narrative shell / external chorus function

Further into the film, another scene marks these sonic lines of space with more force. As some gang members are brought into the police station and transfered to a cell block, the theme song to the film (*Colors* performed by Ice-T) comes onto the soundtrack. It carries across one of the film's few amazing visual scenes as the two gangs – coded with their 'colors' (either red or blue bandanas) – taunt and jeer each other from two adjacent cell blocks. Their voices become a thin cacophany, sonically embalmed in something that is literally shaking the whole cinema: bass. The soundtrack pumps out what in any other context would be an inordinate amount of bass but in keeping with the overall stylistic tradition of hip hop music (where bass is simultaneously a sign of sonic excess and a subcultural token of black cultural identity[9]), the bass serves to energise the song, to foreground it in the film. It is foregrounded for two main reasons:

1 Technically, the subsonic frequencies in the lower range of the song's musical production (particularly the booming synthetic kick drum) are central to the record's mix and fortuitously resonate with most presence in the film's spectral mix, generating a series of earth-shaking pulsations which make the song stand out from the audio-visual screen as much as the initial sound effect of the spray-can.

2 Culturally, this song is probably the most authentic black track in the movie (so much so that Herbie Hancock's score 'pales' by comparison) leaving it to be the most potent conveyor of the socio-cultural scenarios the film presents and addresses.

Textually, the song *Colors* as a 'title track' sums up the film's status as an architecsonic object, splitting the soundtrack into three major modes:

1 *Music soundtrack* – composed by MIDI multi-tracking,[10] the concept of rhythmic syncopation becomes not simply a musical aesthetic, but also a form of technological synchronisation. As determined by the core pulse laid down, all other sonic fragments (beat or otherwise) fall into a line of rhythmic precision. The score is thus less layered and more *fused and integrated*, according its fragments a location simultaneously in time (the music) and space (the mix).

2 *Social soundtrack* – the style of the song is more of a lifestyle factor than a formal consideration, as this is the 'type' of musical sound to be heard in the actual environments of the scenes represented in the film. As 'film music' it communicates more through *reference* than evocation.

3 *Film soundtrack* – the song actually contains all the aural elements of the scene it is attached to, for mixed in with the musical arrangement (digital drums, synth bass line, 3 scratch tracks, strange keyboard sound, Ice-T's voice) are some of the dominant sound effects of the film (gun shots, police sirens, 2-way radios, gang slang, police megaphones – most of which have been unironically sampled from movie soundtracks). The point is that the original song – like many 'gangster-style' rap tracks – features these 'sounds of the urban jungle' in such an iconic fashion. The song is thus a mini-soundtrack for the film, just as the film is an extended scenario of the song.

Panning out from these three soundtrack modes, many fractal relationships between elements and components of the film's narrative become crystalline under conditions of territorial sound and demarcated space. The central narrative conflicts of this 'multi-track' film can be structurally and thematically opposed thus:

realm	THE STREET	THE LAW
domain	outside on the pavement	travelling inside cars
ambience	ghetto-blasters (bass)	short-wave radio calls (treble)
contact	beepers (illegal operations)	walkie-talkie (legal operations)
mobility	soft rumbling low-riders & slow cruising vans (bass)	high-speed squad cars with screaming sirens & screeching brakes (treble)
voice	intoxicated (kids on drugs) indecipherable (gang slang)	exasperated (the hysterical preacher) exhausted (Duval reading rights)

Accepting the above as the key semes in the film's aural narratology, certain formal devices in mixing certain sounds recur. For instance, the rap music generally fades up on the soundtrack, as if we/the police are invading a territory, coming into contact with the very signs used by the gangs to mark that territory: their music. Another case would be the way police sirens are floated both throughout the duration of the soundtrack (often linking, fusing or juxtaposing one scene with another) and without the spatial environment of the spectral mix, symbolising through this displacement that the sound of danger (the siren) occurs and carries anywhere and everywhere. A final example is the combination of Hancock's chase-scene music (upbeat but unobtrusive charges of percussive overlays) with the barrage of sound effects, where the former's full stereo mix is designed to blend with the latter's sensurround crashes and screeches, signifying the chaotic music rhythm of the city.

The above aspects of aural narratology are sometimes mixed, other times isolated, thereby contributing to the dynamic contour of the text, as the thematics come in and out of phase with each other. Most interestingly, the Spectral mix allows for a full experience of the function and purpose of the various thematics by combining spaces in ways that would be impossible to achieve if employing other (cinematographic, literary, etc.) modes of narrative construction. This 'dimensional' approach to mixing is clearly a critical development of what earlier was described as the 'planar' approach to mixing early stereo film sound. As such a para-physical sensation drives the dramatic exposition by manipulating the soundtrack.

In summing up, *Colors* 'performs' and 'realises itself' as an architecsonic object in the following ways:[11]

1 It replicates and simulates the aural environment of its scenic/sonic reality (the street, gang lifestyle, rap music, etc).

2 It is textually enveloped by the orchestration and production of its title song's musical fragments (via the MIDI composition).

3 It accords each and every thematic of its narrative a specific place in its spatial sound mix (via the Spectral process).

4 It privileges sonic presence over visual abstraction (highlighting an ontological observation on the cinema, that sound is always present whereas mimetic codes are based on removal and absence).

5 It foregrounds dynamic flow over formal structure (in that the core energy of its text is eventful: through a dynamic handling of the soundtrack it generates effects more than it constructs meanings).

Drugs raid (Colors)

A final word on *Colors*. While it cannot be underestimated how much textual energy this film derives from the admittedly 'uncinematic' realm of 'musicology' (how music cultures and technology operate in a post-industrial environment, and how popular music in particular has, since World War Two been one of the most complex cultural phenomena), it is possible to view a film such as *Colors* – despite its misleading *visual* title – as awakening *and* being awakened by the sonic potential that cinema has always had but has often been denied.[12] Edged up against the sprockets of the celluloid strip, the soundtrack has made its presence more pronounced over the past fifteen years, when sound developments have escalated in the face of the film-vs-video grain impasse. Bypassing those granular debates, the film soundtrack instead revitalizes approaches to sound which, for numerous industrial and cultural reasons, cinema infrequently considered during its first half-century. The point is that the new technologies have not 're-invented' cinema nor have they granted film unheard and unenvisaged capabilities. Simply, various developments in film sound (and only a very small percentage have been mentioned here) have made it difficult for the soundtrack to *not* uncover ground lightly trespassed in years gone by.

Colors – not only as a showcase for the Spectral Recording system but also as a demonstration of advanced aural narratology ('dimensional mixing', 'psycho-diegetics' and 'architecsonics') – redefines the cinematic experience, and hence the so-called cinematic apparatus, by manipulating and communicating to the audience in ways previously unheard of (sic). Irrespective of how film criticism and theory grapples with such a dimensional redefinition of the cinematic apparatus, the film industry has set into motion the mechanisms to produce a cinema experience along these lines, a point proven by the industrial development of Dolby Stereo, and THX throughout the world. *Colors* then is neither 'just' a fancy, sonic spectacle, nor a playful, technological experiment. Far from being stranded as a hi-tech oasis, it is a drop in an ocean of sound waves.

This aricle is excerpted from a chapter titled "The Architecsonic Object" taken from an in-progress work: *SONIC CINEMA – Technology, Textuality & Aural Narratology in the Cinema.*

PHILIP BROPHY

1   Noise reduction systems were not new at a professional level
(the DBX system being a major competing force in the market
of professional recording hardware) but the Dolby system –
invented and patented by Ray Dolby in England in 1966 – found
its greater success on the domestic front which by the end of
the Sixties had branched into three main streams of portable
hi-fi music consumption: (a) transistor radios, (b) audio cassette
recorders and (c) 8-track cartridge machines installed in cars.
Where the Sixties increased portability, the Seventies brought
increases in fidelity and reductions in signal-to-noise ratio,
respectively: (a) the change from AM to FM, (b) new chromium
dioxide tape coatings, and (c) more compact audio cassette car
systems that eventually replaced the more bulky 8-track format.
It is not by coincidence that these developments catered to the
youth market which by the late Fifties was being recognized
more and more as a separate and major demographic spread by
the recording industry. The increased 'mobility' of Sixties' youth
subcultures (rejecting the 'home' in favour of beaches and cars)
went hand-in-hand with the portability, compactness and
increased fidelity of the above improvements. To youth culture
in general, music needed to be bigger, fuller, more 'real' – hence
the success with which Dolby was marketed to the growing
audio cassette market in the Seventies. But why all this talk of
the youth market? Well, once Dolby was established here
(notably through Japanese hi-fi companies en masse employing
the Dolby system in their new cassette recorder designs) it was
not long before film sound picked up on what was a well-
founded fetish for fidelity – especially considering how the
demographics of both the recording and film industries were
overlapping. The first heralded films to employ the Dolby system
were rockumentaries or rock related films (*Tommy* (1975) *The
Grateful Dead Movie* (1976), etc) and after what was a virtual
showcase for the Dolby stereo process – *Star Wars* (1977) – was
viewed as the way to go for increased soundtrack clarity. For
an overview of Dolby's initial rise in film sound applications see
Charles Schreger, 'The Second Coming of Sound' *Film Comment*,
1978. For an account of how the Dolby system was initially
presented to the film industry see 'Dolby Encoded High Fidelity
Stereo Optic Soundtracks' in the 'Film '75' issue of *American
Cinematographer* (September 1975). For a technical account of the
features and characteristics of the Dolby noise reduction system,
see Ioan Allen, 'The Production of Wide-Range Low-Distortion
Optical Soundtracks Utilizing the Dolby Noise Reduction
System' *SMPTE Journal* v84 September 1975. For technical
observations on the ensuing developments of the Dolby system
as applied to stereo optical soundtracks since 1975 see Dave
Robinson 'Dolby in the Cinema' *Studio Sound* September 1976;
Ioan Allen, 'The Dolby Sound System for Recording *Star Wars*'
American Cinematographer August 1978; and David Robinson 'The
CP200 – A Comprehensive Cinema Theater Audio Processor'
SMPTE Journal September 1981.

2   Technically, stereo film sound goes back a long way – especially
if one considers the use of live music to accompany silent film
prints! But even as early as 1941, *Fantasia* – itself a milestone in
sound-image experimentation – was released in 'Fantasound'
stereo, a system involving a 4-track magnetic soundstripe which

effectively set the trend for most 3-channel playback audio-spatial designs: three tracks carrying information to be played left, right, centre, plus movement between and spatial combinations of all three, and a fourth 'control track' to align the volume relationships between the other three tracks in the 3-channel playback. Many other films after WWII, in line with the onslaught of widescreen presentations, were designed to make the cinematic experience visually *and aurally* greater than watching television. Unfortunately, as Cinemascope had become the major widescreen process by the late Fifties, the development of stereo filmsound was retarded by its early catering to Cinemascope's employment of a special discrete 4-track magnetic soundstripe. The incompatibility between the magnetic sound stripe and celluloid footage – due to (a) monosound having always been printed as an optically-printed track running linear to the celluloid footage, and (b) the faster rate at which the mag stripe deteriorated – prevented widespread projection, as only 35mm projectors with either special or optional magnetic sound heads could play early stereo mag-striped prints. Dolby's main contribution to stereo film sound in the Seventies was not simply its fidelity in recording and playback, but more so the industrial viability of its process which capitalized on existing projector/amplifier/speaker set-ups around the world, thereby presenting a cost-effective system to the film industry. (The Dolby optical print is encoded with four bilateral 'lines' of sonic data matrixed into two which – after decoding – are sent to the 3-channel sound system in the theatre in much the same way as the Fantasound process detailed above.) As such, further stereo film sound exploration was equally determined by this factor as it was dependent on the increased fidelity Dolby brought to the recording and playback. For an informative introduction to the history of stereo film sound, see Michael Arick, 'The Sound Of Money – In Stereo!' *Sight & Sound* v57 n1, Winter 1987/88. For a more technically detailed overview see John G Frayne, Arthur C Blaney, George R Groves & Harry F Olson, 'A Short History Of Motion Picture Sound Recording in the United States' *SMPTE Journal* v85 July 1976. For a specific analysis of the technological relationships between the stereo film sound of Fantasound, Cinerama and Cinemascope, see Hazard E Reeves, 'The Development Of Stereo Magnetic Recording for Film (Parts I & II)' *SMPTE Journal* October and November 1982.

3   Accepting that theatre is not simply the written made spoken, but an arena for *vocalised* dialogue, acoustics have generally been the prime province for conveying theatrical effect: the stage may be visually and spatially removed from immediate eyesight, but the audible levels of the actors' voices must be maintained. While the introduction of sound film in the late Twenties was treated as a fad that divided film criticism into technological (sound=invention of realistic cinema) and artistic (sound=destruction of silent cinema) sides, it is often overlooked that sound may have set dramatic film back on a course of *theatrical mechanics* due to its reinstatement of the human voice in the narrative space. Even today, most films privilege the human voice above virtually every other aural and sonic consideration. Perhaps this is why films foregrounding either musical scores or sonically explosive soundtracks (apart from receiving little 'literary-derived' critical respect) afford the more

total *cinematic* experience – a realm where the spoken word is drowned out by its own soundtrack.

4   Established theatre acoustical design had been viewed by recording and mixing engineers as a prime inhibiting factor in the greater development of high-fidelity film sound ever since the widescreen/stereo explorations of the early Fifties. Unfortunately, the Academy of Motion Picture Arts & Sciences had set a standard in 1938 for the electrical reproducing characteristic of projected film sound in theatres. Informally called the 'Academy Curve' it stipulated that projected sound in American theatres should compensate for a 'roll off' (ie softening in volume level) of the upper frequency range of the soundtrack because both the acoustics in many theatres and the capabilities of the optical soundtrack were deemed incapable of accurately replaying such frequencies. (This standard of course affected how engineers and mixers would approach their final film sound mixes: forced to monitor their final mixes *without* the higher frequencies, they would consequently *boost* those frequencies which, in turn, would invariably cause *distortion* in the transfer from the final mixdown to the optical printing of the soundtrack.) The 'Catch 22' here was that these observations were based on late 1930s technology *plus* the then-existing state of psycho-acoustical subjective responses (ie. theatre patrons from the Seventies onwards have experienced much higher-fidelity sound at home). The 'Academy Curve' appears to have remained as stubborn a fixture as the architecture of many cinemas – at least until the mass revamping of theatres by the Dolby system in the late Seventies. Apart from the technical articles on Dolby mentioned above, see Mark Engebretson & John Eargle, 'Cinema Sound Reproduction Systems: Technology Advances & System Design Considerations' *SMPTE Journal*, November 1982.

5   A few technical notes are needed here to explain firstly the usage of the terms 'spectral' as applied here, and secondly – and more importantly – why exactly the Spectral process *is* the next major step forward in film sound fidelity. Firstly, the term 'spectral' refers to the means by which the noise reduction process analyses the signal to be processed, ie. by spectral analysis: breaking up the range of potentially recordable frequencies in order to analyse any incoming sound so as to only employ noise reduction on the frequencies of that sound requiring actual noise reduction. This means that sounds are treated by the SR unit in a manner akin to the human ear's ability to selectively 'mask' various frequencies in relation to each other. Secondly, the Spectral process is the means by which Dolby got around what was both its major breakthrough and its major stumbling block: the stereo '4-2-4' matrix processor. For over a decade now, technical debates have taken place over the pros and cons of matrix signal lines (where two SVA tracks on the optical soundtrack are matrix-encoded to become 4 signal lines sent out to a configuration between 3 main playback channels) and discrete signal lines (where there is a number of tracks corresponding to the number of channels). It has generally been agreed upon that *discrete* lines (ie. separate lines) allow for the best spatial definition in final theatre playback. But with the extreme clarity with which the SR unit encodes the recordable frequency range, the matrix-encoding becomes better defined (as the SR noise reduction is also used in the optical transfer,

which then means that clearer spatial definition is effected in final theatre playback. For a comprehensive analysis of the specifications of Dolby SR noise reduction, see the special supplement prepared by Dolby Laboratories in *Studio Sound* July 1987. For details on how Dolby were leading up to the breakthrough of the Spectral process, see Richard Elen, 'Down At Dolby Labs' *Studio Sound* March 1984. For interesting guidelines for how composers should consider Dolby noise reduction, matrix-processing and speaker monitoring, see Ron Pender & Tim Leigh Smith, 'Music For Film' *Studio Sound* May 1986; and Tony Spath & Dave Harries, 'Music Mixing For Dolby Stereo' *Studio Sound*, October 1989.

6   The bigger the screen gets and the more it curves around, the more incompatible monophonic and rudimentary stereo film sound becomes, as the focal points of sonic emission are virtually rendered static and constricted by the dynamics of the widescreen's meta and internal movement. For an informative and succinct history of widescreen processes and presentations see Rick Mitchell, 'History of Wide Screen Formats' *American Cinematographer* v68 n5 May 1987. See also Michael Arick, *op.cit.*

7   Technical credits related to the final film sound mix:

MUSIC

music score	Herbie Hancock
additional score	Ice-T & Africa Islam
additional music	Capitol production Music/Ole Georg
music editing	Carl Kaller
music consultancy	Gary Goetzman & Sharon Boyle

SOUND

sound design	Randy Thom & Gary Rydstrom
sound recording	Jim Webb
music recording	Mark Wolfson
sound re-recording	Randy Thom, Tom Johnson & Jack Leahy
supervising sound editor	Ronald Jacobs
sound effects editing	Ken Fischer, Robert Shoup & Marian Wilde

8   A literary translation: 'the central themes of the narrative are symbolically reflected in the formal and plastic qualities of the film's construction.' I could easily say this – but it wouldn't tell us anything about the core area of symbolic production, the soundtrack. In fact, reading *Colors* as trite and shallow because of its skeletal thematics and banal social realism is not unlike dismissing novels because they haven't got any pictures on their pages. *Colors* is a film predicated on and privileging sound. To not realize this amounts to aural illiteracy.

9   The lineage of Caribbean music is founded on bass: from ska (the Caribbean distortion of East Coast R'n'B) to reggae (the latter being the first major instance of subsonic bass intruding upon white rock's favoured mid-range aural spectrum) to black disco (which continental Europe technologically colonized into Eurodisco and sold back to white America) to the eventual bass explosion in Eighties' hip hop. This explosion is regional: booming drum machines, pounding disco bass drums, cheesy subsonic synthesiser bass lines and creative distortions of bottom-end effects travelled from the East Coast (the New York

state of electro, rap, hip hop, Latin hip hop) throughout the nation (Chicago house and acid, Detroit techno, Miami bass) and over to the West Coast (LA hard core rap and jack-beat swing). And on it will go. Remember: bass can rock your whole body; treble just gives you a pain in the temples. While the history of film sound privileged the tinny, scratchy timbres of the spoken word, Spectral Recording is *made* for bass – that subsonic dark continent which Sly & Robbie (on their song *Boops*, 1988) stake and title thus *'Bass . . . the final frontier'*.

10   MIDI stands for Musical Instrument Digital Interface. It became the dominant means of studio-recording for pop music in the mid Eighties, replacing 'multi-tracking' which in the late Sixties became the norm for assembling temporally dislocated sounds into a finished, pseudo-real time composition. MIDI effects a very different compositional process. Through storing all required sounds digitally (sampling) and composing/orchestrating them in temporal relation to each other (sequencing), the 'performance' of a digital mix happens in real time and with perfect (inhuman) timing. Also see Alan Durant 'A New Day for Music' in this volume.

11   If this analysis seems too alien in its rhetoric (by favouring aural and audio metaphor) there is not much I can provide as compensation. To articulate sound involves realising it. Experiencing *Colors* involves listening to it as much as watching it – a mandate which acknowledges the legacy of sound-image fusion in the cinema. While it is probably unlikely that one could now take in *Colors* in the form of its original presentation (70mm, THX Sound, Spectral Recording), the stereo Hi-Fi VHS video release (Warner Bros. Home Video) will more than ably demonstrate all the points I have made about the film's soundtrack above – but *only* if one watches the tape wearing headphones to fully experience the shift in spatial dimensions in the mix.

12   The sound in *Colors* is industrially warranted by its aim to hit its target market. *Colors* attempted to be the Eighties' *Rock Around The Clock* by incorporating a stream of youth music into the film's narrative. The point is that since youth music has become so technologically oriented (*especially* contemporary urban black subgenres based on bass) the film has had to follow suit in order to communicate to its projected audience. The commercial failure of *Colors* is too great an issue to ponder here (liberal-minded critics whingeing about drug-related gang violence; postmodernists disappointed with Hopper's telemovie-style direction and Penn's tempered performance; the larger audience demographic being more interested in John Cougar than Ice-T; hardcore rap crossing over into the recording industry but failing to do so in the film industry; etc) but it is safe to suppose that the bottom line of Warner Brothers' gamble in the new JD-gang movie stakes was the soundtrack – the site of commercial exploitation at the nexus of cultural importation (record sales generating film grosses) and industrial exportation (film grosses generating record sales).

SCRATCH AND AFTER
Edit Suite Technology and the Determination of Style in Video Art

GEORGE BARBER

As a rule, in video art, technology is often characterised as self evident or passed over as a 'given'. Usually this is simply because artists are too egotistical to want to share the credit with machines and, not unrelatedly, artefacts seem to be devalued once it is known 'how' they were made. 'Oh you mean you just fiddled with button X to get that . . .?'

Hopefully, from the point of view of the audience, the ideas in video art should be more interesting anyway. Video art is primarily a technological form and thus one is easily able to date and make links between the visual solutions chosen by artists in particular periods. If artists rarely used dissolves in the early Seventies, one is aware that the 'look' of their tape is not so much to do with their 'vision' but frequently, merely a byproduct of what they had access to. Specifically, in Scratch, a mid-Eighties genre of video art, technology played a huge part, not just in a 'making' sense but also as a delimiter of an emerging visual language. However, before elaborating the role of the edit suite in this, I would like to outline a historical context for the genre.

In the Eighties, as far as the fading corpse of British avant garde film and video art was concerned, strung out on the operating table, mouth agape, body limp, there were two blips on the screen where something stirred – the New Romantics and Scratch. The first, pioneered by John Maybury and Cerith Wyn Evans, centred around Super 8 film's image characteristics and mostly involved attitude and a novel no-holds-barred policy on narcissism. The second, Scratch, was more impersonal, throwaway even; it mostly used television companies' product, taped on the newly rentable VHS format, to be re-cut and re-presented with zap-happy glee. Neither of these oscillascope 'highs' had much political or ideological task to which 'weight' might have been attached. And, as it transpired, neither had much chance of living longer than that *certain moment* – except in the world of commercials, there to be hooked up neatly into the visual vocabulary of hip advertising directors, and 'Youth' television programmes. But like all the best Eighties products, the New Romantics and Scratch *felt* good – the independent scene's equivalent of jogging and Walkman culture.

For Merleau Ponty,[1] a fundamental of vision is that, with open eyes, one doesn't *choose* whether to see or not. Vision is an enjoyment in itself, there are no set premises to be fulfilled, even in boredom one cannot help registering 'sights'. Ultimately, seeing has a fascination within itself. Part of the holding power of moving images – film and video – is this flow, technology creating a meta-fascination, one like life itself. Both the New Romantics and Scratch concentrated energy at this mesmeric level, they never really offered anything that would draw one in – other than this eye contact – or go past it. They stayed on the surface. Indeed, frequently the images engendered a feverish passivity that was quite different from the more earnest expectations of what had gone on before in the independent scene. At the time, this kind of approach seemed fresh, weirdly unpretentious in some ways, enragingly so in others. Part and parcel of the Eighties high points was that they ignored the independent 'establishment'. They made their own context, pitching themselves successfully at pop magazines and papers who, in typically English style, were actually sick of pop – their very *raison d'être* and only too pleased to write about something else. Yet the rupture with the past, conceived in these terms, has been most misleading for criticism.

In fact it now seems that the New Romantics and Scratch inherited and drew in quite a logical way from the past, even if the makers never troubled themselves to find out much about it. The New Romantics explored the myriad permutations of how 'beautiful' one could make a film image – lace, snow, reflections, over- and under-exposure, wind machines, flowers etc; while Scratch, with its customary light-fingered approach, spent more time hustling the rules of how pictures go together, searching for aesthetic moments that had gone underrated and unappreciated when the stuff was first broadcast on TV. Furthermore, both movements concentrated almost exclusively on shots containing people. But in retrospect, it appears that the New Romantics especially only ever had formal concerns. In this sense, it could be claimed that these were the *same* ones as those of the previous generation of film makers, say of Peter Gidal or Nicky Hamlyn. Whereas one group searched the smallest matrices of their chairs or bathrooms, the next generation did much the same with the faces of their best friends. Plugholes in virtual silence gave way to pretty pouts to Maria Callas.

In terms of artistic methodology and ideology, both the

New Romantics and Scratch felt very European, very French in fact. Baudrillard would perhaps be pleased but probably he'd be more so with the go-ahead entrepreneurs of television that have now perhaps inadvertently taken over the mantle of the avant-garde. They alone have realised the full power of fragmentation, the full force of Modernism – just pictures from all over the world, all the time, all day, all year. And as far as any television or video goes, never mind the avant-garde or otherwise, it's all about pictures referring back to other pictures.[2] Specifically about Scratch, he'd probably see it as the condensed version of an evening's entertainment, the collapsed version, and he would be right. Seeing things faster than they go on in real life *was* Scratch – the same old impatience as that shared by Fillipo Marinetti, James Dean or, more contemporarily in Britain, the country based BMW-driving lager lout.

Nevertheless, both the New Romantics and Scratch have often been seen as just a reaction – as much in their profile and swanky confidence as anything else – to the stodginess of the British late Seventies independent scene. If anybody can agree about anything, it would be this characterisation. For example, from Mick Hartney, an amusing anecdote epitomising the scene then: Hartney once had his work rejected by David Hall – the Iman of British Video and co-founder of London Video Arts[3] – because he committed the cardinal sin of using music 'and it was Brian Eno as well, who was pretty cool then by any standards, music was just "out", you see. . . .'[4]

The Early Eighties

Britain is famed for its artists a) not knowing much about each other, and b) not knowing much about the artists of other countries. We have no cafe society and seem to dislike, even ridicule, those who attempt to 'manufacture' dialogue. Video magazines like the British *Independent Media* or the Dutch *Mediamatic* have not only poor readerships but seem to generate wilful disinterest. I mentioned earlier that the New Romantics and Scratch seemed more European. I would place this too with another point, the importance of night clubs in both scenes. Having social centres is rare in British art. Neither movement would have gelled so fast or indeed become a recognisable cultural 'blip' had it not been for the way in which everyone knew everyone and their work on the circuit. Not unnaturally, upon seeing other people hitting similar visual conclusions, enjoying the same image tricks, one inevitably grows in confidence and becomes caught in an exciting creative pull. Namely, being part of something, having an identity, a 'job to do', so to speak. For the previous generation, and I assure the reader I write with no malice – surely one wouldn't really think of making a film of a chair or bathroom unless one was in a lot?

Night clubs, then, helped ground an aesthetic for both the New Romantics and Scratch – one of 'visual pleasure'. For the New Romantics, it was held in the long unedited stares of beautiful people out into the audience, poses, set lovingly and dressed with rich fabrics. In Scratch, the idea arose, as in Bowie's *The Man Who Fell To Earth* (Nicholas Roeg, 1976), of a consciousness where images and images, pumped in on banks of screens, could be fed to people with no effort to explain them or make them 'mean' anything – a new line in televisual surfaces. More fundamental too, Scratch looked its best in nightclubs rather than screenings, clubs were its spiritual home. But be that as it may, it wasn't until 1985, upstairs at the Fridge in Brixton in South London – 'the Freezer' – where a club run by Bruno De Florence fully set down the potential of Scratch. At its best for about seven months, various makers would turn up with their latest work and sit around while a sizeable crowd – who'd probably never even heard of independent videos – watched their handiwork on banks of old DER monitors, some upside down, some even, artistically of course (what else?), on the blink.

At the same time, in the late Seventies and early Eighties, art colleges and community resource centres started to unpack the first 'decent' video edit suites – the Sony Series V. And as far as Scratch goes, this was probably as important as any of the cultural contexts outlined above.

The Sony Series V

In the Seventies, the sort of edit suites used in colleges, such as the Sony Series IV and others, were so bad that it's difficult to believe that anybody would have bought one. To use one today, one would need beta-blockers. They had no instantly variable visual search – offering instead a totally laborious process: stop, unlace, fast forward, stop, relace, see picture, wrong one, stop, unlace, fast forward, stop, unlace, see picture, too far, stop, go back, stop etc etc. And you hadn't even found the bit you wanted, never mind tried to edit it – that comes much later in the running order. Hours would go by and very little would be apparent to show for it.

However, if one thought this was bad, the original Sony Portapak was worse. Nancy Holt's *Underscan*, an early American classic of video art, was just about right. That work was a cinch for a Portapak, roll bars were its bread and butter shot. (In 1978, I actually felt physically sick from watching footage I'd shot on one.) In short, it suffices to say that, prior to the Eighties, using grant aided sector equipment in Britain was not for the impatient but only for the very determined.

Editing was central to Scratch – and *being able* to edit – precisely what it appeared the first 'edit' suites weren't very capable of. So, in this prosaic way, the first wave of 'decent' technology did indeed help delineate an aesthetic and make achievable the first truly edit based video form; in much the same way as the invention of Acrylic paint allowed the possibility of Hard Edge painting. But obviously, like a dialogue, the way people were thinking concentrated the fixation, amalgamated aspects of both into an attainable visual approach. Further, the Sony Series V had one trick, and still does, that sets it apart from all the others. One can edit *live* – even the latest U-matic SP (Superior Performance) suites, and certainly not machines of higher professional standards, can do this. This facility more than any other shaped a lot of the work, especially mine.[5]

Take a fast edited tape, full of choice moments, with no dreary shots. Movement is everything, cut pans to pans every time, Copy it. Now you've got two tapes. Keep the copy in the recorder and press play. Press play on the player also, making sure one tape is slightly ahead or behind of the other (it doesn't matter which). Next, with the edit button, located top right, bang out shots as you go (with the right hand), pressing END when you've had enough (with the left hand). There's no stopping involved. It is possible to perform, depending on how fast you want to go, forty or more edits in *one* minute like this – use the music as a guide, if you need one. (Obviously, a few of them will contain 'flash frames' which will need to be patched up but generally it's a precocious way to edit.) Moreover, because one tape is slightly ahead, one gets strange tapestry-like patterns developing, repetitive repeat edits that start to renew, remind, recapture moments that have only just been on the screen. This effect is the definitive 'look', the 'cutting edge' of Scratch, the technical ability to reawaken memories of a shot just gone, a process so fast that you enter oblivion or, paradoxically, a *fast stasis* – life between edits, video that keeps referring back and back to itself.

For me, this facility on the machines seemed to be tailor made to the kind of visual sequences I wanted to work on at the time. It also introduced 'chance' and many conjunctions of the images that Scratchers achieved would just never occur to anyone sitting down with a log of the tapes. This is much the same way in which graphic computers can be asked to randomise the colours of an image, often producing striking combinations that no artist with a palette would be likely to think of. But the point is, to make forty edits or so on anything prior to the Series V would just be a long day's work, suddenly with the Series V, it took half an hour. At this stage, shock alone primed a genre, one of the 'edit-happy'.

Soon, other technological developments fell into the hands of Scratch video makers. First, 'Mixing'. In London in the early Eighties,[6] mixing, ie being able to mix two tapes onto one, became more available. One could make up, say two hours of chance edited material on two separate cassettes, then, at the mixing stage, introduce treated colours, 'posterisation' and other distortions. Afterwards, back on the Series V, one could cut down the best moments of these composite tapes. The final cut would look very complicated – alive and fresh.

Thirdly, the invention of the music computer/sampler had a role. By 1982, Hop Hop music was well established (incidentally the late Pat Sweeney coined the term 'Scratch Video' in 1984, comparing it to New York's Hip Hop scene) and by 1986, Greengate music computer/samplers and equivalents seemed quite commonplace, bought by the same fame hungry people who perhaps only a few years previously would have been buying synthesisers. (Prior to this, these devices existed but were only for the privileged few – the Fairlight is probably the most famous, but only rock stars had them.)

In parallel, as these new technologies were percolating through to various kinds of creative people, significant and similar changes were underway in the world of ideas. Quoting across cultures and cultural forms became a sunrise industry. In forms such as Pop, Fashion, Sculpture, Architecture and Cultural Studies, themes and emphases cross fertilised and video embraced these developments. Again a convergence of technology appeared perfect for this task. Machines such as the Greengate matched the aspirations and helped consolidate an avant-garde video style.

In practice, it became possible to musically repeat stolen voices and small phrases of dialogue, quoting in an exciting and rhythmical way (see for example my tape *Yes Frank No Smoke*[7]). Sound *bytes* or noises could be stored on disk and a music track (see for example the door slamming/helicopter sequence in my *Absence of Satan* tape[8]). Thus, after the sound was perfected, the pictures could be synched in place. Of course, you could have done something similar on an edit suite but it would have taken much longer and could never be quite the same – although Gavin Hodges, John Dovey and Tim Morrison (aka Gorilla Tapes) amazingly produced all the sound inserts and mixes on their *Death Valley Days* tape on

low band U-matic. The then current technological sophistication made dynamic a simple idea, which probably wouldn't have surfaced without it. Indeed, this narrowing of video and audio technologies continues apace today and it is quite likely that eventually a world timecode standard will be established for all machines, both video and audio, expensive and cheap. With this, one could freely edit, adjusting either picture or sound and make videos with the advantage of as many as eight, sixteen or even forty-eight sound tracks.

Video montage in Gorilla Tapes' Til Death to Apartheid *(1986)*

In relation to Scratch, the improved standard of edit suites also gave respite to the long standing intimidation of video artists by technology itself. Often it wasn't that artists had different aims to dominant TV culture but that, in fact, they couldn't realise these as 'properly' as they wanted to anyway since they were not given the chance. Video artists felt that they could never do anything they really wanted to because they just never got on the right equipment, all the new devices were always that bit out of reach.

Suddenly, with Scratch, a group of people made most of one part of the process – editing – and appeared to hit solutions and gain familiarity with a few tricks that the dominant scene had never thought of and, in many ways, could never think of.[9] The business itself always saw Scratch as 'post-production' and, as such, assumed it cost the earth. The movement highlighted the fact that, up to then, the business never 'played' or in any way endeavoured to really see what their equipment could do. For them Scratch became something of

George Barber's
Absence of Satan
(1986)

an early indicator of a new zone, later to emerge as a whole new electronic *sector*, satisfying the ever-expanding 'image treatment' needs of current British television. Soon, 'image processors' were all facilities houses talked about, whether they had them or not – Da Vincis, Paintbox, Harry, Ava, Space Ward, Pluto, Abekas, etc. For today's TV you simply can't make anything look contemporary without them.

After Scratch

I would now like to look at the effect of technology on the British independent video scene – post-Scratch – and raise a few technology issues, and their implications, within the history of video art. In the early days of video art, because of technological limitations, a large body of work came into being that had a doubly distinct difference to television. Obviously, it had completely contrary aims and, frequently, more abstract themes – Illusion, Reality, Space, Time, Texture etc but then again, with the benefit of hindsight, one can see links across such widely differing artists as Brian Hoey and Tamara Krikorian, or Vito Acconci and David Critchley. Compared to television, their work looked quite different, it looked 'wrong' from the very first frame. Often, because of the stronger Performance connection in earlier video art, it had a much more playful and ingenious approach to just 'what is possible with video'. A lot of contemporary video art, including my own, has a much more contrived and predetermined feel; as if it's trying to hit similar rhythms of interest, pace and development that broadcast TV has, only differently.

Recently in Britain, one of the most encouraging developments is that there is now regular Channel Four, Arts Council, British Screen and British Film Institute money being provided for the making of short, eleven minute or so independent film and video art tapes. It would be irrelevant for me to become involved in too lengthy an analysis of what this all means for the video tradition in Britain, for only a part can be explained by technology alone. I would like to choose one of these tapes – Sera Furneaux's *Canvas* (1988) – to make a few points concerning technology's impact but they could be illustrated with reference to many other tapes.

Canvas consists of six sections where women stand frozen, for a couple of seconds, in poses reminiscent of Greek statues. The piece deals with the themes of Time, Perception, Illusion, Reality, Space and Light, key themes from Video Art's tradition, and handles them well and skilfully. One enjoys watching. Yet, it could almost be a perfume ad – specifically the *Simple* ads (a brand of soap and hair care product). In these ads, classical music plays languidly while a group of women barely move against a clutch of wonderfully composed sets – in fact, the same script. In itself, this shared plot, or *mise en scène*, shouldn't really matter, it is after all just the way the two 'look' – there *are* different imperatives at work – but this problem never seems to get resolved or stops corrupting a viewer's response. The problem is that, although it is no greater than what is happening in other cultural areas, video art, as a tradition, seems to be suffering from the depletion of all its previous definitions and areas.

One takes it for granted today that mainstream incorporates the best devices of the avant-garde but this process itself fractures all the time since the avant-garde itself now, by virtue of Channel Four initiatives etc, often finds itself with access to the same equipment as the commercial sector. Today, at a point of technological equivalence, an apparent commonality of access, artists flounder in a dilemma, perhaps created inadvertently by the machines. As the 'look' of everybody's material inescapably becomes more homogenous – technically fine, in spec, no drop-out, all broadcast quality, all sharp, the same sense of pace – it becomes even more likely that any astute commercial eye is going to be able to seize on solutions or novel aspects spotted in any video artist's work. Secondly, coming from the other direction, making anything in an 'amateur', 'wild' or 'unprofessional' fashion becomes just a choice – jerkiness and graininess are now merely a cute aesthetic, a retro excursion. Furthermore, once upon a time, the business wouldn't have had the open-mindedness to wade through the 'amateurishness' or graininess to get to the idea. Now it does. I would contend, therefore, that the basic fixed process of incorporation has rapidly accelerated in the Eighties, so much so that I think it is beginning to enforce a kind of stagnation or, at least, a lack of confidence on the part of video artists as to what it is their work might be aimed at or based on. In the worst possible scenario, it is as if they have no possible role (and, in this case, the future for video art will perhaps be dominated by a return to the gallery, coupled with a retreat from television and screenings).

Scratch's famed burn-out and burn-up can also be seen as related to the technological equivalence and understanding it held in common with the TV establishment. Style, ways of doing things, the agitation of video grammar, suddenly, and not unrelatedly, became an issue and occupation for the commercial sector – a zone to colonise for broadcast TV's own sense of renewal. Today's video artists were never going to be satisfied being the unpaid R&D department of big business. But when that business, in true Baudrillardian fashion, led by the Pop Video/Youth programming division, became more used to experimenting, playing, trying out new technology – ultimately, in effect, taking the mantle of visual playfulness over from artists to itself, this just about put video art on an endangered species list. The Pop Video/Youth sector, and the opening titles and station idents on TV, are now where people find delight and recourse to the kind of visual enjoyment that they might have once found elicited by video art. The need for a purely formalist experimental video art seems gone. (I might cite here the explosion of 'New Narrative' work in Europe funded by innovative TV channels such as the French Canal Plus, including Monika Funke-Stern's *Mit Fremden Augen*, Bruce Romy's *La Ciancee*, Alain Jomier and J. Le Tacon's *Extrait De Naissance* [all made in 1989].) Many of these tapes have admittedly ingenious production values, indeed one rarely sees video looking better but, given the nature of their writing and its combination with its visuals, little else remains but the production values themselves. One just assumes it is how *Play for Today* will seem in four years time. Certainly, no sense of radicality, Video Art or *difference* to TV is engendered. Indeed, worse than that, often the stories' character models: aggressive thugs, tarts, maids, mad scientists, transvestites, the blind, the 'mixed up' (usually woven together in a semi-Surrealist mode with minimum dialogue), are virtually indistinguishable from narratives long felt outmoded by television itself.[10]

In many ways the *absence* of technology probably influences video artists today as much as its presence. Going back earlier in this chapter, the reader might have had the impression that anyone today can zoom into video studios and make things, that perhaps money doesn't come in to it. Clearly, for most video artists, most of the time, work stops when the grants do. But be that as it may, even with grants, artists are not going to get hours playing with the *most* sophisticated hardware and yet often, as a video artist, these are precisely the ones one would love to work with. One of the few who has had such access is Cerith Wyn Evans, who received £60,000 from the British Film Institute to make *Degrees of Blindness* (1988). It is a surprising tape and a fine argument for the creative use of hi-tech machines but this level of financial support is rare, to say the least.

As I mentioned before, there now exists a commercial sector that daily 'experiments' with image treatment and novel ways of putting images together.[11] In an inversion of the accepted flow, artists are not immune from taking from this industry either, watching innovative TV also creates ideas, different aims, different pursuits, maybe, but requiring the same hardware. Even though artists have easier access to better basic equipment today, and more of it, the traditional sense of exclusion goes on. Working within a technological form, one cannot restrain a natural curiosity to experience the latest forms but unless one has big grants, the situation remains essentially as it always has been, with most video makers feeling that they never gain access to the equipment they would really like to. To be precise, perhaps one's sense of what is possible with basic set-ups is hampered anyhow by a feeling, however misguided it may be, that the opportunities available with these machines have been well covered in earlier video art. (For example imagine if the first generation of video artists had had the easy access to VHS that the contemporary one does – the widespread existence of VHS has virtually done nothing – there are no samizdat networks of tape makers, no folk-type developments and no explosion of Neo-Neo-Realism).

In sum, as technology gets more and more elaborate, and the grant aided sector slimmer and slimmer, the kinds of things artists would like to do, itself to some extent fed by what is happening on television and in the work of more fortunate artists, grow further and further away from what is possible in their position. It is in this way that the absence of technology results in the numbing of the contemporary video art scene and, ironically, the situation is probably no different to that which existed in the days when artists had to struggle to get hold of any equipment.

However, it is not all gloom, ideas are what must always

count in the end, not budgets or hardware – however much one knows the situation is more complicated than that. Secondly, it may be simply that present video technology is somewhat out of step with the video artist. If one looks to the world of music a very different history exists vis a vis technology, the simple reason being that the market for DIY music technology is gargantuan compared to the market for people who want to make their own videos.

In the mid Sixties, all you needed to make a hit record was three people with guitars and a drummer with drums. By the mid Seventies, the Pink Floyds of this world needed five articulated lorries just to 'fulfil a fixture'.[12] In the Eighties the situation continued, essentially the same, but with different focuses. When bands like Frankie Goes to Hollywood wanted to make a record – we're told it was too expensive to even think of playing live – they apparently needed budgets of a quarter of a million just to cut five minutes of record time. Thus, compared to the golden era of the Beatles, the technology of the following decades became preposterously out of step with the bedroom hopefuls. But the pendulum is swinging back – manufacturing breakthroughs have not only reduced machine prices, they have collapsed them. Digital drum machines currently sell at around £300, as little as eight years ago they cost thousands. It is the same for practically everything else. Nowadays, it is inspiring to hear the amount of 'home made' music that is in the charts. Bands such as 808 State, 49ers and Black Box have had great success with records such as *Pacific State*, *Touch Me* and *Ride On Time* (all 1989). They work on easily available machines but still come up with good tunes. They really don't need anything super-tech, they know exactly what they can get out of their own equipment and play to its strengths. The older bands, still staggering under the weight of the usual yen hardware fiestas – David Bowie, Phil Collins etc – don't really sound better, just different.

Maybe by the end of the Nineties, video edit suites will not only be affordable but so too will much of the *rest* of the standard video-making environment. Perhaps it's just that no one gets the chance to practise making video art day in, day out, that leads so much of the present stuff to be so awkward and not quite 'there'. Anyway, however one defines them or sees the future, it remains that there have been certain tendencies at work in the Eighties that have led to the slow contracting of space in which to work. At the point where you'd think that there would never be an easier time to make one's own stuff, curiously few want to.

In conclusion, one would think technology should make it easier and easier to do what one really wants but it seems to hide, to do little more than take people further and further away from themselves – at any rate, that is how the argument usually issues from a particularly nostalgic English intellectual position. In Video Art specifically, this usually gets expressed as, 'people just get carried away with effects'. I would never agree – though there will always be bad artists – and would cite Scratch as a prime example of where available technology *was* made the most of, where people just got on the machines and 'did things'. They jammed, winged it and made it up as they went along. It would take a philistine to say it was 'just effects' pure and simple. One only has to look at broadcast television to see its legacy, of how Scratch and the arrival of the first decent edit suites combined to instigate a more edit based video form. In parts of television, the grammar of editing and visual language have irredeemably changed, copying over the excitement of the Scratch scene.

In this way, it is perhaps only when the latest wave of image processing technology filters down to being affordable, that artists will again be unconstrained, unintimidated and original. The Australian artist Peter Callas is a good case in point. In *If Pigs Could Fly* (1987), he ingeniously hitched up three 'low-tech' Fairlights in a way that allowed him to do the bulk of his artwork at home. With everything stored on disk, it could simply be loaded over on to one inch tape and smartened up at the final edit. In general, I think it is to his working methods and to others like him, combined with a renaissance of the video art installation scene, that one would look for the energy of the video art of the Nineties. However, the days of just switching on a video camera and doing things 'live', with no editing, or urge to be succinct, might make a comeback but only as a 'quote' within a larger historical succession – like pitched roofs or a dome on new buildings – the form can never re-find its original purchase. The inexorable trend, as paralleled in other creative forms, outwardly demands more and more technical expertise to revitalise tradition. In the general escalation of technological dependence, video art plays its assigned role quietly, just the odd person still beavering away amidst the indiscriminate landscape of Postmodern Corporate Culture. The artist peers out, swamped by a vast TV industry.

GEORGE BARBER

1   See M Merleau Ponty 'Eye and Mind' in Harold Osbourne (ed) *Aesthetics* Oxford, Oxford University Press 1972.

2   This has been taken even further with video art referring back to video art – Mike Jones and Simon Robertshaw's *Towards A New History of the Origins of Video Art* (1981) for example. Here, the opening water footage of the *Hawaii 5-O* TV series is amusingly cut to refer to the universal video art cliche of videoing water.

3   Now London Video Access.

4   Related at an ICA talk as part of the 1989 Piccadilly Film and Video Festival chaired by Jeremy Welsh.

5   See my contributions to *The Greatest Hits of Scratch Video Volumes One* (1984) and *Two* (1985).

6   The American Video Art scene had all these things earlier and, of course, so did British broadcast stations.

7   *The Greatest Hits of Scratch Video Volume Two* track four.

8   *ibid*, track two.

9   However, it must be acknowledged that Dara Birnbaum in *Kojak Wang* (1983) or, really, any of John Sanbourn's early work, arrived at a metronomic editing style before any of the British Scratch makers. At the time though, it didn't connect up with clubs or magazines and in general hung onto its independent 'Art' status. The British, coming later, took it in a much more low brow direction, frequently using disco music and consciously striving to make a name with superficiality.

10   Obviously, some of my own works such as *Taxi Driver 2* and *The Venetian Ghost* may be felt to fall into precisely this kind of area. Yet I would argue that via humour, 'in' references, and especially the writing itself, breaks with dominant modes of television are clear. Further, when *Taxi Driver 2* was broadcast on Channel Four in December 1987, a member of the public came into the Channel Four Video Box to say that it was the worst video he had ever seen and that his uncle made better ones. I must be getting something wrong.

11   For example, the astonishing work of the TV design company, English Markell Pockett, which does numerous links and opening titles on British television.

12   Punk is obviously an exception here, but being anti-technology was part of its thrust.

7

INDUSTRIAL LIGHT AND MAGIC
Style, Technology and Special Effects in the Music Video and Music Television

PHILIP HAYWARD

Introductory Note

As its title suggests, this chapter principally discusses aspects of the visual 'track' of the combinative form(s) of music video and music television. More specifically still, it provides an account of the manner in which successive developments of visual effects technologies have been utilised to develop *spectacularity* as a key element of the form's appeal. In this manner, this chapter's analysis will engage with Fredric Jameson's contention that, in the advanced capitalist culture of the late Twentieth Century, the 'urgency of producing fresh waves of ever more novel-seeming goods . . . assigns an increasingly essential structural function and position to aesthetic innovation and experimentation'.[1] Discussion of the particular genres and styles in which this tendency has been most marked will in turn lead to an examination of the nature of such aesthetic 'innovation' and 'experimentation', both with regard to music video itself and its convergences and divergences from more traditional trajectories of cultural innovation.

Cultural Contexts

Watching a mass of music videos back to back is like watching a sample of films from the early period of cinema, say from 1906 to 1912. During this period, different forms co-existed side by side – some of which can now be historicised as early precursors of the so-called 'mature' Hollywood form, some of which can be seen as outmoded examples of preceding styles, some as bizarre juxtapositions of sophisticated and 'primitive' and some as simply odd, aberrational or incoherent. Like early cinema, a significant body of music video also possesses what we might term a pronounced *narrative abandon*, in the sense of a zestful recklessness about its construction which often signifies the youth of a medium. But unlike early cinema, which existed *prior* to the development of Hollywood-style narrative into a globally dominant form; the music video's eschewal of narrative results from its constitution and operation *outside* the narrative systems of commercial film (and television). Instead of narrative, the form is premised on patterns of (audio-visual) textual flow which more precisely resemble the music of its soundtrack.

Although music video has developed a number of clear generic styles, and, in the case of MTV America's chart dominated playlist, a degree of stylistic homogenisation; music video as a general form has seen a continuing renewal, development and divergence of styles and use of contemporary visual effects. Unlike classic Hollywood film, and in an exemplarily Postmodern manner, it merges and crosses its own 'mainstream' with its own avant gardes. Established pop stars are just as likely to appear in 'experimental' videos as new or little known artists are to appear in studiedly formulaic work. Like early cinema, the music video scene is also marked by the sheer volume of textual production and by the prolific production capacities of its producers; as Patrick Goldstein remarked of music video director Russell Mulcahy, (he) 'cranks out rock videos the way Mack Sennett used to polish off two reelers'.[2]

Similarly, like early cinema, the broad field of music video encompasses such a diversity of individual texts and styles that it resists broad generalisations. But instead of this plurality being necessarily negative, as somehow indicative of formal *confusion*, it may well be that the music video field offers a situation akin to that Dana Polan asserted for pre-Hollywood narrative film, whereby early cinema can be seen to evidence 'some of the greatest complexities of cinema before its unfolding into a cinema of easy action'.[3] Analysis of the music video on its own terms reveals a wide range of textual forms and styles precisely *because* of the lack of rigid formularization of its textual production.

Like early cinema, which was also, within its own technology and institutional contexts, advancing and experimenting with lighting, colour, sound and camera technology and forming various visual and narrative styles out of experiments of their use – music video can be seen to be actively experimenting with its technology and possible combinative *grammars*. Indeed, in its orientation towards formal novelty and surprise, it can, like certain parallel strands of Video Art, TV Advertising and animated graphics, be seen to effectively embody an internal 'research and development' project. The 'results' of this project manifest themselves in both its own texts and in other forms of audio-visual culture. It thereby constitutes a form of avant garde less concerned with the pursuit of aesthetic purism than formal experimentation and the exploration of 'state of the art' visual effects for their own sake.

Unlike early cinema however, it is unlikely that the exploratory-experimental project of music video will eventually 'arrive at', and thereby *deliver*, a stable form. In one sense, this is due to the fact that the music video already represents a form of *easy action* – one which is primarily non-narrative, premised on repetition, flow, motif and variation in the visual track in a manner analogous to that of the musical. But it is also no accident that the music video sits at the end of the high period of classic Hollywood Realist Cinema, a period when one significant tendency of feature production appears to show the form shifting from a style heavily derived from bourgeois realism into a phase marked by a variety of Postmodern attributes.[4] This is of course even more marked in television with its plurality of narrative and realist forms, witness for example the variety of traditionally anti-realist techniques used in recent American television drama series such as *China Beach, thirtysomething* or *Moonlighting*.[5] A number of these modes and styles, such as textual bricolage, a tendency to narrative fragmentation and an elaborate use of visual effects, are also increasingly evident in the broader audio-visual culture of television advertising, trailers, programme packaging and the like.

The significance of the broad audio-visual culture within which the music video operates was emphasised by the programme notes for the (New York) Museum of Modern Art's 1985 music video show. These argued that audiences could relate to the form 'since they are already familiar with the visual vocabulary, which relates to computer-animated station logos and to the "special effects" found in television advertising as well as in Stephen Spielberg and George Lucas's films.'[6] The latter precedent is particularly significant for the style of visually spectacular videos discussed in this chapter. If the music video follows the general cultural orientation of contemporary audio-visual culture, its concern with spectacularity also closely parallels another more specific form – the Science Fiction and Horror 'SFX' film genres which came to prominence in the late Seventies. These (sub)genres were inaugurated by the success of films such as *Star Wars* (1977) and *Alien* (1979) and continued throughout the Eighties in a series of popular (and diverse) movies such as *Ghostbusters* (1984), *The Fly* (1986) and *Batman* (1989) (and saw their most explicit music video parallel in Michael Jackson's *Thriller*, directed by John Landis in 1984).

As the title of the leading Hollywood special effects company 'Industrial Light and Magic' suggests, the commercial success of these genres was substantially premised on the exploitation of the 'wonder-factor' generated by successive elaborations of special effects technology. As this chapter will attempt to argue, a similar concern with visual spectacularity has also motivated producers of the music video and, in a significant range of music video genres, lead to a similar reliance on successive innovations in effects technologies to stimulate and retain audiences.

Impact Aesthetics

As many previous commentators have pointed out, music video has both a *pre-history* in a range of filmic contexts and a range of immediate precursors in the form of various television music shows, pre-recorded inserts and 'film-clips'.[7] But insofar as we *can* locate a decisive origin for the form, and thus its *era*, it is in 1975 with the production of a promotional video to accompany Queen's *Bohemian Rhapsody* single. Although this is now widely accepted as a point of origin, its significance is perhaps more complex than has been previously assumed.

Conventional readings have identified the crucial aspects of Queen's *Bohemian Rhapsody* video as its demonstration of the extra promotional function the music video could serve over and above radio airplay, advertising, guest appearances on television and the like, in promoting sales. As is now widely known, the British record company EMI decided to produce a (then) big budget promotional video for *Bohemian Rhapsody* after the single 'peaked' in the mid 'Top Ten' of the British singles charts. EMI Records had made a substantial investment in the band by this time, but had not managed to translate this into major singles success, with the group's two previous singles *Killer Queen* (1974) and *Seven Seas of Rye* (1974) only getting into low chart positions. The company was therefore keen to achieve a sales and promotional 'breakthrough' with this third single.

The unusual step of making a special promotional clip *after* the recording had apparently peaked represented a promotional gamble by the label. This gamble relied on the specific nature of British television at this time and the status of the BBC's weekly pop show *Top of the Pops* as the only significant popular music programme on television and thus a highly significant promotional platform for singles sales in the British national market. The pivotal status of the *Bohemian Rhapsody* video as a marketing device derives from its production for screening on *Top of the Pops* to promote a band who *could* have simply mimed in the studio in the standard manner. The video was specially designed to secure maximum viewer attention (and product-image *retention*) through a visual track which was markedly more varied, sophisticated and carefully orchestrated to the specific music than the relatively formulaic presentation offered by *Top of the Pops*'s (in-house) production team. The clear aim of the video was to provide a visual *impact* for the song which would distinguish it from the other singles featured on the show and in this it was highly successful.

Though Bruce Gowers' video for *Bohemian Rhapsody* attempted to produce its visual impact through dynamic visual imagery and editing, its images clearly derived from the associated traditions of live rock performance and visual packaging. The lighting and studio effects in the video for instance, derived heavily from those uses of stage lighting, dry ice etc common to rock performances – and indeed a substantial proportion of the video simulates such a live performance. The visual quality of the quasi-operatic sections also recalls live stage performance in its dramatic lighting but is further influenced by the dramatic and inventive album cover designs popular for heavy rock and 'progressive' acts in the early to mid Seventies.[8] But perhaps the most original and individually effective visual images, which signalled the 'special' nature of the video, were those ostensibly 'high tech' visual effects which used feedback to extend and distort images of singer Freddie Mercury and the band in a manner only previously familiar to British TV viewers through the similarly 'high-tech' opening visual sequence(s) of the BBC Science Fiction show *Doctor Who*.[9]

As far as can be ascertained from available sales statistics and industrial analyses, the company's gamble paid off in spectacular fashion, with the television screening(s) and a general popular 'buzz' over the video helping revive sales and push the record to the number one position, where it stayed for nine weeks. Following industrial recognition of EMI's successful use of this promotional strategy, a number of other British companies explored the use of such promotional videos during 1976-77 with this activity noticeably gaining pace in 1978-79 when various 'New Wave' bands were signed and developed by major labels. While videos made for acts such as The Sex Pistols or Stranglers primarily reinforced their established images, music videos for other acts such as The Boomtown Rats played a major part in *transforming* their image.[10]

While it was perhaps Mallett's collaboration with David Bowie on his *Ashes to Ashes* video (1980) which first established the lavish (and lurid) video post production effects now common in music video production, it was another type of music which was to have a more significant impact on the style of high budget music video productions made in the mid to late 1980s. This style was particularly associated with the director Russell Mulcahy and the small group of British bands such as Visage, Spandau Ballet and Ultravox who were briefly termed: 'The New Romantics'. Mulcahy first developed this distinctive style in 1981 for Ultravox's *Vienna* single, a costly production whose locations (Vienna and London's Covent Garden Piazza), lavish interior sequences, costumes and overall visual style complemented the lofty sub-operatic aspirations of the song's arrangement and lyrics. As Mulcahy has subsequently emphasised, the significance of 'New Romantic' acts such as Ultravox was that 'the music was very rich and was a joy to put images to.[11] Directors such as Mulcahy used this aspect of the music to give their videos a correspondingly more elaborate and richer visual quality than had previously been commonplace. This in turn brought more attention to the video as a form-in-itself and as Mulcahy has also emphasised, 'I don't know whether it [ie. New Romantic music] helped the British Record Industry but it definitely helped the British video industry'.[12]

Though significantly *filmic* in its imagery (with Mulcahy even blacking off the top and bottom of the screen to imitate the television image of a cinemascope film print), *Vienna* set a stylistic precedent for a range of video productions which embraced a similar combination of high fashion style photography, the use of glamorously dressed figures, moody evocative locations and atmospheric visuals. But like the music fashion itself, the New Romantic phase soon exhausted itself. With an increasingly standard production of music videos by record companies to promote *successive* rather than *significant* releases, there was also a corresponding acceleration in the use and diversification of styles to create an impact upon the viewer through either their deviation from established styles and/or their innovatory use of effects or images. This produced the classic Postmodern situation referred to in the introduction to this chapter, where as Jameson argued (in 1984), the 'urgency of producing fresh waves of ever more novel seeming goods . . . now assigns an increasingly essential structural function and position to aesthetic innovation and experimentation.'[13]

Significantly for this analysis, the popularisation of a new series of artists in the period 1983-5 coincided with both the expansion of television exhibition outlets for music and the introduction of the sort of video edit suite technology described by George Barber elsewhere in this volume.[14] This period saw both the ascendancy of the American MTV channel and the introduction of Channel Four's ninety minute long *The Tube* as a significant and more adventurous and diverse alternative to the BBC's *Top of the Pops*. During this period a number of artists came to the fore, at least partially, through their record companies' skilful exploitation of television air time. In this competitive environment, novelty and spectacularity became increasingly important aspects of music video production. These were attempted through the use of a number of different elements, often, in the case of high-budget productions, combined in a single tape, and included the use of:

a) Ornate studio sets, such as in Duran Duran's *Union of the Snake* (1983) or Kim Carnes' *Voyeur* (1983).
b) 'Exotic' and/or spectacular locations, such as in Duran Duran's *Rio* (1982) or Jessie Rae's *Over the Sea* (1985).
c) Complex choreographic displays, such as in Elton John's *I'm Still Standing* (1981) or Olivia Newton John's *Physical* (1981).
d) Pronounced filmic imagery such as in The Human League's *Don't You Want Me* (1981) or Spandau Ballet's *Musclebound* (1981).
e) Extracts from feature films (for tracks also featured in film soundtracks), such as in Giorgio Moroder and Phil Oakley's *Together in Electric Dreams* (from the *Electric Dreams* soundtrack) (1984) or, more unusually, in the homage to director Nick Roeg in Big Audio Dynamite's $E=Mc^2$ video (1986).
f) Use of recognisable celebrities, either as characters in narrative sequences, as in The Eurythmics *Who's that Girl?* (1983 – with its galaxy of glamorous stars) or Tracey Ullman's *My Guy* (1984 – with its guest appearance by Labour Party leader Neil Kinnock); or else occasionally, as additional 'inserts' (as in Ray Parker Junior's *Ghostbusters* [1984]).
g) The erotic spectacle of female models used as – 'dancers' (in innumerable videos); recognisable individuals (as in Billy Joel's *Uptown Girl* [1985] featuring top model Christie Brinkley); sketchy narrative presences (as in ABC's *Poison Arrow* [1983]); anonymous decorative elements (as in David Lee Roth's *California Girls* [1985]) – or even anonymous fragmented physiques (as in ZZ Top's *Rough Boy* [1986]); or else, more unusually, imitating musicians (as in Robert Palmer's *Addicted to Love* [1986][15]).[16]

In addition, the period 1983-5 also saw the emergence of another spectacular aspect of music video production, the increasing foregrounding of high-tech images and special effects *as style*. This led to the production of a cycle, or rather series of mini-cycles of music video texts, discussed in detail in the following sections, which showed a fetishistic preoccupation with post-production visual effects. Their arguable *excess* has supplied us with particularly intense demonstrations of technology employed to produce dazzle and impact – a return to childhood wonder akin to that aimed at by *Star Wars* et al and which bypasses concern with textual profundity in favour of technological 'magic'.

Spectacular Technology

The years 1984-5 were pivotal ones for music video. During this period the American MTV (Music Television) network developed into a major broadcasting service with a significant share of the national youth audience and prompted the spread of other music video programmes and services on national network and local television. This in turn prompted American record companies to move to a far more routine production of music videos to accompany single releases than had previously been the case.[17] The period was also a significant one for the introduction of a range of new image processing and effects technologies, particularly various types of animation, graphics, video editing and matting.

With regard to animation, the Eighties saw something of a renaissance of the form in general, most notably in films featuring computer animation such as *Tron* (1982) and *The Last Starfighter* (1984), various TV advertisements and, more recently, a mix of animation and live action in the highly successful *Who Framed Roger Rabbit?* (1988). In the early Eighties, music video provided a significant area for this development. Annabel Jankel of London's Cucumber Studios, producers of animation videos for singles such as Elvis Costello's *Accidents Will Happen* (1979) and The Tom Tom Club's *Genius of Love* (1981) has for instance, characterised the opportunities offered by music video production as reviving experimentation in animation after fifty years of domination by Disney aesthetics.[18]

Due to various factors such as the size and fragmentation of the American record market, no *one* video produced for broadcast on MTV and other outlets can be observed to have had the same dramatic effect on national record sales and subsequent industrial strategies as the original broadcast of *Bohemian Rhapsody* on BBC television. A number of videos produced for the American market during 1984/5, such as The Car's *You Might Think*, did however attempt a similar strategy to EMI's original promotional ploy, attempting to attract audience attention and product 'buzz' through a video whose visual composition and effects stood out from the flow of music video material on services such as MTV.

In order to create a spectacular video and produce a strong 'product image' for the group, the record company invested $250,000, a relatively high budget for this period, in the production of a video directed by Jeff Stein and extensively post produced by the New York animation company Charlex. The video used a combination of post-production techniques including Paint Box effects and sophisticated video mattes produced by the Ultimatte video compositing system[19] – a system which, according to its manufacturers 'makes it possible to [seamlessly] composite . . . virtually anything . . . smoke, shadows, transparent objects, individual strands of hair . . .'[20]

The video's elaborate composition process eventually required two and a half hours of post production for each second of the final video.[21] These techniques were used to create a scenario where singer Ric Ocasek pursues a beautiful model by metamorphosing into a variety of startling precisely visualised forms such as a human headed fly and a giant King Kong scale figure who eventually grabs her from her flat. The video, still striking in its image techniques some six years on, thereby both introduced advanced animation techniques into a popular cultural context and provided an additional aspect to the group's image through their association with the high-tech images and the sort of visual imagination evident in the visual track.

Early screenings on MTV and NBC's *Friday Night Videos* in March 1984 attracted immediate attention to the video and helped the single to number three in the national charts – both a higher position and one achieved more rapidly than either the record's radio airplay or band's national standing suggested. The video thereby at least partially fulfilled its intended function of boosting the band's somewhat flagging singles career and indeed went on to serve as an additional promotion for the band by winning a series of music video prizes. In this manner, *You Might Think* can be seen to have further elaborated on *Bohemian Rhapsody's* original high impact promotional strategy by demonstrating how innovative special effects work could produce a greater impact than use of rapidly standardised music video conventions. In fact, Queen themselves, pioneer of the music video as promotional device, turned to an animated video for their 1986 single *A Kind of Magic*, using a more traditional kind of animation mixed with live action. Made on a budget of approximately double that of the Cars' *You Might Think*, the *A Kind of Magic* video nevertheless failed to deliver a similar degree of promotional impact to either the Cars' promo or their own previous *Bohemian Rhapsody* video (with the single peaking in the mid Top Ten of the British charts – as might have been expected).

A similar level of high-tech impact was achieved in the same year as Charlex's success with *You Might Think* by the group of young British video makers who developed the rapidly edited form of video collage known as 'Scratch Video' by using new forms of edit suite technology such as the Sony Series V.[22] Although the majority of scratch video pieces produced during 1984/5 were not specifically made as record promos, the majority were set to contemporary music, most often the style of American dance music known as Hip Hop, and were usually of three to four minutes duration (standard music video length). Drawing on the 'impact aesthetics' of the music video form, these video collage pieces were initially screened at fashionable night club venues before a number of them were made commercially available on video compilation cassettes. From the beginning, individual scratch tracks and the two highly influential compilations, *The Greatest Hits of Scratch Video (Volumes One and Two)* were packaged and promoted in a manner akin to music products, or music video cassette compilations, rather than as either video art or independent film releases (an aspect reinforced by the inclusion of the Duvet Brothers' scratch video treatment of New Order's highly popular 1983 dance track *Blue Monday* on *Volume One*).

The release of the first compilation in early 1985 in particular, had a rapid and significant impact on styles of both music video production and television advertising.[23] The producers of the video for Paul Hardcastle's number one hit *19* (1985) for instance, overtly copied the style and visual 'breaks' of various tracks off the *Greatest Hits Volume One* compilation, most notably the brief *War Machine* scratch. The prominent and prolific team of music video producers Godley and Creme, themselves former members of the highly successful British band 10cc, also drew on early Scratch techniques in a more creative fashion in videos for tracks such as Frankie Goes To Hollywood's *Two Tribes* (1984). Their video for Howard Jones' *Life in One Day* (1985) also adopted a rapid collage technique in a promo which wittily appeared to scramble transmission signals from a live *Top of the Pops* appearance by the artist with images from other channels. The cross fertilisation between the scratch and promo reached its logical conclusion in 1988 when Rik Lander, a former member of The Duvet Brothers, produced a scratch video promo for M/A/R/R/S' highly successful *Pump Up the Volume* record, the first sampled collage single[24] to reach the number one spot in the British singles charts.

Various animation techniques, scratch video edit suite assembly and the other styles discussed further below, all engaged with the fascination of new developments of image technology as *spectacular* in themselves – a fascination with *technovelty*, the 'how-did-they-do-it' factor, the charisma of the gizmo . . . This factor soon came to dominate a particular approach to music video production. As Cucumber Studio's producer Rocky Morton lamented in 1987, when talking of pre-production meetings with clients, 'a lot of times you present an idea and the last thing people want to talk about is the idea, all they want to talk about is the technique . . . they expect some sort of "magical" film'.[25]

By 1986/87, recognition of the increasing importance of the *technovelty* factor resulted in an increasingly self conscious reference to such aspects in music video productions. One result was a brief flurry of what we might term *retrotech* productions, the deliberate pastiche use of dated visual effects aimed at a knowing audience. In some cases these *retrotech* effects were simply produced to complement the *retro* styles of the song's music track (such as the video for Danielle Dax's 1987 single *Cathouse* which complements its 'psychedelic' update of R 'n' B riffs with its 'dated' use of image feedback effects); while in others it lead to more sophisticated referrals back to earlier traditions of television pop music production.

Classic examples of such referential videos include Diana Ross's 1986 hit *Chain Reaction*, which re-created the blurred black and white video images and studio sets of Sixties American music shows such as *Shindig* and interrupted and juxtaposed them (via a 'chain reaction' in the studio control room) with colourful late Eighties MTV-era images. Significantly, the award winning video also re-created Ross's own performing past and musical styles. These presented her as a virtual simulacra of her earlier self, a slimmer, more styled, more perfectly shot version of images of her from the period. In a similar, though perhaps more modest vein, the video for The Pogues' 1988 single *Yeah Yeah Yeah* similarly recreated Sixties monochrome video images and the studio sets of the British Sixties music show *Ready, Steady, Go* only to contrast them with gaudy colour sequences designed to emphasise the song's exuberance, impact and contemporaneity . . .

In a complementary response to this tendency, BBC Television's *Top of the Pops* show produced a similarly referential pastiche for The Time Lords' appearance on the show in May 1988, miming to their single *Doctorin' The Tardis*, which later reached the number one position. The record itself was a virtual showcase of postmodern popular music composition, employing all the fashionable techniques of pastiche,[26] bricolage and mode retro, to combine a music riff and melody line derived from Gary Glitter's 1972 hit *Rock and Roll (Parts 1 & 2)* with lyrics and sound effects referring to the long running BBC science fiction series *Dr Who*. When a band, or rather performers substituting for them, since it was primarily a studio record, mimed on-air in the studios, the show's producers processed the video images into colour reversals which both resembled classic *Top of the Pops* visual effects from the Seventies, the sort of image manipulation used in various of the *Dr Who* title sequences[27] and the negative image technique used to signify the Daleks' exterminating rays in classic *Dr Who* series.[28]

With audiences becoming increasingly used to visual innovation and experimentation as a standard factor in music video production, video producers became increasingly aware of the need to update formats and utilise various aspects of the *technovelty* factor in order to attract significant attention to the visual track. Such an awareness was not only confined to the production of music video texts themselves but also the wider broadcast contexts of music television. By 1987 for example the American MTV channel, which in 1986 alone had generated a $48 million operating profit,[29] was beginning to feel the impact of competitors in the US market, with over ninety other national and regional music video services competing for a share of the market.[30] The majority of these services had simply imitated MTV's visual styles and packaging more or less wholesale. The combination of popular music and the dynamic visuals of the music videos themselves were therefore no longer a distinct property of the original channel. In order to keep its market primacy, MTV reviewed its format and subsequently revamped its packaging. This move was designed to increase the impact and appeal of its visual packaging of music videos and can therefore be seen as an attempt to create a visual impact and spectacularity *supplementary* to its established programming – an attempt to saturate their service with the spectacularity conceived of as a prime attractor to audiences.[31]

This revamp, significantly designated 'Operation Light Switch', primarily involved a range of visual re-packagings. Along with the re-modelling of the channel's basic studio sets by the New York architectural firm Site Projects, MTV also introduced 'electronic environments' for its veejays,[32] animated by video Paintbox systems, re-designed station idents[33] and brief 'art breaks'. The art break format was an innovation for the channel and comprised eye catching animations or visual effects sequences designed to function as discrete textual units *without* the specifically *promotional* function of either the music videos themselves or the channel's own idents or veejay sequences. In contrast to the mixed reception accorded to the channel's flirtation with electronic veejay environments, the art breaks were recognised as a significant and prestigious addition to the channel's service. As Paul Allman put it, the 'class acts are the art breaks, paid for by MTV and produced by big-name artists from different disciplines'.[34]

To any conventional aesthetic standards derived from Fine Art traditions, the 'art' status of these breaks was of course highly contingent, being premised on the sequences' relative aesthetic autonomy rather than any traditional project, context or apparent address to a transcendent aesthetic function. Such developments can be seen as direct consequences of the increasingly hi-tech and Special Effects context of the video material played by MTV itself. Similar developments were also adopted by other shows and services presenting music video material. Channel Four's *Chart Show*, for instance, adopted a distinct style of video graphics packaging (including informational graphic overlays) and also, for its third series in 1988, featured an introductory computer graphics 'pinball-jukebox' sequence which incorporated specially designed mattes which allowed the television programmers to insert different music video images into the standard sequences for successive shows.

With the introduction of the MTV Europe satellite service in August 1988, such visual concerns were developed from the inception. Careful consideration of such formats was particularly important to MTV Europe since the company was well aware of the commercial failure of its European satellite predecessor Music Box (whose music video programming was absorbed into the Super Channel satellite schedule shortly before MTV Europe's 1988 launch). During MTV's first year of European transmission, the service paid particular attention to dynamic visual packaging. Director of on-air presentation Jonathan Klein commissioned thirteen companies to produce 10-30 second 'art break' sequences on budgets ranging from £3,000-£18,000, with the only stipulation that the producers should use any technique 'you've always wanted to use but thought it too wild for television'.[35] Though the shift from using pre-produced promotional music videos to the commissioning and screening of video 'art' pieces is perhaps an initially surprising move for a commercial television service, it parallels the interplay between the role of the video artist and music video producer which increasingly occurred in the late Eighties and saw established video and computer graphic artists such as Joan Logue, Zybigniew Rybcznski, George Snow, George Barber, Rebecca Allen etc. producing music videos and blurring the distinction between the two spheres.

This tendency was taken even further by MTV Europe in April 1988 with the introduction of their *Ultratech* show. This was a new half hour 'programme', transmitted twice a week, which developed the dynamic visuals of MTV Europe's specially commissioned idents into a long format programme accompanied by a continuous *techno* music DJ mix (produced by Dave Dorell). The aesthetic base of *Ultratech* reflected the concern with impact, attack, surprise and disorientation which had variously inflected developments in Rock, Rap and House music in the Eighties – as Klein emphasises '*Ultratech* is a bit brutal, it's very confrontational television',[36] what critic Willem Velthoven has described as *hardcore* television.[37] As the name suggests, *Ultratech* was not conceived as just a collection of semi-abstract sequences but also as a dynamic showreel of the latest in (ultra) modern image generation and processing techniques – a foregrounding of state of the art techniques as a cultural form in its own right.[38] This association of rapid transitions of images and impact aesthetics with a quality of *ultra-contemporaneity* recalls the association of dynamic images and sensations which characterised Futurism, and just as Marjorie Perloff has characterised Postmodernism as a 'cool Futurism',[39] so Klein has characterised his original commissions as 'cool TV art'.[40] As he also emphasised, 'We see *Ultratech* as a very global idea because there is no language, there is no plot, there are no characters . . . It's just sound and light, TV taken down to its essence'.[41]

Aesthetic Innovation

The development of post-production and image processing technologies received fresh impetus in the late Eighties with the introduction of digital editing and effects systems which offered a series of improvements on previously available technology.[42] One improvement was their ability to produce multiple image overlays and image processing without the 'generational' deterioration of quality which occurred with analogue technologies. Another was the greater ease with which such manipulations could be produced, previewed and combined. Although access to fully digital editing facilities was too expensive for even the highest budget music video productions in this period, 'transitional' technologies such as the Ampex A64 system[43] first began to make a significant impact on music video production during 1987/88. One early

example of a video which utilised the distinctive abilities of such systems was the promo for Johnny Hates Jazz's *Heart of Gold* single (1988). This used digital effects to distort the video's source visual sequence and render it in a style which resembled the multi-polaroid collages produced by artists such as David Hockney in the late Eighties.

Neneh Cherry set against John Maybury's distinctive graphics (1989)

Though the particular approach used in *Heart of Gold* was not widely copied in subsequent music videos, a number of distinct generic styles began to emerge in 1988/89. These included a cycle of music videos such as Boy George's *No Clause 28* (1988), Sinead O'Connor's *I Want Your Arms Around Me* (1988), Neneh Cherry's *Buffalo Stance* (1988) and Technotronic's *Pump Up the Jam* (1989); which combined multiple mattes (giving a succession of superimposed image planes) and complex animated graphic backgrounds. Videos such as these use the multiplicity of images and image planes, various kaleidoscopic and image multiplying techniques and rapid image transitions (both within frames and between them) to give themselves a particularly intense and elaborate 'high tech impact'. Echoing Klein's remarks on the *confrontational style* of *Ultratech*, British director John Maybury has, for instance, described his video for Boy George's *No Clause 28* as 'an assault course of colours and shapes, with different images fighting to the front each time the video is viewed.'[44]

Maybury's comments should not however be understood as purely a statement of personal artistic taste or preference. The production of music video texts which feature complex, disparate and rapidly superceded images which require *active* (re-)viewing on the part of their audiences is, increasingly, an industrial imperative. The function of a 'promo' is to attract attention and 'hook' audiences in its own right – thereby also drawing attention to the video's music track. Since the advent of MTV and the commercial retailing of music video compilations, producers and directors have increasingly seen music video as having a sustained cultural circulation. This factor in itself necessitates compositional considerations. As David Byrne emphasised in 1987, 'videos are replayed a lot so they have to be multi-layered'.[45] Maybury elaborated on this with regard to his work on videos such as *No Clause 28*, emphasising that,

> *I feel it is my duty to enforce a longevity . . . I want things to have a life beyond the initial moment – by having multiple passes* [image layers] *on a video, viewers should still be noticing new elements when they view it for the sixth or seventh time.*[46]

This concern with elements such as multiple image layering, spectacular image compositions and dynamic transition, emphasises the *competitive* nature of individual video's attention-seeking amidst a prolific field of production. Starting from the premise that 'the ability of a music promo to withstand or invite repeated viewings is central to selling a song', Robert Krey has emphasised how a video's success in attracting and sustaining such multiple viewings is 'the reward for cinematic [sic] innovation'.[47] This emphasis on the 'rewards of innovation' returns us of course to the analytical project of this chapter. Krey's emphasis supports Jameson's contention that aesthetic innovation has increasingly assumed a structural function for the culture industries. But in accepting this characterisation, we also need to consider the nature of the 'aesthetic innovation' taking place.

One of the difficulties of applying Jameson's formulation to a specific area of cultural production is that 'aesthetic innovation' is as much a critical perception as it is an empirically verifiable cultural tendency. It is, for instance, both less tangible and less identifiable than its associate tendency, *formal* innovation. Experiments with style and genre and/or the constant revision or diversification of formal attributes cannot be seen to evidence, *per se*, aesthetic innovation (and thereby demonstrate its 'structural function'). While music video has been characterised by a continuing project of formal experimentation and innovative uses of successive generations of image effects technology, we need to consider whether this in itself can be observed to have lead to a progressively innovative *aesthetic* base for the overall form.

With regard to the particular styles and genres of music video detailed in this chapter, we can characterise their distinctive aesthetic attributes in terms of: their orientation towards what has loosely been termed 'impact aesthetics'; an associated preoccupation with the use of new technologies for novel image effects; and, increasingly in recent work, a conscious multi-layering of the visual image. The combination of these does not however constitute an innovative aesthetic *in itself*. The fetishisation of new generations of technology, what I have termed the *technovelty* factor, can perhaps be seen as distinctive to, or at least particularly pronounced in, music video. Again though, it does not in itself constitute a primary aesthetic for the form. Similarly, the music video's dynamic visual images are not innovative in themselves but rather the latest manifestation of formal tradition(s) in a new cultural context. Their variously influential predecessors include, for example, the clashing montages of Eisenstein; the 'dream-like' progression and juxtapositions of Surrealist Cinema; the rapid image transitions of television advertising; the sophisticated visual style of magazines such as *The Face* and *Blitz*; and the dynamic visual conventions of live music performance and disco lightshows.

We can however begin to perceive the development of a new *decorative* aesthetic in those series of multi-layered texts which appear to invite multiple (re)viewing. Synchronised to a soundtrack, these texts feature a distinct organisation of visual elements composed as a multiplicity of surfaces, flattened to the picture plane. They therefore deviate significantly from other contemporary developments of contemporary hi-tech image media and, in particular, the shift towards 'virtual' or 'cybernetic' spaces that are not representational but rather entirely generated and 'illusory'. By contrast, the multi-image layers of videos such as *No Clause 28* or *Buffalo Stance* constitute simultaneous multiple montages which require different responses to foreground and background levels and associations than conventional audio-visual media texts – one where the spectator is more loosely structured into the visual image (progression) than has hitherto been the norm for most forms of cinema and television.

This approach to visual composition is in itself a product of the use of newly available technologies within a media project neither concerned with representational realism, nor narrative logic, nor any preconstituted discourse of image organisation. Nor even, with the advent of sampled 'impossible' vocal techniques such as those featured in Black Box's international hit single *Ride on Time* (1989), notional fidelity to achievable human vocal performance. The enabling effect of technology in contexts such as this is to offer a transformation in both the nature of visual and sonic composition and its interrelation. It thereby offers a radical reconfiguration of the nature of the apparently representational image, and, in the case of videos featuring mimed performance, the actual human origination of the vocal sound as performed activity.

With music and the visual tracks of music video productions increasingly utilising digital sampling, production and editing techniques, it has been possible to see a gradual complementary *dovetailing* of the two activities over the last five years. While music videos such as Rik Lander's promo for M/A/R/R/S' *Pump Up the Volume* have used video edit suite technology to produce visual collage tracks for sampled music singles, it is only recently that such sampling and purely post-production technologies[48] have been used to produce both visual and music tracks. Perhaps the most notable complementary use of such technologies to date has been that pursued by Colin Scott of the British video production duo Stakker. Under the name 'Humanoid', Scott produced both a sampled music track, entitled *Stakker* and an accompanying visual sequence. Like Stakker's two *Eurotech* programmes for MTV Europe's *Ultratech* slot in 1988,[49] the visual track principally comprised images generated on a Fairlight computer and subsequently re-mixed and processed on more sophisticated video graphics systems. Unlike the duo's *Eurotech* programmes (and the subsequent versions which appeared in 1989), which were produced and circulated as video (ie *visual*) art pieces, *Stakker* was released as an audio track. The record became a minor hit in British clubs and the singles charts in early 1989, with the video supporting it as a promo in the conventional manner.

With the complementary use of technologies to provide audio and visual tracks for music videos, the possibility obviously opens up for music videos to be *integrated* in their production – ie to be produced as one artefact rather than as the visualisation of a pre-constituted form. The development of an integral relation between visual and audio media has of course been the aim of a number of avant garde artists over the last century. Various approaches to combinative and mutually reactive audio-visual equivalence have been pursued. Some of these, such as Schoenberg's notions of visual equivalence, have been largely theoretical. Others, such as Oskar Fischinger's abstract visualisations of preconstituted music tracks (such as his series of *Studies* or his famous *Komposition in Blau* [1935]) have been pursued in a more or less programmatic fashion. But it is with new developments of computer technology, particularly MIDI interface,[50] that such exercises in visual equivalence have reached a new degree of (potential) sophistication. Works such as Zbigniew Rybczynski's visualisation of Paganini's *Capricci # 24 for Violin* (arranged for synthesizer) illustrate the potential of new technological processes. This piece, made in 1989, develops a precisely coordinated (re-coded) visualisation of its music track by measuring the duration of each musical note as stored on the synthesizer. As Rybczynski emphasises, using this method of measurement makes it 'easy to measure video frames to be exactly in synch with the music. Every note . . .'.[51]

Due to the time and budget required by such production practices, this procedure is unlikely to develop as anything but an occasional method of music video production for the foreseeable future. Other developments of technology and practice do however offer an even greater degree of equivalence between music text and visual. In the past, groups such as Cabaret Voltaire and the Severed Heads have attempted to produce video and music work as part of an integrated group activity. Similarly, video artists such as Paul Garrin have attempted to produce visualisations of pre-constituted music tracks whereby changes in the sound directly trigger new images and visual transitions.[52] Scratch video makers such as George Barber have also reworked 'found' sound elements and their visual contexts in producing highly integrated audio-visual texts.[53] New technologies currently offer the potential to produce an even greater integration of visual and music composition and production. As Martin Raymond has emphasised, developments of voice-to-image interfacing now mean that a range of contemporary visual effects can 'be done by the singer/musicians themselves – microcomputers harnessing, cutting, reversing vocal patterns to produce comparable video effects from stored or real time effects loops'.[54]

MIDI derived technologies are now rapidly facilitating the production of new forms of audio-visual metamedia which merely await a cultural context within which to operate and circulate before they develop into a distinct *cultural* medium in their own right. Depending on a complex set of economic and cultural factors, these integrated audio-visual forms could be produced and circulated in a variety of ways. They could be developed and promoted as simply more sophisticated versions of conventional music video promos, distributed and exhibited as video art pieces[55] or otherwise be packaged, promoted and asserted as an autonomous form.

This brief survey serves to emphasise how, in the specific cultural context of pop(ular) music and music video, the combination of highly competitive commercial forces and successive developments in technology has provided a dynamic motor for audio-visual development and innovation. This in turn suggests that the judgement with which Charles Berg concluded his historical survey 'Visualizing Music: The Archaeology of Music Video'; that 'building on a rich legacy that goes back to the prophecies of Edison, the music video format possesses artistic, cultural and economic potentials that have only begun to be tapped,[56] was not only fundamentally correct, but perhaps rather inappropriately modest about the achievements of the form to date. Despite the form's continuing misfit with traditional cultural paradigms and assumptions of value, it is apparent that it is no longer tenable for cultural criticism to neglect such a vibrant and prolifically productive area of (popular) culture – one which arguably represents the most distinctive form of audio-visual production to grace the late Twentieth Century.

1   Fredric Jameson, 'Postmodernism, or the Cultural Logic of Late Capitalism' *New Left Review* n146 July-August 1984 p56.

2   Patrick Goldstein 'The New British Invasion' *American Film* May 1983 p17.

3   Dana Polan 'Jacques and Gilles: Reflections on Deleuze's Cinema of Ideas' *Art & Text* n34 Spring 1989 p25.

4   For discussion of various aspects of this phenomenon see the various articles in *Screen* v28 n2 Spring 1987, particularly Philip Hayward and Paul Kerr, 'Introduction', pp2-8 and James Collins, 'Postmodernism and Cultural Practice: Redefining the Parameters' pp11-26. For a discussion of an individual film in these terms see Giuliana Bruno, 'Ramble City: Postmodernism and *Blade Runner'* *October* n41, pp61-74.

5   For a discussion of *Moonlighting* in these terms see Philip Hayward, 'How ABC capitalised on Cultural Logic: The *Moonlighting* Story' *Mediamatic* v2 n4 June 1988 pp185-188 reprinted in Manuel Alvarado and John O Thompson (eds) *The Media Reader* London, BFI 1990 pp265-274.

6   Barbara London and Keith Johnson, programme notes to *Music Video: The Industry and its Fringes* show, New York Museum of Modern Art, September 1985. For a review of this show see Joan Lynch, 'Music Videos: In a Museum Setting', *OneTwoThreeFour: A Rock 'n' Roll Quarterly* n5 Spring 1987 pp104-108.

7   See for instance Charles M Berg, 'Visualizing Music: The Archaeology of Music Video' *OneTwoThreeFour: A Rock 'n' Roll Quarterly* n5 Spring 1987 pp94-103.

8   See for instance the range of album cover designs produced for EMI's Harvest label in the early to mid Seventies.

9   Since its introduction in 1963, with title sequences designed by Bernard Lodge using a new technique called 'howl-around', the series' title sequences have had twelve re-vamps designed to keep their visual effects up with current technical developments. (See Sue Griffin 'Who Dares Change' *Invision* n15 August/September 1988, pp18-19 for a further discussion of *Dr Who* title sequences.)

10 In 1979 The Boomtown Rats were a punk band with R & B inflections who had achieved limited chart success with two previous singles released in 1977, the year of the British punk 'explosion'. *Looking After Number One* and *Mary of the Fourth Form*. Their 1979 single *I Don't Like Mondays* was however something of a departure for the band both in musicial terms, being slower, more complex and arranged; and in projecting a new image for the group via its accompanying video. Directed by David Mallett, the video's multiple sets of geometric image compositions, rapid edits and general 'tone' reinforced the new 'older' market orientation of the band and contributed to the record becoming their best selling single.

11 Russell Mulcahy interviewed in the BBC2 documentary *Video Jukebox* broadcast in 1986.

12 *ibid.*

13 Fredric Jameson, *op cit.*

14 See George Barber 'Scratch and After: Edit Suite Technology and the Determination of Style in Video Art' in this volume.

15 As Andrew Goodwin points out, the 'female models who adorn the set to mime the performance of guitar, keyboard and drum parts are one of the most explicit statements pop has made

regarding its essentially visual nature. We are not asked to believe that these women actually play these instruments . . . what is offered is visual pleasure almost unrelated to the usual codes of pop performance . . . these images are the culmination of a pop industry coming to terms with the visual imagery that lies at the heart of pop meaning'. Andrew Goodwin 'From Anarchy to Chromakey: Music, Media, Video'. *OneTwoThreeFour: A Rock 'n' Roll Quarterly* n5, Spring 1987 p19.

16   It should also be noted that the male body is now frequently used for similar purposes, see for instance Belinda Carlisle's *I Get Weak* (1988) or Malcolm McLaren's *Something's Jumping in My Shirt* (1989).

17   There were however a number of significant music videos produced in the USA in the mid 1970s, including Captain Beefheart's one minute long TV advert for his *Lick My Decals Off, Baby* (1970), various film clips for 'underground' acts as Devo (eg *Secret Agent Man* [1976]) or The Residents (eg *Land of a 1000 dances* [1975]), the ultra-low budget video produced for Commander Cody's *Two Triple Cheese, Side Order of Fries* (1979) and the more lavish music video produced for Mike Nesmith's *Rio* in 1977 which prefigured a number of later stylistic developments in the medium.

18   Annabel Jankel, interviewed in *Video Jukebox* op cit.

19   'Ultimatte' is an electronic visual compositing system which was originally developed as a video previewer for film matte composite photography (and was first used for this purpose on the feature film *Battle Beyond the Stars* [1980]. Subsequent to its introduction in this context, it has been used extensively as a video post-production device in its own right.

20   As stated in advertising copy for Ultimatte's full page advertisement headed 'Ever Wish for an Ultimatte in your Switcher?' *World Broadcast News* November 1989 p43.

21   For further production details see Roma Felstein 'To the Frontiers of Creativity' *Broadcast* November 1984 p27.

22   See George Barber *op cit*

23   See for instance the series of Amplex ads produced for British television in the mid-Eighties.

24   For a discussion of sampling technology see Alan Durant 'A New Day for Music? – Digital Technologies in Contemporary Music Making' in this volume.

25   Rocky Morton interviewed in *Video Jukebox* op cit.

26   Despite the fashionability of pastiche, it should be noted, as Theo van Leeuven has pointed out to me, that stylistic pastiche in music goes back much further than postmodern popular music, to Stravinsky, Satie and Poulenc for example. Also modern 'easy listening' arrangements can be seen to fit into this category. What is new about pastiche in contemporary music is its particular rationale and the particular cultural legitimation of this.

27   See Sue Griffin *op cit.*

28   The music video for the single, also played on *Top of the Pops* in subsequent weeks, used low budget special effects and props as an ironic comment on the low budget set designs and props habitually featured in the *Dr Who* series.

29   As cited by Jane Harbord 'Europe Pops the Question' *Invision* n15 September 1987 p14.

30   For further discussion of MTV's competitors in the US market, see Maria Viera 'The Institutionalization of Music Video'

OneTwoThreeFour: A Rock 'n' Roll Quarterly n5 Spring 1987
pp80-93.

31   For a more detailed account see Paul Allman 'MTV – A Fad
      Gone Bad' *Invision* 25 September 1988 pp34-35.

32   On air comperes, a term derived from the radio designation
      D J – 'disk jockey'.

33   Brief sequences identifying the station and animating its logo.

34   Paul Allman, *op cit*, p35.

35   Jonathan Klein, cited in 'Cool Art of wild MTV idents'
      (unattributed) *Invision* n20 March 88 p6.

36   Jonathan Klein, cited in Willem Velthoven, 'Pump Up The
      Picture' *Mediamatic* v2 n4 June 1988 p175.

37   Willem Velthoven *op cit*.

38   Amongst the best received of the *Ultratech* programmes were
      the two produced by Mark McLean and Colin Scott under the
      group name of Stakker (which gratified Klein's artistic
      aspirations for his product by being subsequently exhibited on
      the international Video Art circuit). These two programmes,
      Eurotech I and *II* took the *brutal confrontational* approach to a high
      extreme with strobe-like rapid editing produced by the duo
      generating basic shapes and patterns on a Fairlight 6000
      computer and subsequently doing more complex visual mixes
      and processing on Encore or Mirage video effect computer
      systems.

39   Marjorie Perloff *The Futurist Moment* Chicago, University of
      Chicago Press 1986 p195.

40   Jonathan Klein, cited in 'Cool Art of wild MTV idents', *op cit*.

41   Jonathan Klein, cited in Velthoven *op cit*.

42   For a discussion of aspects of digital technology see Alan Durant,
      op cit and Jeremy Welsh, both in this volume.

43   George Barber has described the Ampex A64 as 'a clever piece
      of niche marketing' which is 'essentially a digital recorder with
      two disks'. 'You can record up to sixty seconds on each disk –
      then mix them, re-record something onto *one* of the disks and
      mix again – on and on and on. It is true that it *is* digital, but it
      is in the middle . . . you certainly need tape machines, as all
      you can do is work on *small* sections of your video at a time,
      slotting them into place'. (From a letter to the author.)

44   John Maybury, interviewed in Toni Rogers 'Clause and Effect'
      Invision n24 July/August 1988 p7.

45   David Byrne interviewed in *Video Jukebox* op cit.

46   John Maybury *op cit*.

47   Robert Krey, 'Music Promos: Thinking Visually' *American
      Cinematographer* April 1984 p81.

48   See Alan Durant *op cit*.

49   See footnote 36 (above).

50   See Alan Durant *op cit*.

51   Zbigniew Rybczynski cited in Paul Allman 'Zbig Noise',
      Videographic v1 n2 August 1989 p13.

52   See for instance his visualisation of Ryuichi Sakamoto's *A Rain
      Song* (1986).

53   See particularly *Yes Frank, No Smoke* and *Absence of Satan* (both
      1986).

54   Martin Raymond, 'Hard Disc' *Videographic* v1 n7 January/
      February 1990 p6.

55   As indeed Stakker's two *Ultratech* programmes for MTV Europe
      – *Eurotech I* and *II* – were, subsequent to broadcast.

56   Charles Berg *op cit* p101.

8
POWER, ACCESS AND INGENUITY
Electronic Imaging Technologies and Contemporary Visual Art

JEREMY WELSH

What Can It Do? How Much Will It Cost?

As we approach the end of the century, the practices of Art and Technology, which once seemed to emanate from widely diverging discourses, move ever closer together. However, this convergence is really nothing new, as we were reminded by a recent exhibition devoted to Leonardo da Vinci at London's Hayward Gallery.[1] Interestingly, the exhibition not only demonstrated Leonardo's breadth of vision, encompassing both aesthetics and engineering – the intuitive and the analytical – but also applied some 'state of the art' Twentieth Century technology to Leonardo's ideas, using computer techniques to bring to life some of his inventions.[2]

Aside from extraordinary individuals like Leonardo who can encompass both art and science, there has always been the presence of technology of some kind in the background of artistic production. From the invention of oil paint to the invention of 'Harry' – one of the most powerful tools of digital image production and manipulation – it has never been solely the vision of the artist that has determined the progression of art. However, the situation we face now is so intrinsically different that we can make a distinction. What we can say is that in previous periods of art history, at least up until the development of cinema, technology's role has primarily been that of developing and perfecting materials. The artist's concern, at the technical level, has been to do with *technique*, with the ability to manipulate and transform materials. Photo-mechanical media represent a transitional phase in which technology comes to play an increasing role in the process of creation, but one where there is still a material base that can be acted upon directly and materially.

With the advent of electronic media, the material is abolished to all intents and purposes. Technique is no longer the ability to manipulate material but the ability to manipulate technology. The artist using these new tools may have concerns that are apparently the same as Carravagio's – the manipulation of colour, light and shade, the creation of realist images that portray and comment on the world at large – but the methods of production are entirely different. These artists do not arrange molecules of paint upon a flat surface, they arrange small quantities of electricity in a system that ultimately fires electrons at a charged screen which then glows to produce the appearance of an image. The question of technology's impact upon such art is not one of 'whether', but 'to what extent' technology determines what an artist may or may not create.

Again, this is not a new idea. It is simply that the process has been accelerated substantially and that technology has come to occupy a highly visible position within the creative process. While it can certainly be maintained that the invention of oil paint was what made oil painting possible, any discussion of oil painting itself will focus on the artist's use of it and not the stuff itself. The special qualities of the medium used need to be taken into account, and the artist's approach to dealing with its specific problems, but the question of how or whether to attempt to make art out of oil paint is not something one need be concerned with.

However with computer technologies and electronic media such questions can and will be asked. Although the photograph has now largely been granted the status of art object – notwithstanding traditional art historians who will refute this – the electronic image, the television image, the computer generated image, still exist, possibly will *always* exist, in a disputed territory which, however artful, is not quite 'Art'. The fact that what is seen is entirely the result of a technological process and that any 'magic' in the image can be attributed to the power of the machine or its software (or its inventors and programmers); means that an evaluation of the image within the traditional discourses of art criticism becomes deeply problematic. The status of the 'artist as genius' cannot be maintained since what is most impressive is the power of the machine the artist used. The role of the artist is therefore changing and the creative process changes with it to become one of problem solving: Genius is exchanged for Ingenuity.

The first problem is this: consider a specific item or technology in terms of what it can do and determine whether or not it is useful, whether or not it allows scope for an idea to be developed and communicated. The second problem is to decide whether the specific qualities of a piece of technology are, in themselves, interesting enough to build a work of art upon. The third is to identify a technology capable of doing what the artist wishes it to do and the fourth is to make it do what the artist wishes to do even if this contravenes the intentions of its inventors.

These four problems are all prior to the actual making of a single image and there are numerous other problems to be overcome before the work can be made. A question central to the discussion of Art and Technology is whether technology enables or determines what the artist may do. Does it represent limitless possibilities for creative expression (as much advertising copy for high-tech hardware suggests)? Or does it impose a set of restrictions which must inevitably limit the horizons of the artist and thereby circumscribe the territory of Art? The answer often lies not with the technology itself, nor with the ability of artists to master and exploit it but with the entirely practical questions of Money and Access. Obviously, the most powerful technologies will tend to be the most expensive, so access to these technologies will also be expensive. This in turn means that acquiring the skills and experience necessary to exploit these technologies will be expensive. The question then becomes not 'Can X machine do what I want it to?' but 'How long will it take and how much will it cost for X to do Y?' and 'Can I afford it?'.

The importance of this question shifts according to the level of technology under consideration. If we position digital editing systems like Quantel's Harry at one end of the scale and home computers and low cost video equipment at the other, we can examine the shift in Access-Power ratio between them. If Harry does offer virtually boundless possibilities for the construction and manipulation of complex digitally produced images, then this boundlessness is, to a large extent, 'notional'. At this moment almost no-one can possibly afford to experiment with it long enough to find out what the whole range of its capabilities (and therefore its limitations) are. Conversely, the Commodore Amiga, a powerful micro computer originally produced for the domestic market but increasingly used by artists and designers, is cheap – with a top of the range model costing the equivalent of a short day in a Harry suite – and accessible but lacks the enormous power and flexibility of high end computer imaging systems. While Harry and other machines like it retain an almost mystical status for many artists who can only dream of using one, the Amiga, as its name suggests, is an accessible and friendly tool which, with ingenuity, patience and determination, can be pushed to give more than it has apparently got. It is interesting to speculate whether the gap between the capabilities of high end professional systems and low cost domestic educational or semi-professional ones will gradually close, or whether the rate of development at both ends of the scale will ensure that even as 'high street' technology increases in power and sophistication, the advances made at the leading edge of technological development will continue to accelerate more rapidly.

Technical advances in video image production are, almost without exception, being made in the commercial sector and most especially within the field of 'Videographics' – what used once to be called television design. The few exceptions to this tendency have occurred in the USA, where the crossover between Video Art (non-commercial and grant aided) and commercial, or commercially funded, production is more fluid than in Britain. A few artists like John Sanborn, who once described Video Art as the R & D (research and development) division of broadcast television, and Zbigniew Rybczynski, known for his technically dazzling video productions, have been able to work with High Definition Television recording systems and extremely powerful three dimensional graphics computers. But in general, it is in the field of videographics that we see the standards being set for formal innovation in the production of electronic images. The use of Harry, which allows for multiple layering of digitally recorded images without loss of image quality, is almost entirely concentrated in production of graphic 'stings' for television stations, television commercials and pop videos – all of which are short form.

Britain, and London in particular, occupies a leading role in the development of the style and the visual language of Videographics. The pre-eminent exponents are, for the most part, young artists and designers who have emerged from centres like Dundee's Duncan of Jordanstone College of Arts and who have grown up with video machinery and computers. What we are seeing is the development and refinement of a sophisticated visual language that took up where confrontational and deconstructive forms like Scratch Video left off.[3] This language, like much contemporary visual culture, takes for granted the 'game' of quotation and cross reference, absorbs the signifiers of cultural history, plays cat and mouse with the viewer's cognitive powers and indulges unashamedly in the pleasures of the electronic text.

Although Video Art claims to have elaborated alternative ways of using television, these may turn out to be more marginal than we previously thought. It is quite clear at present that the real shifts in our perceptual framework are being brought about by developments within mainstream media culture, through forms like videographics, some pop videos and commercials and television drama as typified by the non sequential and fragmentary narratives of *Moonlighting*, *thirtysomething*, etc.[4] All of these forms obey the logic of a technology whose promise is to deliver more information, more rapidly, more accurately and in a more absorbable and attractive package.

So if the logic of high technology is locked into the imperative of a market led media culture, then perhaps the arena for the expression of alternative content is to be found elsewhere – not in the 'virtual worlds' of electronic simulation nor in the seamless visual aerobatics of digital video post production, but in other approaches to technology. The following section looks at a few examples of artists' works that exploit technology in particular ways that are not tied to the 'more is better, faster' logic of digital media. What they have in common is that, in each instance, the choice of technology used has been central to the making and/or presentation of the work. Not simply in the sense that a given technology would offer the best way of making the work but in some cases that it could *only* be made through the use of this technology.

Some Examples

There are two important factors governing the choices of technology used by the artists in the following examples. Firstly, each has chosen a technology or set of technologies whose specific capabilities enable the full realisation of an idea; secondly, all have some form of privileged access to such technology. In the case of Viola and Snow, their status as artists is such that they can command the kind of institutional and corporate support that provides access. Through his collaborations with Nam June Paik and the Japanese musician and actor Ryuchi Sakamoto, freelance editor Paul Garrin has developed strong links with New York facility houses and produces his own work as an artist in commercial 'down time'. The Theys Brothers miraculously produced *Die Walkure* on a miniscule budget, relying on the patronage of the Belgian TV station RTBF (which allowed them free access to studios when not in use). A similar form of sponsorship in kind also enables Finnish artist Marikki Hakola to produce her works on similarly modest budgets.

See You Later: A Film by Michael Snow (1990)

The first work I want to discuss is not video and was not made on a computer. It is a film but one which neatly encapsulates a discussion of the Art/Technology relationship. It carries forward many of Snow's concerns from earlier films like the famous *Wavelength* (1967) – the experience of cinematic duration, slowing of time, an examination of minutiae – and, like many avant garde films, it places process in a prominent position so as to either deconstruct or demolish illusion. The film consists of a single take inside a room in which a man (Snow himself) gets up from a desk, puts on his coat, walks past a woman at another desk and goes out of the door. In real time the whole action would last for thirty seconds but here it is extended to last eighteen minutes. The action is seen in extreme slow motion but, at the same time, with an almost hallucinatory clarity. The blur that normally occurs with slowed down film or video is entirely absent because it was shot on a high speed camera and the effect it gives is somewhat akin to seeing a large and sumptuous colour photograph metamorphosing before one's eyes. The film is clearly an example of a work that could only be made using a particular piece of technology and, whilst the technology certainly determines what is possible within the film, the film also defines a use for the technology, so idea and realisation exist in equilibrium.

Passage: A Video Installation by Bill Viola (1987)

This work by Bill Viola has in common with Snow's film an interest in extreme manipulation of time but, in this instance, it is achieved by the use of video rather than film. A video recording lasting one hour is played back on a one inch VTR with variable speeds, allowing it to be played at one eighth of its normal speed. So an hour of time is stretched to become eight hours, and the subject of the tape – one hour at a child's party – is stretched to last the equivalent of a working day. Viola has described the use of video slow motion as a 'temporal magnifying glass', the implication being that the closer you look the more you will see. Such an attitude could hardly contrast more with the 'three minute culture' aesthetics of pop video and tv commercials but, interestingly, both use technology in their own deliberate ways to provide 'more' of something.

Yuppie Ghetto: An Interactive Video Installation by Paul Garrin (1990)

Garrin is a New York video artist who uses video as a direct confrontational medium, employing the entire arsenal of digital post production, but turning it back to fire scattershot volleys at the values and hypocrisies of the media and the establishment. His recent work spans the range of technologies a video artist might use – shot on an 8mm video

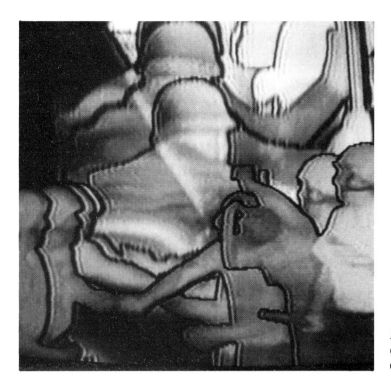

*Images from Paul
Garrin's* Yuppie
Ghetto *(1990)*

camcorder because it is small, light, discreet, and can be used almost anywhere, but edited on broadcast quality one inch equipment with digital effects allowing the construction of multiple layers of mattes. For his 1990 installation, the video material was transferred to laser disc for interactivity and instant playback.

The centre of the gallery space is lit by a harsh white spotlight and at the end of the room opposite the entrance is a breeze block wall sprayed with graffiti, and a barbed wire fence behind which is a video monitor showing the image of a large guard dog. Above this enclosure, a surveillance camera scans the space. As the viewer enters the room, the dog takes notice and becomes progressively more agitated. By the time the viewer is at the centre of the room, the dog is lunging forward, snarling and snapping. When the 'intruder' stops moving, it gradually calms down again, until another presence in the room causes it to respond once more. On the wall behind the dog/monitor is a large projected image of the interior of a room in which well dressed people are mingling at a cocktail party. Matted into the large picture window are images of rioting crowds and police.

Every stage and each level of this deceptively simple work relies upon the specific qualities of a technology or set of technologies. The video 8 camera allowed the artist to shoot the action from within rather than from a detached viewpoint, so the riot images have an immediacy that would be diminished had they come from a more 'objective' source. The technology controlling the interactive monitoring/dog is a Apple Macintosh computer that uses information from the surveillance camera to determine which segments of a laser disc are to be played back. Software for this system was developed by Canadian computer artist and musician David Rokeby who has been experimenting for some time with movement activated audio installations. This was Garrin's first experiment with interactive video and, by his own admission, it only scratches the surface of what will be possible with systems of this kind. What is especially interesting is that interactive multimedia systems like this will become increasingly commonplace, cheap and accessible, being based upon the micro computers like the Macintosh, the Amiga and IBM PC. The CD revolution in recorded music is now spreading to video and to data storage through CDV (compact disc video) CD ROM (audio visual data storage on compact disc for computer based interactive teaching applications) and CDI (compact disc interactive which will combine digital audio, video and data storage in the same medium).

Song of My Soil II: Die Walküre: A Video by Frank and Koen Theys (1989)

This ninety minute production is the second in an ambitious proposed series that will, if completed, commit Wagner's entire Ring cycle to video – not as a neutral recording of operatic performances, but as a contemporary electronic interpretation on the Wagnerian ideal of the *Gesamkunstwerk*. The primary tool used by the Theys brothers is the television studio – not a single item of equipment, but the whole system of studio production and post production. Electronic mixing, superimposing and keying (selective montaging of segments of separate images) are used extensively to build up a multi-layered and multi-dimensional simulated space within which the opera is portrayed.

Die Walkure is remarkable in a number of ways. For video art production it is extremely long, complex and wildly ambitious. As an interpretation of high opera it is more than a little unconventional. As an exploration of the possible uses of studio and post production effects as narrative and dramatic devices, it has no counterpart. The intention of the Theys Brothers was to find an equivalent for Wagner's *lietmotiv* system and what they devised was a series of effects and images that would recur in the production and take on that function. The tape was entirely shot in a studio and all of the sets, backgrounds and scenery were electronically keyed in behind the action. Bizarre composite images transform parts of bodies into architectural forms, create collisions of separate realities and produce illusions of space and perspective that would be impossible on a 'live' stage. Performers fly through the air, bodies merge into one another and metamorphose into androgynous or hermaphrodite forms, landscapes slide around like sheets of ice laid one on another.[5]

The site of power in the narrative, the God Wotan, here observes the actions played out by the mortals and his warrior maidens, the Valkyries, not through the disembodied omniscient consciousness we would traditionally attribute to his status but on a screen – a glowing segment of wall like the giant monitor screens of science fiction movies. The role of the screen as embodiment of power, as the site of struggle, triumph and failure, is reinforced throughout the production. Video noise – the 'snow' of an untuned television screen, is used to represent fluid elements, chaotic, formless energy, space or matter. There is no sun in this world – all is lit by video light, diffuse, directionless and endemic, flattening the visual realm into a series of planes, areas of charged colour that define a space that is entirely synthetic. And the performers are not, for the most part, characters with developed, individuated identities, but are ciphers, icons. Icons more precisely in the sense that an icon is a small graphic symbol on a computer screen which, when acted upon, causes a change in the state of the screen to occur. The performers, the electronic space, the graphic objects that form the architecture of this electronic space are all more or less equal, are all design elements in the compositional vocabulary of the artists.

Milena's Journey: A Videotape by Marikki Hakola (1990)

Finland's foremost video artist Marikki Hakola has a painterly approach to the use of video effects which gives her work a richness and sensuality that is almost akin to the quality of woven fabric. In particular she exploits the use of dissolves, superimposition and various forms of keying – the electronic equivalent of photomontage – to create multi-layered images. Colour, form, texture, movement and stillness are all manipulated to create atmospheric and often haunting episodic works that lift the viewer out of the mundane and everyday into an imaginary realm. In *Milena's Journey*, Hakola takes a classic theme for the film or video maker and, like the French video artist Robert Cahen, of whose tape *Juste Le Temps* this new work is reminiscent, she adds an extra layer of magic to the theme of the journey.

Using effects, she transforms the visual field of *Milena's Journey* into a fluid and dreamlike landscape in which distortions and aberrations of spatial and temporal perception combine to provide an almost hallucinogenic quality. The successive layers and strands of imagery are blended together so seamlessly that the work literally flows – reminding us once again of a specific 'liquid' quality that is exclusive to video and sets it apart quite clearly from films. It is no accident that the combination of water and light so often becomes the subject of video art since the precise visual qualities of reflected light in water are in some sense a visual metaphor for video itself.[6] What Hakola manages to do is to create this sense of liquidity through the simultaneous manipulation of several layers of image; a perfect blend of aesthetic vision and applied technological form.

Epilogue

The Art and Technology debate will continue and will always cause contention. There will always be those who maintain that Art is, by definition, a unique and hand made object. Equally there will be those who proclaim the death of painting at the hands of some new medium, process or procedure. Neither position is a realistic one to adopt. What seems certain is that electronic technologies will continue to penetrate every level of our culture, from production to distribution, and that new technologies will call forth new responses from artists anxious to use them. Paintings will be produced on video screens and printed out onto canvasses by giant paint jet printers but they will also be made on easels in private rooms, with sable brushes and watercolours. Computer graphics will deliver ever more sophisticated computer games, educational environments, simulated journeys, virtual experiences and new forms of visual representation that will provide artists, critics and lookers alike with an ongoing subject of debate, research and pleasure.

What is important from the cultural viewpoint is that we continue to have and, indeed, augment and extend, a situation in which artists like those discussed above have the opportunity to explore possible uses of new technology. Such opportunities allow the true potential of such technologies to become apparent, as they are used to convey depths of experience and meaning which are beyond the scope of information use and corporate propaganda. To ensure this continued cross fertilisation of art and technology, we need a number of factors to be in place. Starting from the bottom up, there needs first to be a well established and well resourced educational sector that will allow individuals wishing to work in Art/Technology the time and space to develop both technical skills and a personal style or vision upon which a substantial art practice can be built.

Beyond this first level, there needs to be a properly funded and effectively managed production sector that allows artists access to the tools of production outside the normal constraints of a commercial budget. This, in essence, has existed in Britain in the form of the subsidised film and video workshop sector but as these workshops go into rapid decline as a result of the withdrawal of subsidy, we are faced with the real likelihood that we will be back where we started twenty years ago before the workshops were established.[7] Thirdly, since any 'independent' workshop sector will always be based on less than state of the art technology, there needs to be a far sighted policy of patronage on the part of manufacturers and commercial production houses to provide artists with access to the highest levels of technology.[8] Fourthly, public funding resources need to be developed to meet the challenge of supporting the Art of the Twenty First Century.

In Britain it is unfortunately the case though that public funding policy is still barely equipped to deal with the demands of the decade we have just left behind. Resources continue to diminish and, instead of searching for imaginative ways of directing more finance and patronage into areas like Art/Technology, the funding agencies seem to be hell bent upon pushing their responsibilities back onto their clients or over into the corporate sector. In the USA, a scheme like the innovative 'On Line Program'[9] can function because:

a) People who knew what they were doing negotiated terms with the commercial sector; and

b) Artists can command grants – which are not tied to the apron strings of a Channel 4 editor, a BFI producer or an Arts Council Committee – which give them a degree of financial muscle sufficient to produce effectively on a professional basis. Such schemes benefit both artists and their patrons alike.

Current government policies which, in turn, become public funding policies, seem to be predicated upon the principle that we will only have the Art we can afford and that what we can afford is not much. If it costs more, then we will either not have it or try to pull the price down. Instead of this negative attitude, efforts should be made to raise the money.

Our scientists suffer from exactly the same problem, brought about by short-sighted funding policies. Scientific research, technological innovation, high quality education and forward looking cultural policies do not come cheap. But a society that chooses not to afford them chooses an intellectual and cultural impoverishment that will, in turn, have an adverse effect upon its status as an industrial and commercial force. While support for Art and Technology programmes may not be a panacea for our various economic, social and political ills, it would nevertheless – as one plank of a well constructed platform of technological, educational and cultural policies – secure us a position close to the cutting edge of technology for the Nineties and beyond.

Notes

1   'Leonardo Da Vinci: Artist – Scientist – Inventor', held at the Hayward Gallery (London), Spring 1989 (sponsored by the IBM Corporation).

2   For a brief discussion of the contemporary relevance of the exhibition, see Richard Wright 'Videographics and Allegorical Knowledge: The Epistemology of Leonardo' *Mediamatic* v3 n4 Summer 1989 pp196-197.

3   See George Barber 'Scratch and After: Edit Suite Technology and the Determination of Style in Video Art' in this volume.

4   For discussion of *Moonlighting* in these terms see Philip Hayward 'How ABC Capitalised on Cultural Logic: The *Moonlighting* Story' *Mediamatic* v2 n4 June 1988 pp185-188 reprinted in Manuel Alvarado and John O Thompson (eds) *The Media Reader* London, BFI 1990 pp264-275.

5   For further critical discussion of this see Gerard Lakke 'Song of my Soil – The Walküre' *Mediamatic* v3 n3 Spring 1989 pp151-157.

6   Also see George Barber 'Scratch and After', footnote 2 in this volume for another perspective on this.

7   I do not wish to cast myself as the Prophet of Doom, but this danger is something that has concerned me for some time and, for a fuller discussion of this, I would refer the reader to my articles 'Mixed Metaphors, Broken Codes' *Video* Montreal Artexte 1986, and '20 Questions, or, Leaving the 20th Century, Again, At Last' *Variant* Glasgow January 1990.

8   In the USA, the 'On Line' program developed by Media Alliance in association with facility houses in major cities like New York and Chicago has allowed artists to gain 'down time' access to high tech facilities at a fraction of the commercial cost. It should however be stressed that the level of grant aid they enjoy is considerably higher than is the case in the UK, so their 'down time' costs would still look expensive from the viewpoint of many British video artists. The video workshop situation in the US is also worth mentioning in passing; specifically the Experimental TV Workshop in Owega, New York, which was established in the late Sixties by Nam June Paik, among others, and has pioneered the development of image processing technologies made by and for artists. This 'DIY' approach to technology has never really taken hold in the UK.

9   Described in note 7 (above).

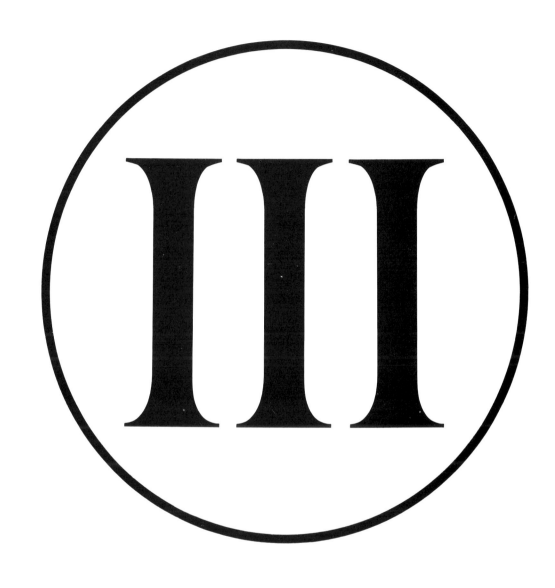

CONTEMPORARY
TECHNOLOGIES AND THE
REALIGNMENT OF CULTURE

9
ART BYTING THE DUST
Some considerations on time, economy and cultural practices of postmodernity

TONY FRY

Anyone who has studied the visual culture of modernity, even in a most cursory fashion, is aware of the massive burgeoning of the image and the technologies of its production in the modern era. Whole domains of signs were brought into being (and Being) and disseminated in all directions. Modern art was both an element and product of this milieu. The electronic image and the net its technology casts has, and is, changing this situation. Images are being created, captured, transformed, stored and managed like never before. Although still only partially established, and unevenly geo-economically evident, new image technologies have already changed the conditions of possibility of production of both art and the artist for ever. The very ground of culture has shifted. This means that art, as we have known it and have often been told throughout the 20th Century, is over. While this statement has always echoed a crisis in culture, what it now marks is a major change in art's materiality. But this does not imply that art will disappear for, like an old soldier who might be dead, it never fades away. Why? What can support such wild and general claims being made? I am going to answer these questions from three complementary viewpoints which cut across a number of contemporary cultural and economic theories.

The argument presented will attempt to work against the idea of a teleological model of staged development. The basic implication of this model is that history unfolds from a historical point of origin from which it moves away in ever more progressive forms. As the dominant mode of thought and narrative structure, such evolutionary thinking has permeated all domains of historical discourse in both the arts and sciences. In place of this established framework, which is common to many theories of history, I will adopt one which is closer to Thomas Kuhn's notions of paradigm formation and paradigmatic shifts.[1] This can be schematically characterised as the displacement of what, up to a given moment, is regarded as the best explanation and ruling idea by another one, which becomes deemed superior, and thereafter held to be more acceptable to a specific or general intellectual community. In this context created, it is possible to view the cultural consequences of advanced techologies without the assumption that earlier modes of technology will simply go away as either artifice, process or cultural determinants. Historical change, located within such a critique, can be approached, understood and analysed in a frame of difference, rather than as a marker on the lineage of progess.

From the non-teleological perspective, the new is neither celebrated nor lamented as the end of the old (which either continues or returns, but not necessarily in its original form). Certainly qualities of 'the new' can be brought to an ethical evaluation of object, process or use. This cannot be done, however, on the basis of values wherein the new is posited as good in itself. Ethics themselves do not exist at the end of a road of moral development. They also are ensnared in a web of difference. The pursuit of ethics, from a number of contemporary philosophical positions, has actually shifted from reductive discovery to pragmatic construction. From this, an anti-foundationalist point of view, ethics have to be made in particular circumstances, rather than assumed to be able to be found in the metaphysical spaces formed by the Enlightenment as 'truth'. This means they do not exist outside a circuit of relative legitimation – in other words, ethical values have to be in place for ethical values to be created.

The Chronopolitical Nexus

The chronopolitical is a useful idea to bring a non-evolutionary model of change together with the materiality of the cultural lifeworlds in which change is taking place. It describes the historical co-existence of multiple social, economic and political moments and their cultural perceptions.[2] The chronopolitical is thus an inseparable mixture of actual, imminent and materially affective fictions.[3] Living in its lifeworld is life at the end of teleological history – it has a real reality, with a substance of confusion and contradiction, which limits the prospects of material change. However, this is only knowable through immaterial forms, as either interpretations or as fictions, which in turn become the basis for the production of representations of the world.[4] Thus in one direction we face the certainty of a reality of which we cannot have certain knowledge, while in the other we encounter optical representations, taken as reality, which are grounded in the simulacra of a commodified terrain of appearances. It is as if there were an opaque glass between us and reality, through which we see a blurred image that prompts us to speculate on, fantasise about and attempt to authoritatively project that which we do not quite discern. Our knowledge, with its restricted perceptions, therefore cannot bring into being a mirror of nature – a reflection of the world. What we can do, what we actually do is let loose an unending stream of competing impressions. It is into this 'hell of images' that for the last four hundred years the philosophers of the metaphysical tradition have peered, with, at their side and slightly to the rear, the assembled host of artists.

The knowledge seeking subject stands before the paradox of the world – which is to be before all that is in and out of sight, contemplating the terror of the unknown, of the unknowable reality or the terror of the loss of the unreality of real representations. Such terror follows from coming to know the facticity of the myriad surface appearances of representations that represent nothing but themselves. Hence it is possible to view much contemporary life as the living in the hell of images.[5] In this environment of sign saturation there is clearly a problem of an information overload, which in turn can make any notion a singular and correct course of action very problematic indeed. Equally in this paradoxical situation the consequence of unchosen direction, of doing nothing, are just as fraught. The rising cultural proliferation of the medium of video provides a good way of putting flesh on these observations.

Paul Virilio writes of the video missile – the video eye at the tip of the warhead which enables a pilot or ground controller to guide the weapon to its target. He argues that a fusion occurs between eye and weapon.[6] People die daily around the world as a result of their attempt to capture the image in the war of images. This struggle is on a primary, if immaterial, front in almost all wars of sought liberation, it is another registration of the eye and weapon fusion. In a recent issue of *Time Australia*, for instance, we find illustrations and information which make the significance of the VCR weapon clear in circumstances of conflict as diverse as: its use, by the *mujahedin* (who have eight video units) in Afghanistan to project its battlefields into world media space; its use by Cayapo indians in the Amazon rain forests to create imagery to internationalise their struggle; its use in Burma, Chile, Israel, Eastern Europe, Sri Lanka and Vietnam as an underground communications tool, in the hand of forces in opposition to regimes in power, to circulate information inside and outside the country.[7] In some ways reported events are in advance of Virilio's futurist inflected theory.

True to chronopolitical circumstance, many other consequences of VCR culture in the third world are also made clear by the same article. Viewing (often in communal situations) and making video is now commonplace even in remote areas of the Third World. There are, for example, over 100,000 video lending outlets in India.[8] Although more controls upon the circulation of video tapes (be they political, pornographic or commercial mainstream) are being enforced than ever, these are now almost, if not totally, impossible to regulate. The very technology itself negates structures of control. Copyright in other words is virtually defunct.

Just-in-time economy and culture

Post-Fordist developments in labour processes are one particular domain in which the chronopolitical translates into observable practice. Not only does this mean that the multiple moments of the organisation of production methods become a feature of the system itself but that causal relations can no longer be usefully thought of in terms of the lineages of effects that were presented by earlier characterisations of a cultural superstructure being driven by an economic base. Notions of social being determined by a real materiality are contested by ideas of the driving force of 'the reality we know' as ungrounded representations. The exploded world of signs delivered by modernity can be argued as modality of bringing the social into being/Being that have grown in significance over the past two centuries. The inventions of the novel, the poster, advertising, photography, the illustrated press, film and so on to the laser disc and video are thus all elemental to history of this, the rise of the power of the sign and its industries. It follows that the emergence of the ontological reality of a sign world has been gradual. This is contrary to the impression given by some structuralist and post-structuralist writing that culture, representation, information, immateriality, or any other name of the world of appearances, has only recently acquired a directive influence upon the forms of social being in the world. Causality, or for that matter effect, in this understanding is not just dumped into a teleological chain of events. What is being indicated is that (like genetics) there is a general elemental condition which exists, and that can be representationally referred to, in which difference is constituted. To address or to evoke this condition is not to totalise, the chronopolitical is not a theory of society, rather it is a refusal of difference as a doxa. In addition, to intervene to shape the world is not to effectively engineer reality, for it cannot be reached, but rather it is an attempt to manage, and even police, appearances of difference we know; with the result, usually, that more differences of being in plural time are produced.

The 'just-in-time system' is one subset of post-Fordism. It is a mode of the organisation of production developed in Japan which turns crisis management into the heart of the system. It is a designed labour process that rests on:

- market feedback used immediately to direct production, this in terms of variants of product form and output volume;
- the manufacturer setting up a power structure upon which supplies are dependent;
- the constant measurement of worker output and corporate specified product quality;
- a compliant workforce and a plentiful supply of young and healthy replacement labour;
- the delivery of materials, the drawing of stock components in product assembly, the fulfillment of orders.

All of these activities become done *just in time* as a way of keeping the capital inventory and labour costs as low as possible. Running everything on the edge of crisis, doing everything at the last minute, always being in a rush and workers ever being disposable, and so on, is not a consequence of the system. It *is* the system.

Besides the creation of profit, the aim (which is almost but never fully realised), is to produce a work culture devoid of resistance to managerial control. The pragmatic of just-in-time is based on action to defer crisis, but, in contradiction, it is itself a registration of crisis, a crisis of living on the edge, thus of being in a state of advanced anxiety.

The culture of just-in-time is one location of postmodern chronopolitical life that is constituted by corporate capital culture to sustain itself and extend its sphere of influence. Viewing the totalising impetus of this culture can take us into an examination of some of the features of the new materiality of postmodern/post-fordist futures. Like, for instance, the arrival of mass produced product difference, as it is delivered by 'new technologies' which break with standardisation. Specifically, this is a situation which is increasingly becoming possible with the flexible manufacturing methods which use systems of advanced multiprogrammed machine tools, robotics, older designed machines with fast 'make ready' (the time it takes to set a machine up to perform a particular task) and labour trained to be adaptable.[9] What is in prospect here is the expansion of the hyperconformity of difference. This is to say that, as the pluralism form and style increases, as the technological system becomes more sophisticated and with the continued eclectic raiding and reconstruction of postmodern design practice, product sign and periodic time will become ever more disengaged. In such a chronopolitical configuration of the objects of the seen space of everyday life, the old and the new, the authentic and the unauthentic become increasingly difficult to identify. It is not that the latest 'developments' take the world over but rather that the end of the rule of teleologically directed style makes *seeing* any distinction between past and present much harder. Here then out of the shifting nature of materiality, with its rupturing of reference from representation, we have the arrival of an immateriality, of a plethora of information without the verification of the eye. This situation, which will be returned to later, provides one way of approaching the changed conditions of creative thought. Conversely, the reverse direction can be considered and followed. This is the recoil from whatever gradation of life on the edge one experiences, into the space of the particular, into what Christopher Lasch calls the minimal self.[10]

What the space of the minimal self mobilises can be understood as the result of a particular creative drive, it can be viewed as an imagined small and comfortable retreat. This not in order to establish a secure place from which to resist, or manipulate, the drift of a de-individualising dehumanising corporate culture but rather as somewhere to hide. Fleeing into this space is an attempt to find or create a certain, redemptive self and self controlled safe environment which, although in the world, is felt to be outside it.

In some ways the minimal self's creative drive is the reverse of the dynamic of the modernist's critical or conspiratorial relation with the agency and expression modernity. The ego does however form a bridge. Rather than a vanguard breaking new ground, in the belief that history can be pushed or pulled forward, there is the attempt to find reassurance in recoveries, especially of the primordial. Postmodernism's attraction to primitive and classical art, its reinvigouration of expressionism through to its rediscovery of minimalism, these are all indicators of the desire to retain faith in an essence of prime creativity. The objective is to establish a nexus with the idea and appearance of tradition by making associations with marks of origins and bringing these together with claims, both old and new, of the expressions of 'the creative'. The result is a simulated lifeworld, a bogus teleological back projection and a historicist modernism without direction or dream.

Creativity and the creative beg comment at this point. Perhaps of all that has been demolished in the critical passage of the trinity of postmodernist, poststructuralist and deconstructive theory, it is creativity which stands alone almost unscathed. It still circulates as an unexamined category, a taken for granted, a springing forth of the marvel of the human spirit when all else has been designated dead. The 'man', the subject, the author, art, all have been moving in a cycle wherein they are diagnosed as terminal, fall, are laid to rest and are then reborn. Creativity meanwhile seems to run on full of health. Furthermore, it is called upon by all ideological factions, from restructuring manufacturing capital to Derridean deconstructionists, as the solution. It's what the moment (whatever the moment) needs in order to conceive, deliver and adjust to a new future. Even more generally, creativity is essential in dealing positively with any situation in which we find outselves. It is however not a constant – it changes as we change and as our conditions of existence alter. It cannot just be unproblematically evoked or instrumentally called into service. The technologies and circumstances of the production of culture indicated here are, for instance, going, or rather already have, changed the nature of creativity. The materiality of imagination/assemblage/bricolage are all altered by the way in which information is stored, recalled and pushed around. Creativity therefore invites a good deal of inquiry and rethinking.

Depending on specific circumstance, the artist moves between poles of cultural difference, a semi-private imaginary territory of disengagement and the market place of cultural commodities. Movement then encompasses the traversing of the dysfunctional spaces, which evidence the abandonment of modernity's project of universal development, to entering the wealth centers at the rich end of widening local, national and international material inequality. In such a setting the artist can appear as a bricoleur (which is always the case) who takes what s/he can from wherever s/he can on a journey of chronopolitical wanderings. Creative production is not quite like that, judgement or direction (even as recoil) always creep into the schema.

Designed art as the art of chosen inscription

To understand the production of art at the end of tradition, which in our lifetime means art at the end of modernism, requires, as the postmodern debate has shown, a careful consideration of the idea of history and the notion of ending. Rather than just thinking ending as the arrival of the finality of a fixed chronological moment, it can also be thought as a slow and indecisive process of internal decomposition that leaves in place numerous deposits of us, in us and with us – all with a considerable and complex afterlife.[11] In this context all figuration is prefigured. This is to say that the design element of the production of a work of art, the compositional, now exists prior to the management of form of, and on, the picture plane. Techniques of assemblage, like montage and collage – which not only juxtaposed different aesthetics but also different historical moments, were the precursors of what is now the general condition of production. They also now exist as just another of the available mode of inscription, in the non-developmental chronopolitical unpatterning of the production of art at the end of tradition, at the end of style. Furthermore, with greater recognition (after Foucault) of an expanded view of the aesthetic, which exposes it as the textuality by which the world is known, we have another form of ending of art. This by the crumbling of the frame in which art is held and thus made discrete. To make the argument a little more tangible let's contrast two very different examples. The first in some ways is a return to art of the minimal self; or perhaps to art as a lingering fragment of a residual pre or early modernism; or maybe art as parody (which of these it is depends on the subject in place – the who and the where of the chronopolitical loci of encounter).

The second example is the art of the expert system. This places the artist before the keyboard as a manager of information. Besides being able to be characterised as a cultural projection of an emergent leading edge of a technology, which can produce an image in any genre in order to fit any design regime, it also marks a primary transformation of the conditions of production.

Simulated art at the termination of the grand romantic tradition of aesthetic elevation and judgement is the first example. This is the hyperreal art of the art of the Baudrillardian 'Precession of Simulacra'.[12] It is an art of simulated models, which fakes origins or plays with them as parodies. It is the craft of an art of being crafty, of being self deceptive or of deceiving others by aim or default. Design here is the mobilisation of appearances to present an art which can lend a lie to the disappearance of art, as such it is an act of attempted salvation after death. The simulated therefore stands between the absence of the real and the desire for it. Conditions of production can of course be inducted into the illusion as either part of a known falsehood or as a space of unwitting seduction, except, as Baudrillard points out, the end of the real is also the end of the reference for illusion.[13]

The inscription of simulated art is not only about maintaining a world of appearances of the continuity of art nor just about a recuperation of a certain class of object in order, in part, to code a certain class of subjects. It is also about the replication of the role of the artist and associated romantic models of free thought and creativity. If there is no authentic product there is no authentic producer – fake would not be a fake without the faker. However, things are never as neat as they can be made to seem. If art has slipped out and become part of the aesthetic fabric of the world's textuality then the artist has not so much disappeared but merged with all other producers of culture – put another way, anyone who produces this textuality of the world is an artist. Questions start to fall out of this cluster of observations in profusion:

> Can we talk of the value of the simulation, and thus of the value of the fake?
>
> Has not exchange value, whale like, swallowed up all other values?
>
> How can we think of and identify the art?
>
> Is it not that the artist and art have not disappeared but rather that it is no longer possible to identify either?
>
> Does not this mean that what we are presented with as art and artist is but a parody?

And so the listing and picturing can go on.

Now to example number two which throws up the same, and more, questions and is really a reworking of example one in a different context. Under consideration is the state of the art of the technology of the conditions of production of simulated art and its futures. The technological ensemble in play is a mixture of the digital scanning of visual information, expert systems, numerically controlled robotics and post-electrostatic colour spray photocopying. The unfolding scenario is of an ability to reproduce an image, which is either computer generated or not, in a simulated form in any genre that is desired. Which is to say any image, say a photograph, can be materially reconstituted in any form in any moment of the history of art. Now I am not saying such a technology is currently up and running and without limitations (but it undoubtedly could be if sufficient desire and investment were directed at its realisation by corporate culture).

Walter Benjamin's seminal essay, 'The Work of Art in the Age of Mechanical Reproduction', shows that the aura of art was lost with the arrival of the technology of early modernity.[14] What, in its age of electronic reproduction, the technology of late modernity has managed to do is to lose the materiality of already despiritualised art altogether. So now all that remains is memory, which is accompanied and prompted by the immateriality of simulations of art. Hence art never fading away but living on after death.

The implications of contemporary technology and culture, aspects of which are already partly in place in the world of product and labour process design, is that the artefact is not where the action is. Craft skill, while still a significant registration of human centeredness, now also lives in a chronopolitical space alongside the arrival of immaterial practices which then marginalise the artefact, in favour of information, as the aim of production. Drawing/visualisation, for instance, leaves the drawing board and becomes an exercise performed, via menu, digitising pad and software, on the screen of the computer's monitor. The creation of forms are thus liberated from the activity of their rendering and registered as informationally malleable simulations.

More significant, however, to the present concerns of this exposition is the relocation of the evidence of creativity and its changed nature. Creativity has impacted with information, quantification and the management of conditions of the possibility of assemblage. This is to say that creative invention, in many emergent settings, is less a matter of the conception and expression of form than it is of the organisation of the conditions in which form can appear and be selected. It is not implied that the only kind of determinate information is technical, the socio-cultural is, for instance, equally able to be inducted as directive. Neither is it suggested that there is an appropriate aesthetic to accompany new technologies (which would be just another echo of base and superstructure modelling). It follows that computer art, as a genre of art making, is but one genre option which itself is but a sign of an early and limited, if retained, moment of the technology as it transforms itself.

Once more the changes sketched are not posed as overriding, neutrality is not inferred; for the chronopolitical is clearly a terrain of power and contestation. Neither is the individual producer vanquished – information based creativity no doubt still invites marks of difference and the signature. Besides the rise of the immaterial, its technology, culture and version of creativity within a chronopolitical frame, I think the changes indicated will produce a further breaking up of the art making community. This in turn will create more classes of visible and invisible art and artists as well as a deepening crisis of the identification of the role of that artist who works outside the currently self defined and public identity of art and cultural production.

In my final comment, as elsewhere, the problems of thinking a future that is not in front of the present are evident – old ways of thinking shine through, they are not easy to discard. But if we are to live in chaos we have but two choices: the minimal self that hides or the new self, whatever and whoever that might be, who makes a space and life in the hell of images.

1   Thomas Kuhn *The Structure of Scientific Revolutions* Chicago, University of Chicago Press 1970.
2   Masao Mivoshi and H D Harootunian *Postmodernism and Japan* Durham (USA), Duke University Press 1989 pxvii.
3   *ibid*
4   See special issue on Immateriality *Design Issues* v5 n2 1989.
5   Paul Virilio *War and Cinema* (trans Patrick Camiller) London, Verso 1989 pp31-45.
6   *ibid* p83.
7   Lisa Bever 'Subversion by Video' *Time Australia* 11 September 1989 pp68-73.
8   *ibid* p70.
9   See John Mathews *Tools of Change* Sydney, Pluto Press 1989 pp10-85.
10 Christopher Lasch *The Minimal Self* New York, Norton 1984.
11 See, for example, Gianni Vattimo *The End of Modernity* (trans Jon R Snyder) Cambridge (UK), Polity Press 1988.
12 Jean Baudrillard 'The Precession of Simulacra' *Art and Text* n11 1983 pp3-47.
13 *ibid* p24.
14 Walter Benjamin 'The Work of Art in the Age of Mechanical Reproduction' *Illuminations* (trans Harry Zohn) London, Fontana/Collins 1973 pp204-254.

A NEW DAY FOR MUSIC?
Digital technologies in contemporary music-making

ALAN DURANT

In discussions of music, the relationship between art and technology has been an especially problematic issue during the 1980s. New modes of music-making, especially sampling and sequencing, are stimulating musical forms that exploit techniques possible only with recently available kinds of digital musical equipment; and in doing so, the new musical technology can be thought to add to and diversify existing musical genres. Alongside such changes in musical style, 'reproductive' aspects of digital music technology are transforming conditions under which *all* types of music now circulate. Compact disks (CDs) and digital audio tape (DAT) affect, for instance, the size, kinds, and social characteristics of audiences likely to exist for different musical styles, and so also the revenue that can be collected by the music industry on them – in this way moulding that industry's plans for capital investment and selective promotion. Such overall restructuring of music production and distribution in turn governs the resources available for, and the social profile of, even those kinds of music which have no direct connection with digital music technologies at all. Beyond this, such changes in music production gradually alter how people (including people not actively involved in making music) think about music's aims, styles and properties, setting up different standards of excellence and musical ideals to be aspired to, and challenging many existing practical ideologies of music theory, technique and education.

   Collectively, these changes create conditions for what amounts to a new kind of digital musical *culture*, or interlocking set of conditions and relations in which the sounds of music are produced, circulate and are understood. What in particular makes these changes add up to such a shift of musical 'culture' is that they concern not only the direct outcomes of the new digital production processes themselves – particular records and performance styles – but also more general relationships between writers, performers, forms, and audiences which exist in contemporary music considered as a whole. Despite difficulties with the word 'culture',[1] the use of the term in this context captures the sense that digital music technologies are currently re-ordering a system of interrelated means and relations of music-making; rather than simply bringing into being a specific music sub-culture within continuing and relatively stable relations of how other areas of music are made, distributed and perceived.

These issues are made especially topical in the context of broader interests in art and technology by a further common idea: that contemporary popular music's means and relations of production are exemplary or prototypical of directions for radical cultural practice. This problematic image of radical importance – as an alternative, procedural model for cultural production – follows from thinking about contemporary popular music as typically mixing together two usually conflicting characteristics: small-scale, collaborative production (often independent of access to financial or cultural capital available only in a cultural mainstream); and potential access to 'mass' 'popular' audiences (e.g. by way of chart success), while remaining loyal to more specialised audience constituencies in existing music sub-cultures.

So far, consideration of the development of digital music technologies has taken place less in terms of a general musical or cultural transition they are bringing about, than of particular practical innovations the technologies allow, or questions of law they raise or problematise. Representations of the changes tend to divide into four principal areas of interest:

■ *Performing and recording techniques, and product evaluation and promotion.* In trade and musicians' magazines, journalism stresses the novel capabilities of each new machine but often describes them in ways which seek to maximise continuity with known and current ways of doing things (in order to remain user-friendly for a readership in the process of relatively rapid musical re-education).

■ *Legal and economic issues surrounding music use,* especially in Britain, in the context of the *Copyright, Designs and Patents Act,* 1988, and its addition of 'moral rights' (including a 'right to integrity') to existing provisions for civil litigation in cases of infringement under the earlier *Copyright Act,* 1956. Given the coincidence of a new music technology and new copyright provision (in which the 'moral rights' give an author the right to be identified as such, and the right to object to distortion, mutilation or other modification or derogatory action concerning a copyright work prejudicial to the author's honour or reputation); such legal discussion is concerned with matters of clarification, as well as with critical commentary and arguments for reform.[2]

- *Originality and creativity in 'art'*. Discussion, in media and cultural studies, of who is *responsible* for music devised in the new production conditions leads into arguments over who should enjoy the status of 'artist' or 'author' (arguments corresponding to early debate of the cinematic auteur in 1950s film criticism), or whether successive stages of automation of music-making processes have effectively dehumanised musical creation, undermining its essential attributes. This second possibility is sometimes then taken to necessitate fresh political priorities involving resistance to new music technologies (e.g. in the British 'Keep Music Live' campaign), based on the idea of a subordination they enforce to dictates of advanced consumer capitalism.[3]

- *Attitudes towards 'art' and its cultural significance*. Such discussion focuses on issues of the *aura* of individual works or texts. These questions are often investigated through re-readings of arguments from Walter Benjamin's 'The Work of Art in the Age of Mechanical Reproduction',[4] re-examined in the context less of conditions for a historical shift in art from ritual to politics, than of interest in notions of postmodern culture. Such discussions lead quickly to a watershed between the view that digital music technology most clearly illustrates the postmodern cultural condition (and implicitly celebrates it); and the view that prevailing forms of use of the new technologies are in fact in the service of an older, Romantic ideology of the arts.[5]

Insofar as generalisations across these different areas of interest and argument have been made, they mainly concern what is seen as the crisis of *authorship* which it can be claimed the new methods of music-making bring about. Each of the four kinds of discussion referred to above offer a different perspective in this debate. But two clear difficulties appear to beset virtually all current attempts at generalisation. First, with the exception of promotional and review literature, discussions tend to be vague on matters of practical detail; they are rarely anchored in close attention to the music-making techniques they claim to be about, or to the terminology and relations of work which will define whatever new conditions of music emerge. Second, discussions tend to be vague on questions of interpretation. This is despite the fact that debate over the imputed general cultural significance of, for instance, collage and pastiche in House, Hip-hop and other new musical forms, inevitably depends on views about how interpretation takes place at all (regardless of whether what is in question is interpretation of social styles or directions considered as symptoms of cultural transition or development).

Taking these blockages in current argument as starting-points, the descriptions and comments which follow seek to do two things. First, they review briefly the history of digital sampling and sequencing, and in doing so seek to show how 'established' concepts and terminologies of music-making have been redefined as parts of – to take another deeply problematic word which current musical changes nevertheless demand – a new musical 'literacy'.[6] Second, the descriptions introduce discussion of implications of recent changes in musical production as regards more general arguments about the role played in changing musical cultures by technical innovation.

Historical context

Given the scale and difficulty of current arguments over music and technology, it is immediately necessary to try to place recent developments in their larger historical context. Only by doing this is it possible to get an idea of what large scale change in music might be like (cf the consequences for music culture which followed the development of synoptic scores or the invention of the gramophone).

Even the sketchiest historical study of music shows that dependence in music-making on technology is not by any means a new, or regionally or culturally limited phenomenon. Changes in the technology of music-making regularly correlate with changes in ways of making, distributing and thinking about music. In this sense, virtually all forms of music-making are dependent on some kind of deliberately designed and specialised equipment or technology.

Musical instruments of all periods and places, for example, show deep interconnections with technology of one kind or another. While the gamelan is often cited by Western musicians and audiences as a symbol of communal 'naturalness',[7] mechanically it depends on the calculated refinement, over time, of sonorous properties constrained by more general social conditions of production. Similarly with Western 'folk' instruments. The Bronze Age Irish horn, the lyre, the flute, the Fender Telecaster guitar, and any other instrument you care to think of, all have histories related to ideas of what they should sound like and when and how they should be played, as well as to economic and technical conditions of how they can be manufactured. So too – only more famously – does the piano, with its complicated history of design modifications during the nineteenth century. The history of musical instruments is always, in this sense, a history of technology; and contingencies and idiosyncrasies of such history form a major part of a musician's relation to a particular instrument (as dramatised, for example, in Patrick Suskind's monologue of a demoralised double-bass player: *The Double-bass*[8]). What prevents peculiarities in the specific instrumental histories from being widely acknowledged is that they are often obscured for modern listeners by performance rituals and conventions which make such history invisible; for example the 'standard' dress-style and layout of the classical concert orchestra, which regularises the complex individual histories and capabilities of its instruments into a single, corporate musical instrument for the conductor to play.[9]

What is true in this respect of instruments is also true of technologies of amplification, recording, transmission and reproduction. The pianola, gramophone and cassette-player all developed in complicated histories of invention, production and diversification of use, constantly modified in response to changing patterns in commercial demand. The modern, multitrack tape-recorder, for example, provides a clear instance. Current computerized multitrack recording, editing and mixing facilities developed out of early refinements in day-to-day practice in early studio recording techniques, such as the use of microphones close to instruments to increase control over relative volume levels in mixing, and the use of 'dry' recording environments so that reverberation could be added selectively after the recording itself. From these early techniques of separating the recording process as far as possible from modifications that might be made subsequently, followed experiments during the 1940s with sound-on-sound overdubbing, bouncing recordings from one track or machine to another; leading in 1952 to the Ampex 8-track recorder build for the guitarist Les Paul.[10] In the late 1960s, full multitrack recorders appeared (16 track, 24 track) partly in response to rapid expansion in the popular music industry of the early 1960s. In doing so, they restructured studio working relations by increasingly involving the recording engineer in complex manipulations of the raw material provided by musicians.[11] Deferred decision-making led to important compositional inputs from traditionally 'non-musical' studio personnel. This has redefined what is understood by 'composition' by altering working relations, and *techniques*, on the basis of changed opportunities presented by characteristics of the *technology*.

It is of course clear in these various accounts that music is deeply connected with developments of technology. But since technological development – even addition of the simplest new design feature – is usually sought out, planned for, and resourced by human beings in their given social relations, chains of causality in such processes are not easily identifiable. Music is never simply led by technological invention, as is suggested in crude forms of technological determinism.[12] Rather, technological developments take on their particular character only in specific instantiations within prevailing, but also changing, social relations and contexts. They lead to networks of reactions, responses and effects that cannot be predicted merely from the resources or design of the technology itself. This complexity of interrelations restricts possibilities for generalising from history and making predictions about the future, or for formulating unchanging, principled or dogmatic views on conflicts and contradictions in the present. Each of the two most common responses to music technology, therefore, are certainly simplistic. Either (a) the immediate celebration of any 'new age' of machines brought about by each successive gizmo (the Hammond organ; the wah-wah pedal; the Fairlight CMI); linking up music technologies with sci-fi utopianism and teleological ('progress') versions of cultural change, irrespective of conflicting social and economic interests which contribute to shaping that future. Or, (b) resistance to machines as a dehumanising departure from the domain of pure human creativity in sound (or as a replacement of human beings by machines doing their job, as is implicit in those industrial relations attitudes which seek simply to restrict studio overdubbing, sampling and simulation of 'natural' instruments such as string or horn sections).

The question is not, therefore, whether music depends on technology, but what relations exist between different technical and practical elements at play in any changing context of musical production, and whether these relations can be analysed only 'historically' (as a unique, given set of relations) or whether satisfactory generalisations and predictions can be made from them. Attitudes and practical responses to technological innovation in the meantime have to be found by considering cultural consequences of the specific directions in which new music technology stimulates musical activity, while at the same time assessing a balance of interest – which will always depend on a particular view of a culture and its priorities – between the new and expanding fields of activity stimulated by the technology (including new and possibly unforeseen capabilities), and the challenge to economic, legal and labour rights which exist in current ways of doing things.

Recent changes in music technology relate primarily to a general system for the encoding, storage and manipulation of musical signals (digital, rather than analog), and to the standardisation of a system 'language' or set of machine protocols known as MIDI (Musical Instrument Digital Interface). This enables different components in any music-making or recording set-up, such as synthesisers and sequencers, to communicate with each other and with general-purpose micro-processors. In general terms, MIDI communications systems enable, for example, a computer to *control* a keyboard or drum machine, or to *receive*, store and manipulate data (finally, sounds) generated by such an 'instrument' (instruments in this context are often referred to as 'MIDI controllers'). During the time that the musical information (textures, rhythms, melodies, tempi, etc) is stored in digital form, it can be manipulated and edited like other kinds of computer data.

Modern digitally-based musical instruments have their closest antecedents in early synthesisers, which in turn grew out of earlier traditions of keyboard design (such as efforts to develop different voices for the organ), and in experimental electronic music techniques using (analog) tape recorders. Early synthesisers sometimes tried to re-create recognisable, conventional sounds, such as those of the harpsichord or the violin section of an orchestra, sometimes to create new 'electronic' sounds, blending together, reshaping and filtering outputs from Voltage Controlled Oscillators. Monophonic synthesisers (ones which could play only one note at a time) have been almost completely displaced in both professional and amateur use by polyphonic synthesisers (ones which can replicate the 'two-hands' harmonic capability of traditional keyboard instruments such as the piano or the organ). Correspondingly, single-timbre synthesisers have been displaced commercially by multi-timbre ones (with that capability generally made possible by splitting the octaves of the keyboard into different textural or timbral 'zones'). During the development of modern synthesisers, samplers and sequencers, various ways of producing and storing sounds have been tried (including the use of mini loop-tapes triggered by keys). Instrument design has also been refined in terms both of size and complexity (producing more portable and easily-operated domestic and stage-show machines), and of cost (to compete with an established market for electric guitars, and to fit in with an expanding market for home computers, peripherals and leisure-oriented software).

In 1977, onboard microprocessors were first incorporated

into commercial synthesisers. In response to a recognised musical aspiration to chain synthesisers together, so that one can drive (or sequence) another, some scope for inter-synthesiser communications also became possible as a result of the informal adoption of a Control Voltage standard: one volt per octave. In 1981, perhaps the most significant 'technical' development occurred (symptomatically, not in fact a technical development at all, but a commercial decision); an agreement, at the 1981 Audio Engineering Society, between the company Sequential Circuits, manufacturers of Prophet synthesisers, and the companies Oberheim and Roland, on the question of a 'system standard' that would specify digital music technology protocols (i.e. MIDI). Broader US negotiation followed, leading – though only after disagreement between the US manufacturers – to agreement with and among Japanese manufacturers. By 1983, the protocols were updated to Midi 1.0, a language deemed by its designers sufficiently underspecified to facilitate software innovation rather than simply the use of existing software.[13]

What followed this standardisation of the music-digital interface was then the design and production of a wide range of relatively cheap, digitally-based musical 'instruments' (evidently foreseen from the outset, given that a pricing constraint was allowed to impose design restrictions on the technical specifications of the interface). Many different types of instrument have been devised; a new generation of drum machines, which store pre-defined drum sounds that can be triggered in pre-programmed patterns; samplers – in effect, combinations of a keyboard with a (technically fairly simple) tape recorder – which record and replay excerpts of sound and then allow manipulation of the sounds which have been stored, and their triggering by a command from a key or computer programme; other kinds of MIDI controller based on existing musical instruments (triggering pre-stored sounds by plucking a guitar string or pressing a saxophone key and blowing, etc); and sequencers, which programme and store rhythms melodies, tempi and harmonies, and can be thought of as composing and performing computers (with a commercial diversification of software to be implemented on a range of machines including Apple II, Macintosh, Atari ST, Commodore, etc).

Practical changes as a result of MIDI

Even at the immediate practical level, the changes outlined above, especially if thought of in conjunction with CDs and DAT, permit several apparently different avenues for innovation and influence:

- *New composition and editing possibilities*, involving samplers and computers;

- *New personalised listening possibilities*, by linking MIDI editing capabilities to commercially produced records or tapes in suitable DAT and CD formats, enabling listeners to re-mix records and tapes as they play them

- *New mixed-media possibilities*, such as MIDI stage-lighting systems for performance, or by use of an agreed SMPTE (Society of Motion Picture Technical Engineers) code; a digital timing signal/code to link a music track with a video track, harnessing together developments in music editing with video soundtrack editing.

Each of these directions is significant, and has specific implications. But from the outset MIDI was intended to form part of an increasingly *interlocking* network of digital technologies (it was designed exactly as an *interface*). As well as making possible the foreseen intercommunications between musical instruments and computers, it also contributed to the development of further mixed-media and inter-communications possibilities; not only the use of SMPTE code to link music editing to video editing, but also to ways of producing the sound effects (SFX) likely to be used in such editing (devising them digitally and storing, distributing and accessing them on CDs). Beyond this, too, MIDI developments fit in with far more general directions in longer-term research in digital technologies, for instance towards 'hypermedia' (the merging of sound, image and written text within a single interactive 'mixed media' computer environment).

The scale of technical possibility is evidently enormous; and together, the possibilities symbolise the diversity of implications which can follow from one originally very specific innovation. What is needed therefore, in order to get beyond reflex responses of extreme enthusiasm, paranoia, or bewilderment, is attention to the precise ways in which any given technical device affects existing relations of musical practice, as well as how connotations and conditions of reception of music are affected as a whole. From such case studies, generalisations about the influence of technology on music may be made; but limits on possibilities for generalisation are also likely to become evident, especially as regards views on any overall, single cultural significance of the changes.

Roughly speaking, the digital production technologies described above have led to three main types of practical musical innovation:

Samplers give access to an extended range of sounds that can be used in music-making and provide ways of using those sounds not physically possible in (non-digital) live performance. This extension to the sounds available in music-making comes about in two main ways. Firstly, it is possible to use pre-set sounds (textures stored in memory and loaded from disk) and to layer, or combine, such sounds – superimposing textures to create new orchestral voices. Such pre-set sounds can be conventional musical sounds, such as a particular guitar, trombone or drum sound; or they can be conventionally non-musical sounds and sound effects, such as birdsongs, roadworks or water dripping. Widely available commercially as computer software, pre-set sounds can also be modified by use of a patch editor and librarian programme to create new and personalised pre-sets, and so an individual sound catalogue. Secondly, sounds which have been defined either by being pre-set on disk, or in a patch editor, can be manipulated. They can be transposed in pitch, for example, even beyond the pitch range available to the sounds in their pre-sampled, 'natural' occurrence. Flute sounds are monophonic when made by flutes; but when they have been sampled, they can be used polyphonically, like a flute *section* which can also play beyond the pitch-band available to actual flutes. Guitars generally have six strings, and therefore play chords with a maximum of six notes; but they can have any number of 'strings' once sampled. Together, the library of timbres and the possible manipulation of sampled sounds can create a preternaturally or artificially enlarged sound world, or set of textural possibilities. In addition they make it easier to combine disparate sounds (such as creating a new 'voice' to play a melody that is texturally a combination of a sampled cello, a dog bark and a pneumatic drill). Similarly, sampling facilitates 'musical' references to the acoustic world (e.g. to noises, voices, speech, etc), and so redefines possibilities for programmatic music and music theatre by enabling music to connect more easily and extensively with sound effects and with drama. More generally too, the range of sounds or textures a musician (or user) can make is no longer limited by technical facility with the mouth or fingers or by how many fingers or mouths human beings have. A woodwind player can in principle simulate an orchestra of sounds, without learning even a keyboard (it is the piano which has traditionally been used for arranging); and a musician can pick whatever she or he finds the most comfortable type of MIDI-controller, based on earlier musical experience and aptitude. At face value then, what this aspect of the technology leads to is easier orchestration and an enlarged and enhanced sound-world.

Composition and editing possibilities

The manipulation of sampled sounds is not restricted to pitch variation. By using the editing functions of composition software, it is possible to create entire musical pieces. This can be done either by writing a traditional score into a sequencer (which generally reads and writes both staff and numeric notation systems), assigning pre-set textures (instruments) to each part and defining parameters such as tempo, then commanding the sequencer to playback – and so perform – the piece. Alternatively, it can be done by playing in real-time into the sequencer, then editing the notated form the machine encodes. Such performance can take place at any speed (with the tempo changed later, using a variable MIDI clock); or it can be keyed-in note value by note value, with the notes assigned a tempo at a later stage.

In relation to the basic material, various editing possibilities then arise. The MIDI clock gives a unique address (like a time code) to each beat or note in the recorded material, making it possible to edit from any given point (and to drop in and out automatically, recycling the section to be edited in isolation from the rest of the piece for rehearsal purposes). After this type of editing, it is also possible to modify the piece, by 'auto-correction' or quantisation (adjusting what has been played to the nearest relevant beat – set by the musician (operator) according to the rhythmic structure of the piece in question); or by modifying the acoustic characteristics of any *single* sound within a composition (e.g. its volume, duration, attack, etc). In some programmes, 'non-destructive quantisation' is possible, so that a quantised form can be compared with the non-quantised form before the latter is replaced. At face value then, what this aspect of the technology leads to is extension and enrichment of traditional compositional processes, by offering solutions to problems of inaccurate, incomplete, or technically impossible performance, and by allowing for intensive scrutiny, manipulation and repair of anything entered into the machine.

Idiomatic possibilities: quotation and musical reference

The textural and compositional possibilities of MIDI sequencers and samplers relate to creating new pieces of music; they can be seen as revisions to existing compositional and performance techniques. But sampling need not only use individually selected sounds (either pre-sets bought as software, or a user's own recordings made with a microphone or line-in recording); it is also possible to mix these two processes by recording directly from commercially available records and tapes. Where this is done extensively, new styles come into being based on the embedding of sections of musical material in kinds of musical collage. Such collages involve the sampling of whole phrases, riffs, melodies, bass lines and drum patterns and fills; and create musical pieces which are quite evidently collages, intended to be allusive rather than 'original', compositions which merely use sampling as a convenient way of acquiring instrumental sounds.

It is significant, in this context, that the MIDI developments of the early 1980s have led to the emergence, in the late 1980s, of musical forms such as House; a hi-energy dance music originating in gay dance clubs in Chicago. This form involves a cross-over, brought about in record production and as a result of mixing by DJs, of elements from earlier forms of disco music with aspects of rock (such as particular guitar sounds). House music is simple enough for anyone to dance to, in any style or mixture of styles, and has a following among both blacks and whites. House records, such as Steve Silk Hurley's *Jack your Body*, Bomb the Bass's *Beat This*, or Lil Louis's *French Kiss*, bring together current digital music technologies with a DIY (do-it-yourself) attitude to music production, and with a specific urban aesthetic and cultural politics based on mixing and rapping – with little concern to respect intellectual property.

The functions of sampled material in House and hybrid idioms, such as the British genre Acid House, may be thought to vary. Three types of function are distinguished, for example, by Goodwin, which he calls 'realist', 'modernist' and 'postmodernist' sampling.[14] In 'realist' sampling, the aim is merely to simulate a particular instrument sound; a short-cut in production. In modernist sampling, juxtaposition of 'quotes' serves to ironise or satirise excerpted material, undermining or redefining its established connotations; or else its allusions show a kind of identification with a particular tradition. Postmodernist sampling is formally similar to modernist sampling but juxtaposes materials in a network of 'texts' which refuse any position of judgement on them; the listener has only a tissue of fragmented references which exemplify a culture saturated with sounds but which prevent interpretative fixities or certitudes. Acid House mixes, from this viewpoint, are sound-worlds or environments made up of selected fragments from a culture's history and formation, and produce a distinct form of musical pleasure largely or primarily invested in cultural reference for its own sake. At face value, what this use of the technology leads to is possibilities for generic innovation.

The MIDI 'revolution' and questions of music literacy

The descriptions in the last section presented 'possibilities'; and at face value, what MIDI technologies offer are extensions and enrichments of existing priorities in musical practice. They supplement, rather than displace, current approaches to performing and composing, and permit complex and rapid manipulations of musical material in ways which build directly on existing ideas of instrument design, notational conventions, recording processes and compositional techniques of allusion and musical reference. It is apparently only in the generic innovations implied by sampled musical collages that signs of major redirection for music are evident.

But such descriptions of 'enrichment' and 'extension' in the modes and relations of music-making nevertheless expose two important areas of unresolved issues. Firstly, there remain questions about the ways in which digitally-produced music is conceptualised and discussed, and how changes in practice are typically accompanied by the development of specialised kinds of musical knowledge and skill; a new musical literacy, in the sense of new ways of construing or 'reading' music and of producing or 'writing' it. Arguably, what is happening is not 'extension' and 'diversification' of the ways people make and understand music, but 'replacement' and fundamental 're-structuring', displacing one regime or paradigm of musical sense (what music is, and why people make or listen to it) with another, significantly different. Secondly, there remain issues regarding the value, if any, of preserving a public domain in musical culture which is available for reverential, ironic, comic or critical reference; a store of shared images, or public tradition and mythology. Such a public domain has existed in previous centuries by default, in the absence of rigorously enforced musical copyright provision and in the context of heterogeneous, regionally and socially varied circumstances of performance and consumption of music. Progressively during this century however, such a domain has diminished, following the setting-up of licensing and collecting agencies such as the Performing Rights Society (PRS), Phonographic Performance Ltd (PPL) and the Mechanical Copyright Protection Society (MCPS).[15] As a result of sampling in particular, the pressure for keeping any recognisable form of public domain has become entangled to an unprecedented degree with questions of copyright, broadening the whole issue of changes in access to music from specific questions of the cost and availability of machines to issues of law and cultural policy.

Each of these two issues is now briefly outlined, before the two are brought together in conclusions which try to assess claims that, in the broadest terms of argument, digital music technologies are bringing about a kind of *democratisation* of music.

New ways of working: a new literacy

Predictably, along with changes in the kinds of machines used to make music, corresponding changes in ways of talking about the music being made have come into being. These involve a combination of terms common in elementary computer literacy with an earlier musical and recording vocabulary characteristic of 1960s and 1970s pop groups – riffs, fills, breaks, intros, fades, tracks, overdubs, etc (a vocabulary made up in turn of a compound of intuitive characterisations of music and borrowings from a more established notational literacy found among session musicians and jazz and show-band players). In this process of redefinition of musical terminology (in which new vocabulary items co-exist with continuing use of the vocabulary among concert performers, music students, amateur singers and pianists), trade and musician magazines and user-groups have taken on the role of disseminating basic technical knowledge, assisted by educational programmes about music on radio and television, and by small changes in school-level music teaching. Together, these channels for the spreading of technical knowledge have built a skills-base in some sections of the population which is radically different from conceptions of music common among earlier generations of musicians.

New ways of thinking about music which remain entangled with the older conceptions can be seen, for example, in the following details of practice:

- New and specialised terms are developing to describe not only rhythms (which have for a long time been informally classified – as on domestic organs with simple rhythm facilities – by musical genre: cha-cha, bossa nova, disco, etc), but also individual sounds, so that they can be recognised and easily accessed from disks which may contain twenty different bass guitar sounds or fifteen door chimes. Often, sounds are named not only by metaphors of their acoustic characteristics ('thin', 'buzzy', 'smooth'), but also after performers, periods, and styles they are associated with. Literacy with regard to pre-sets can become very much a question of knowing bits of music history (of particular bands, records, styles), rather than knowing anything technical about sound envelopes, filters, or instrument design.

- Instructions in composing software are often modelled on tape-machine commands (rewind, record, playback, fast forward, etc), on the assumption that multi-track recorders form a known reference-point for the generation of 'analog' musicians who are currently re-educating themselves for digital technologies. A relatively known operating format is used as a model for conceptualising compositional and editing processes which actually work on a very different technical basis. As ability to 'read music' (or to produce a score) is increasingly displaced by software literacy, it becomes interesting that systems designers often try to allow for combined or mixed literacies (offering both staff and numeric notations, for instance). Similarly, provisions of the software are used to different degrees by different sorts of musician, in a process of uneven change dependent on disparities in knowledge and experience between musicians, as well as between successive stages in any individual musician's experience.

What supports the idea of calling this change in ways of thinking and talking about music the emergence of a new kind of 'literacy' is the sense this term captures of a set of specialised skills and concepts musicians are likely to need to learn, involving both what might be called a 'reading' component (a shift from staff notation to computer notations), and a related 'writing' component (not only 'copying out', as in sampling, but also writing creatively; making up pieces of music). When changes around digital music technology are seen in this way, connections with arguments about other, existing technologies and literacies can be seen. As with those other literacies, the important questions are not so much about the level of skill of particular individuals (and the problems of definition and measurement these raise), but of social distributions of skills among a population. With respect to digital music technologies then, a critical agenda based on this view would have to prioritise assessment of exactly who buys, owns, and uses digital instruments, focusing on patterns in terms of gender, age, general educational background, etc.

The second major area of unresolved issues regarding digital music technologies concerns ways of understanding the role of musical reference and allusion in defining a culture's public images of itself. The amount and type of musical sampling produced or reproduced in public is restricted by legal respect for ownership rights. Details of such regulation determine crucial factors such as how much permissions typically cost, and therefore who can afford to make 'allusive' or 'collage' records (especially if unpredictable risks of, and during, litigation exist). In such circumstances, it is difficult to see how private interest in generating income by licensing use, and public interest in maintaining unrestricted access to materials for making music in the public domain, can be made to coincide.

To see why this should be the case, it is necessary to consider how music (which historically has nearly always been made for specific community audiences, or under restrictive social and economic conditions of patronage and employment) can be thought to have a place in the public domain at all, except, as suggested above, by default. One reason is this. During the Twentieth century, as a result of mechanical and electronic means of broadcasting and reproducing, there has been an explosion in the amount of music people hear, and the range of circumstances in which they hear it (on disk and radio; on personal stereos and car radios; as musak in shopping malls, etc). For the overwhelming majority of people in modern industrial societies, music becomes – not necessarily by choice – a substantial use of time rather than an occasional ritual or spectacle. Since the ears cannot be closed, music becomes also in this process an object of more continuous and enforced 'attention'. In particular, listening to music at social events (such as parties), or while engaged in other activities (driving, washing up, waiting for a train at a station), forges ever closer and more intricate connections between pieces of music and aspects of personal experience, and involves music in processes of self-definition, contemplation and identification. From such experiences follow, for entire populations, not only a high degree of familiarity with a given music and its associations, on account of the scale of exposure, but also a new importance for that music, on account of the increased role in anticipating, defining and recalling personal experience that music (even unwanted music) can acquire.

An additional – and generally unrecognised – issue as regards the 'listening' aspect of any new musical 'literacy' therefore emerges. This issue is less a question of any single individual's musical knowledge or background, than of the shared, collective knowledge of a community of listeners, involving subtle distinctions between meanings and connotations which are simply taken for granted. It is from this (heterogeneous but nevertheless theoretically recognisable) public musical *competence*, or tacit knowledge of musical conventions, that the possibility and potential meaningfulness arises of quoting from musical sound-imagery. To make music which contains specific references to other pieces or compositions is to intervene in a surrounding musical culture, exercising a right of reply to musical discourses which make up our social environment, by re-making, re-ordering, or re-contextualising them, and so commenting on their meanings by changing them.

A public domain for music can accordingly be seen as a kind of store of sounds, or sound data-bank; a repository or resource of sounds and styles that have been made and will be interpreted. Each sound or style has attached to it a variable but largely culturally determined set of connotations and resonances that can nevertheless be re-mobilised for new and different purposes. In present legal circumstances however, such a bank has also to be understood as being made up of many separate accounts that have to have appropriate credits made to them. Uses of music, whether they are made possible by buying, copying or broadcasting a disk or tape, are authorised only on payment of sums of money in respect of the property rights invested in that music. Acceptance of this principle is the basis for the operation of modern music industries, which use copyright law and licensing and collecting agencies to exploit rights and prevent plagiarism or unauthorised use of the results of creative work. It is the maintenance of such rights, in changing circumstances of production and distribution, that enables the music industries to remain big business and to continue to invest in music production on its present scale. PRS (in the UK), for example, collects roughly £100 million annually to distribute to members, and the BBC pays over £20 million annually for its music permissions.

To suggest that music sampling importantly alters the situation as regards music in the public domain, by engaging differently with copyright, is nevertheless not to say that plagiarism, copying and copyright infringement in music are new. Even apart from deliberate copying, there has always been the practical problem that, since individual creativity in music necessarily involves innovating within established genres and styles, the risk exists of repetition, imitation, and thereby, in this century, of copyright infringement. (Many song-writers in fact, openly say they start composing by copying a model, relying on the fact that the final product will inevitably sound different when they themselves perform it.) More generally too, since in conventional Western music there are only 12 different musical notes, to play in any recognisable idiom is also to build from a very restricted range of basic melodic and harmonic materials.

The situation as regards sampling however, differs significantly from this longstanding scenario. Whereas traditional plagiarism infringed rights in musical ideas (e.g. it was the melody and chord sequence of George Harrison's *My Sweet Lord* (1971) which resembled the Shiffons' *He's so Fine* (1963) and therefore allowed Harrison to be successfully sued by its composer); with sampling it is not the idea but the recording itself that gets copied. Infringement involves direct replication of the actual recorded sounds (a difference from traditional plagiarism held to be crucial by at least some litigants, for example by Stock, Aitken and Waterman in seeking remedies against M/A/R/R/S's borrowings from their hit single *Roadblock* (1988) in the number one record, *Pump up the Volume* (1988)).

Given, however, that it is difficult to separate opportunistic cloning from creative collage, sampling presents a new set of legal difficulties. Current legal argument seeks, in effect, to balance two conflicting interests: the legal right of an author or producer to exploit intellectual work (which calls for restrictions on copying), and a public interest in preserving a freedom to quote, allude to, and draw on things in the public domain (many of the pieces of music likely to be sampled will be pieces already saturating the public domain). At present, to adjudicate between these conflicting interests, legal argument relies on notional tests for infringement, such as that of 'substantial' borrowing, and disputable assessments of the amount of skill involved in transforming the original. Significantly, current copyright law does not enforce a *right* of quotation; it merely seeks to create a suitable climate for the granting of permission, by protecting the financial incentives for the copyright owner. The issue which arises as regards the cultural significance of sampling is accordingly how far the commercial exploitation of musical work in capitalist societies can be made to fit with the interests and rights of a general public, since pieces of music are *simultaneously* symbols of a culture's constantly renegotiated sense of its own identity, and yet also commodities made to be exploited for profit. In any discussion of a balance of interest between gains and losses which result from the new phase of music technology, the possibility of increased, active engagement with the musical world through sampling has to be weighed against the more common idea of an enforced retreat from originality into banal mimicry and replication.

Conclusions

As has been suggested above, the political character of technological innovations cannot be read off simply from features of the technologies themselves, nor from the history of the technology's introduction. Nevertheless, many people in and around music would still want to maintain that, thinking through the kinds of development outlined in this article, in broadest terms, MIDI technologies are bringing about what amounts to a major *democratisation* of music.

How far this is true depends on what specialised senses of the word 'democracy' are involved in the discussion.[16] Several distinct meanings appear to be mixed in current debate – and yet another whole field of meaning, concerned with control over sounds in the public domain – is typically absent. In order to work through existing arguments, therefore, it is necessary first to review the main senses in play:

a) 'Democracy' as something which results from cheapness of the equipment (as required, for example, by the manufacturers in their initial definition of the MIDI interface). The claim for democracy in this idea is that everyone can *buy* MIDI, and so have access to the means of musical production;

b) 'Democracy' as something which results from an input into definition of the technology. The claim for democracy in this idea is that everyone can help *specify* the technical protocols of the interface, and so have some control over the characteristics of the means of production;

c) 'Democracy' as something which results from a low or easily attainable skills-threshold for using the technology. The claim for democracy in this idea is that everyone can *operate* music software, and that knowledge in this area is power.

By way of comment on these three senses, it should be said that, so far, it has been the rhetoric of the instrument manufacturers (and of some musicians) that has predominated, especially their suggestion that democracy follows simply because the machines are, by some standards of consumer spending, cheap to buy., If this is all that is required of musical democracy, then that democracy will remain severely restricted by a continuing dependence of musicians on commercial priorities and interests of the manufacturers; musicians are consumers of technology, as well as producers of music. It is often this consideration which prompts the second definition: that democracy results from a say in how the technology is designed. The problem then becomes clearly that the value of any technology relies on opportunities for its use as well as on its own specifications, and that in the case of music such use requires an infrastructure both of performance conditions and of necessary operating skills. This prompts the third definition: that democracy follows if the skills-threshold is sufficiently low, and discourages professional elites. This definition suggests a belief that conditions for DIY production will transform relations of music production by blurring distinctions between amateur and professional; and by way of illustration, proponents of such a view might point to the fact that samplers make orchestration accessible to amateur musicians, and in doing so displace, with boxes of floppy disks, some of the previously widespread need for specialist 'trained' musicians as arrangers.

As regards democratisation of music however, the difficulty with this third definition remains that of how exactly to interpret changes in the relationship between musicians, technicians and amateur users brought about by the levelling foreseen as the result of the low skills threshold. Certainly technical innovations can create new possibilities for people previously excluded from or marginalised in public music-making, such as isolated individuals and musically-untrained computer hackers. But in doing so, they equally undermine established roles for musicians trained in other, continuing traditions of making music. The political character of the innovations depends, therefore, very much on the viewpoint from which they are seen; if you are a paraplegic but aspiring drummer, then MIDI technology is undoubtedly progressive, significantly improving your possibilities for activity. If you're an unemployed drummer, on the other hand, MIDI technology is more likely to seem a manufacturers' plot to take your livelihood away. Either way, what is clear is that unless appeal is made either to a general conception of economics and production, or to an ideology of musical purpose, it is unlikely that any single political content can be attributed to the digital music innovations – especially at so early a stage, and concerning technical developments whose possible uses are so diverse.

There are, in any case, problems beyond the scope of the three common definitions of musical democracy. The usefulness of any of the definitions is restricted by the fact that they are all narrowly concerned with production; they are about encouraging music-making (or, to take an opposing view which questions the aspiration towards 'democratisation') about stimulating a high-volume, low unit-cost domestic instrument market, based on youth cultural aspirations to pop stardom. However this question is resolved, beyond it lie further difficult questions, which require close attention to audiences and to restrictions on the social circulation of musical meanings.

Such issues can be outlined roughly as follows. 'Passive' music literacy (in the sense of awareness of stylistic distinctions) has been significantly extended and modified by two aspects of current technological and generic innovation; the extensive recycling of earlier periods of music in quoted and sampled forms; and increases in the amount of music people typically listen to. But these extensions to popular music 'literacy' have not been paralleled by a related general rise in 'active' literacy, because of the severity of legal restrictions on access to some of the necessary raw materials for digital musical production. In present circumstances therefore, the most likely directions for a musical culture using digital music technologies appear to involve an emerging, practical literacy of production skills which are nevertheless largely *cut off from* the possibility of responding to developments in musical culture with comment expressed in the form of quotation and imitation.

If current changes in music stimulate primarily the purchase of equipment and development of basic production skills, it seems safe to say that no major democratisation of music will take place. For any shift meriting such a description to occur, at least one other, political change would have to be made: intellectual property rights would need to be modified (perhaps by an automatic right of quotation subject to payment on a scale which is not prohibitive from the point-of-view of small-scale independent music production). The real problems in the current phase of change are not those of access to making music – or even of who makes it – but of access to essential raw materials (sounds, melodic figures, etc) and to people who might listen to the wide range of musics that can now potentially get made. The inevitable processes of selection that will determine which music reaches beyond local sub-cultures into the more general public domain depend on the ways in which channels of distribution and transmission are organised and regulated. And since the creation and definition of audiences for new kinds of digital music depend significantly on aspects of social policy, rather than simply on technical capabilities of any particular machine, assessment of the cultural importance or implications of the new digital music technologies has to engage with definitions of musical 'democracy'. These are not only about cost, technical specification or required user-knowledge, but also about more fundamental issues of music's social meanings, channels of circulation, and value.

1   For an analysis of the difficulties surrounding the word 'culture', see Raymond Williams *Keywords: a vocabulary of culture and society* London, Fontana 1976.

2   See Simon Frith 'Copyright and the Music Business' *Popular Music* v7 n1 1987 pp57-75; also Lionel Bently 'Sampling and Copyright: is the Law on the Right Track?' *Journal of Business Law* March 1989 pp113-25.

3   See Simon Frith (ed) *Facing the Music* New York, Pantheon Books 1988.

4   Walter Benjamin 'The Work of Art in the Age of Mechanical Reproduction' in his *Illuminations* (translated by Harry Zohn) London, Fontana/Collins 1970.

5   See J Mowitt 'The Sound of Music in the Era of its Electronic Reproduction' in Richard Leppert and Susan McClary (eds) *Music and Society* Cambridge, Cambridge University Press 1987; also Andrew Goodwin 'Sample and Hold: Pop Music in the Digital Age of Reproduction' *Critical Quarterly* v30 n3 1988 pp34-49.

6   For discussions of the meaning of the word 'literacy', see Kenneth Levine *The Social Context of Literacy* London, Routledge and Kegan Paul 1986.

7   See for example the discussion in Christopher Small *Music, Education, Society* London, John Calder 1977.

8   Patrick Suskind *The Double-bass* London, Penguin 1988.

9   See Alan Durant *Conditions of Music* London, Macmillan 1984.

10 For a detailed discussion of these developments see Paul Theberge 'The "Sound" of Music, Technological Rationalisation and the Production of Popular Music' *New Formations* n8, 1989 pp99-111.

11 See W Schlemm 'On the Position of the *Tonmeister* (Sound Recordist) in the Musical Communication Process', in K Blaukopf (ed) *The Phonogram in Cultural Communication* New York, Springer 1982; see also Edward Kealy 'From Craft to Art: the Case of Sound Mixers and Popular Music' in Simon Frith and Andrew Goodwin (eds) *On Record: Rock, Pop and the Written Word* New York, Pantheon 1990 pp207-20.

12 For counter-arguments, see for example Raymond Williams *Television, Technology and Cultural Form* London, Fontana 1974; see also Stephen Heath, 'The Cinematic Apparatus: Technology as Historical and Cultural Form' in his *Questions of Cinema* London, Macmillan 1981 pp221-35.

13 For a detailed, critical history of these developments, with special reference to the instrument manufacturers and the politics of interested user groups, see Paul Theberge 'Democracy and its Discontents: the MIDI Specification' *OneTwoThreeFour* n9 (forthcoming).

14 See Goodwin *op cit*.

15 For a detailed history of these developments see A Peacock and R Weir *The Composer in the Market Place* London, Faber 1975.

16 For analysis of the general history and a range of senses of the term, see Raymond Williams *op cit*.

11
DIGITISATION AND THE LIVING DEATH OF PHOTOGRAPHY

ANNE-MARIE WILLIS

> The spectacle inherits all the weaknesses of the Western philosophical project which undertook to comprehend activity in terms of the categories of seeing; furthermore, it is based on the incessant spread of the precise technical rationality which grew out of this thought.
>
> Guy Debord[1]

The society of the spectacle which Guy Debord wrote about in 1967 has been a major preoccupation of twentieth century intellectuals. Each have named it differently: Adorno and Horkheimer defined it in the Forties as the culture industry,[2] Baudrillard later referred to it as the hyper-real and the sign economy.[3] More popularist writings, Umberto Eco's *Travels in Hyper-reality*[4] and Stuart Ewen's *All Consuming Images*[5] for example, or to indicate a different tradition, Marshall McLuhan's *Understanding Media*[6] and Vance Packard's *The Hidden Persuaders*,[7] have also sought to comprehend and critique the spectacularised cultural life of modernity. Their encounters may be different, their analyses varied and their conclusions diverse, yet these writers and others like them have all assumed a self-evident object of enquiry. The naturalistic image, delivered by photographic/filmic means, mass reproduced and distributed to large audiences, is taken as a given. Their starting point has been imagery of mass culture. In this sense they have typically placed themselves alongside the consumer rather than the producer. Imaging technologies themselves have not been subject to anywhere near the same level of theoretical enquiry – this has been the province of specialist historians or critics of photography, cinematography, television/video. Current developments in computer simulated image-making make this absence and these knowledge divisions less operable. They also make it all the more necessary to ground theorisations of the visual culture of late modernity in an analysis of the technological. The means of production of 'naturalistic' visual imagery is undergoing a mutation as significant as the invention of photography itself.

The aim of this chapter is to discuss some of the issues raised by the arrival of the new imaging technology of digitisation. In some ways we are facing the death of photography – but as in movie fiction the corpse remains and is re-animated, by a mysterious new process, to inhabit the earth like a zombie. Imagery that looks photographic will continue to exist, but its means of production is undergoing radical changes. Appearances remain, while substance changes. One question is, will we still continue to believe in appearances?

Traditional photographic imagery is based upon the mirror theory of representation, that 'which conceives of representation as the reproduction, for subjectivity, of an objectivity that lies outside it'.[8] Just as this theory of knowledge is coming under increasing criticism, technological developments themselves are also threatening it. Just as traditional categories of understanding are breaking down, so too are the once neat divisions between the reproductive technologies. As is apparent from a number of essays in this book, still photography, video and computer generated imagery, are all beginning to merge. The implications of these changes need to be thought about, for it becomes increasingly less relevant to think about these as separate image producing technologies, particularly to treat them theoretically and historically as if they are discreet. In the past, they were distinct, but to bring an historical understanding into the present and future, they need to be thought of together. In fact a new field of critical activity needs to be opened up which will transcend the previously separate concerns of historians and theorists of film, photography, television, video and computer generated imagery.

The Western philosophical project to which Debord referred implies that the more clearly we can see, the more we will know. The means to grasp, categorise, store and access the world of appearance has been relentlessly pursued. This desire to grasp the physical 'real', to duplicate it in order to know and control it, has been the impetus behind the move towards greater naturalism, speed and ease of production of the visual image. From still to moving, silent to talking, black and white to colour, there has been a double movement – on the one hand to be subservient to a truth assumed to be pre-existent in the visible world and on the other to create a duplicate reality that will be more intensely compelling than 'the real world'. Instrumental rationality does not stop to ponder, means become ends. There is massive unevenness between the development of the means of production of the image and the application of these means to ends of significance. Cultural theorists have come to see the way in which hyper-reality menaces and annihilates the real, with the world of manufactured imagery becoming the instance of first encounter and point of reference for all experience. Those developing image technologies, the computer programmers, the digital engineers, are however still working within Enlightenment categories of dualist thinking such as image/ reality and subject/object. There is no perceived crisis of representation for them as they work hard to extend the reach of the hyper-real by devising ever more efficient ways of producing ever more convincing imagery, yet new developments in computerised image making are being pushed to a limit in which the philosophical categories upon which they are based are breaking down.

Pictures by Numbers

Digitisation is a process which is cannibalising and regurgitating photographic (and other) imagery, allowing the production of simulations of simulations. It enables the storage of images on video disc which can be played back through a television set or computer. Stored pictures can be radically altered by using graphics-type programs and can be transmitted via telephone lines to other computers. Hard copy is simply 'scanned' or the image can be taken directly from video input by using a 'frame grabber' to capture the chosen image as a still. The quality available is that of broadcast video – colour or black and white. Digitisation works by the reduction of the image to picture elements or pixels, each of which is coded by number. The image is reconstituted by each mathematical unit being read and translated into a pixel value. The sharpness, brightness and contrast of any part or all of the image can be altered (the alteration corresponding to a changed mathematical value), it can be cut and pasted, rotated, reversed, slanted or warped. The ease with which these transformations can be made – using menus and a mouse, as on any personal computer – mean that digitised imagery allows much greater potential for manipulation than traditional photography. The potential for extensive image banks and networks, for the instantaneous accessing and reworking of vast numbers of visual images, is enormous.

Of course all photographic imagery is coded in some way or another. Light falling on photo-sensitive material produces tonal variations which can be measured according to the intensity of light, the length of exposure and the degree of sensitivity of the receiving material. Traditional photography can be understood as a process by which a coded version of appearances is produced according to 'the laws of nature', ie, of optics and the behaviour of silver compounds under varying conditions. As every photographer knows there are many optical and chemical choices to be made which affect the final look, feel and 'information content' of the image. The operations of the darkroom processor affect the final image but s/he cannot individually manipulate each grain of silver. With digitisation the alteration of every constituent unit of the synthesised image is, in theory, possible, for each pixel has a precise mathematical value. Any form of image can be digitised, stored, re-used, altered – the original may be video (broadcast or taped), a still photograph, an illustration in a magazine, an original artwork. The need for original 'hard copy' will diminish as still video cameras become more commonplace. Nikon has a sophisticated model for professional applications in 'journalism, government, law enforcement, education, publicity'.[9] Other models are being aimed at the amateur market – Canon's Ion, for instance can store up to fifty pictures on a video floppy disc.[10]

Digitisation is still in its early stages and there are problems to be overcome. Images take up a lot of memory space – the average personal computer at present only has the capacity to store around fifty to a hundred – hardly enough for an archive. Larger systems dedicated exclusively to digitised image storage can accommodate much more. Hard copy can be produced by linking to a thermal printer, but the quality at this stage leaves much to be desired. However, as with computer technology in general, research and development is orientated towards increased storage capacity, image enhancement and cost reduction. Given the breakneck speed of change in this area it is not unrealistic to speculate that still video cameras will be commonplace for both professional and amateur photographers within a few years and that the use of digitised imagery will be widespread.

True or False?

Manipulability of the image and instantaneous access are the major features of digitised photographic imagery. Both of these 'advantages' raise major areas of critical concern. If it can be assumed that the credibility of photography has rested traditionally on a knowledge of its mechanical rather than manual mode of operation, what will be the 'truth' status of images that look convincingly photographic but have actually been constituted from multiple digitised elements and subjected to re-workings by an operator? The traditional distinction between art and photography has rested on the crude, but nevertheless operational, division between the subjective and the objective. Precisely because it was produced by a machine and therefore the product of a regularised and predictable process (the laws of nature again), the photograph was regarded as a more 'truthful' medium.

As Alan Sekula has pointed out, two 'chattering ghosts' have haunted photography – those of bourgeois science and bourgeois art – the one claiming truth for the medium, the other stressing the subjectivity of the operator and hence claiming art's elevated position for photography.[11] But these competing discourses have only worked by remaining apart, bonding themselves to other discourses. John Tagg has argued that the proposal of photography as truth has been sustained by the location of the medium within domains of power and authorised knowledge, such as the law and medicine – photography gained power by its association with these and conversely it has magnified their power.[12]

To put it rather simply, photography's claim as bearer of truth has rested upon two foundations: the empiricist assumptions and understandings of its operation (objective tool for recording reality as it is) and the authority of the institutions that deploy it. Digitisation sweeps away the first basis, leaving only the second. The truth value of the image will become more dependent on use and context. It can be argued that this has always been the case – that the 'truth' of the medium is always asserted in particular authoritative contexts; that viewers/consumers never have before them empirical evidence (ie the referent), that their relation to photographic imagery is based on faith. Sekula's art/science distinction also begins to melt away as all computer stored photo-imagery is in principle capable of being manipulated. Manipulation, once a series of awkward processes borrowed from other media, most particularly painting, becomes an intrinsic feature of the new computer based medium.

Explanations of the ontology of photography which have assumed a clear divide between sign and referent are perturbed by the phenomenon of digitilised imagery. From a semiotic perspective the particularity of the photographic rested on its iconicity and indexicality (the former referring to the resemblance between sign and referent) – the naturalistic quality of photography. This of course photography shared with other media such as naturalistic painting and drawing. Its claim to be more truthful than painting has relied more strongly on its indexicality, the fact that as a sign it is partially produced by the referent. It is as if the scene or object at which the camera was pointed *imprinted* itself on the film. With digitised photo-imagery the viewer will never be able to be sure of this any more – the index will be erased as the photo becomes pure iconicity. In this sense digitisation reverses the history of imaging technologies and takes photography back to the ontology of infinitely manipulable medium of painting. If Paul Delaroche declared in 1839, 'from today painting is dead',[13] now we would say 'from today photography is dead'. And ironically it is a simulated form of painting that is displacing photography.

The Image Circuit

The photographic medium is imploding. At one end it is being electronically programmed out of existence, at the other it is becoming pure (video) data. Its function as data is operationally based upon an empiricist notion of appearance as truth and an implicit knowledge of the photograph's indexicality, yet many applications are now rendering problematic a model of fixed sign and referent and are moving image-making into a circuit of reference in which there is no fixed point of origin or destination. This becomes clearer in considering a particular application of the continuation of the indexical character of photography in its digitilised form – that of the 'photophone' – a device for transmitting still video images. Its makers, the US based Image Data Corporation, promote it as an aid to quality control for companies with widely scattered branches. Instead of sending engineers to different plants to troubleshoot, still video images of manufactured component parts can be transmitted from one branch to another and telephone conferences held to iron out production problems.[14] In this case the image is used as pure visual data, its function being to make the processes of industrial production more efficient. Photography has always served capital, but what is of great concern in the current situation of ecological crisis is the introduction of any techniques which contribute to the increase of industrial production.

As already noted, the assumption of the primacy of the real and of the image as a second order rendering of the real has been the philosophical premise that has underpinned the development of photo and video technologies. Users of the photophone assume that they are looking at an accurate rendering of an object that has a concrete existence. Operationally they are. For example, a still video image of a newly manufactured component is transmitted to engineers at headquarters; they observe a fault and issue instructions for the production process to be adjusted to correct it. We could ask where is the 'real' or the first instance (this linkage is itself contestable) in this case? The components are not 'nature' – they have been manufactured according to an engineer's drawings. Increasingly such design is being done on computers, and digitised imagery could have a role to play here – the image could be altered as an instruction to alter the material object. Leading edge developments suggest that this process could become even more automatic.

The notion of a sign driven economy could become even more literal than the current understanding of it in terms of images driving desire which drive production. What are being referenced here are developments in 'computer vision' in which robots are being taught to 'recognise' digitised imagery. The frightening techno-utopia being striven for here is one in which production robots 'read' the pictures sent to them and produce the object in the image of the image. Notions of the primacy of the material world over the world of images (real versus representation) which have been challenged by postmodern theory are thus being undermined by technological developments themselves. The image versus the real distinction has had its day; a more workable distinction now might be between the immaterial and the material, with a recognition of the ways in which the power and command of the techno-immaterial is proliferating. Imaging and production could be thought of as a circular system with the visual image being (n)either product or origin. The still video image is a nodal point in the circuit. Still video/photography becomes a technology not for recording 'the real' but a means of gathering raw data. In this sense it could be seen as a break in the circuit of the system. It is still attached to it but points outside and captures something external in it in order for that to become part of the metabolism of the system. Such a conceptualisation, though sketched only schematically here, needs to be developed in opposition to those theories that grant primacy to a concrete world assumed to exist independently of images.

There is a rampant literalism that is particularly frightening about a number of recent developments. Imagination, meaning here the mental capacity to visualise things other than as they are, is surely being undermined the more that this becomes the domain of technology. Manipulating an image becomes a question of trying out a series of (admittedly vast) options and combinations. Some low level commercial applications are already in evidence: salons in which you can sample different hairstyles by having them convincingly montaged onto your video image. The same technique could be used by interior decorators – begin with a picture of your room and run it through different style options. These examples are not as trivial as they seem, for they point to ways in which personal/social identity, the psycho-material substance of people's lives, is constructed, here even more literally and with an alarming efficiency compared to the familiar practice of flipping through style magazines. It would hardly be original to say that a major fallout of modernity has been the displacement of identity as that which is rooted in tradition by the commodified identities as lifestyles offered by the marketplace. What is changing however is that the new image technologies make this process more totalising as they do the imagining for you. Imagination becomes reduced to imaging. It is as if the bringing together of robotic production and imaging technologies is inspired by the desire to bring to realisation the dream of changing things with the wave of a magic wand. The terror is that change is reduced to appearance, again the tyranny of the literal, without consideration of social usefulness or ecological imperatives being built into the program.

Hardware and software manufacturers are envisaging potential educational applications of digitisation, for example visual encyclopedias which combine image and text in superimposed windows on the same screen which a user can explore in whatever sequence they choose. Such a program would be a truly open text, constituted differently by each user. It could well be a seductive way of learning, an entry into a fascinating world of self-sufficient appearances and information. But it also reduces the need to interact with materiality, thus certain kinds of knowledges are gained at the expense of others.

The Endless Archive

To move from speculations about the future to applications of digitised photography in the present, it can be noted that state and corporate archives and picture libraries are making use of the new technology. To take one example – the State Library of New South Wales in Sydney. Like many libraries around the world, it is using digital storage to develop its historical picture collection. Last year it sent a researcher to country towns to copy private collections of photographs (such as family albums and the work of unknown amateurs). This is how the archive was formed: original photographs were copied onto 35mm negative from which positive transparencies were made. The latter were then copied onto one inch videotape and then onto video laser disc. The video disc storage system used was Search Tech whose manufacturers claim that on-line access of up to 864,000 pictures in usually less than one second is possible.[15] One monitor displays descriptive text – the user can key in a request for particular subject matter, geographical location and/or date and be given a listing. The search can be narrowed by asking more specific questions or the user can choose to view a particular sub-category of picture which flips by on an adjacent screen. A thermal print can be produced for reference purposes, but this is not sufficient quality for reproduction so the library still provides this from its negative file.

Photographs copied had to be more than fifty years old, not for historical reasons, but because photographs of this age and older are out of copyright. This was a significant issue because all the material in the archive is to be available for public use. Like similar projects there was also the assumption that photography is the means by which social history is made instantly visible; what such an archive is likely to reveal is what people chose to photograph rather than 'what life was like then'. Ironic then that this project which is implicated in a social history of photography was made possible by the very technology which is now annihilating photography.

The State Library is now putting its entire picture collection onto laser disc. Users will be able to find what they want much more quickly and will be able to expose themselves to far more images than by sorting manually through filing cabinets. The storage and retrieval of imagery on video disc changes the very nature of the archive – it no longer has to be a repository of original photographs. The original, which has always had a shaky status for photography, becomes even less significant once the means of producing high quality hard copy eventually becomes available. In this and similar social history projects, it becomes irrelevant that the owners retain their original photographs, for once they are made available on video disc they virtually become public property. Makers of historical fiction films, TV documentaries and commercial publishers are major users of these kinds of collections – they are the agencies that select once private images and reprocess them as public history. Technological 'progress' in this instance serves their interests.

The new technologies make possible the storage and accessing of an endless range of imagery and, because of the capability of transmitting via telephone lines from one user to another, the idea of the archive is transformed into a limitless decentred mirror-maze of images available to be used and transformed in countless ways. The crucial questions centre around to whom this will be available, to what uses it will be put and what effects it will have on production, consumption, work and leisure.

One could imagine the creative role of the photographer diminishing while that of the image synthesiser increases (there are new professions waiting in the wings here). The photographer could become no more than a cataloguer of raw visual data, which then gets montaged and altered by the operator at the screen. The imagery of mass culture is of course already highly manipulated and the photographer only a small part of the 'creative team' that puts together an advertisement or style feature. But current processes of careful lighting, costuming, posing, montaging and retouching could all become more efficient by being performed by the alteration of digitised imagery on the screen rather than the cumbersome manipulation of materiality (models, clothes, layouts/hard copy).

A specifically photographic aesthetic can now be simulated. If the operator at the screen can zoom in and out, tilt or alter the angle/viewpoint from which the photographed object/ scene is 'seen', there is little need for the photographer in the field to do this. Photography's claim to be an independent artform has rested on the definition of a distinctive photographic aesthetic based on the camera's capacity to capture, frame, isolate, show from different angles and reveal detail. All of these effects can now be computer generated and definition and detail can be enhanced from a fuzzy original. Photography loses its special aesthetic status and becomes no more than visual information, and, once data is gathered exclusively by still video cameras, traditional film and paper based photography will have disappeared both as a technology and as a medium-specific aesthetic.

In principle every photograph that still remains in existence could become nothing more than raw material for image banks whose manipulators are free to do what they want with. The technology allows, in fact actively encourages, manipulation – with its menus of endlessly seductive possibilities to colour, tilt, flip, cut and paste, reverse and perform any other number of transformations. The archive and history become ruptured. Pictures from the past can no longer be assumed to be a transparent record of the past. An accumulation of imagery travels forward in time as potential raw material for the continual re-invention of history in the present. Conversely it travels backwards as evidence of the archeology of the technology, thus particular genres, styles, techniques become reference points for photography's own past.

Through constant repetition and appearance in many different contexts, visual images eventually become drained – the *Mona Lisa* is a good example. The 'great images' of the officially endorsed 'history of photography' – Dorothea Lange's *Migrant Mother*, Walker Evan's sharecropper families, Robert Capa's *Death of a Loyalist Soldier*, etc are also showing signs of exhaustion. Genres of imagery are subjected to the same process, for example the golden sunsets of calenders or the sepia toned images of frontier towns and 'old characters' that populate spectacularised history, in books or as cafe murals. Mass culture is greedy for new images; the consumer economy is driven by images which fuel desire. The networking of image banks will speed up the processes of accessibility, cannibalisation, re-animation, and exhaustion of imagery. Copyright law becomes dysfunctional with the proliferation of new image technologies. What is alarming here, is not that 'great images' will be unprotected (here we could also include the entire history of canonised art) – for photography has always been promiscuous. Rather it is that the endless circuit of the creation of desire for commodities – the consumer culture which continues to gobble up the Earth's resources and attempts to induct once distinct and self-sustaining cultures into its logic of self and life as nothing more than that which is delivered via the marketplace – now has an even more powerful means of proliferation.

As indicated earlier, the development of leading edge computer imaging technology proceeds on the basis of continual 'improvement' of means divorced from any consideration of ends; and its applications are assumed to be within the context of corporate culture. Within this culture the division between technology and appearances is ceasing to exist. Earlier writers assumed a technology and an end product and focussed their analyses on the latter. This is becoming less viable. The end of photography is not the end of something that looks like photography, but the end of something which can be considered as stable. In the metabolism of the image/production system it is part of the flow. The specific character of this system needs further analysis and its technological mutations need to be continuously monitored. Such critique needs to be grounded in the inescapable actuality of the techno-immaterial in order to develop knowledges that will contribute to the growth of critically conscious cultures which can be introduced into the system to work like viruses.

Thanks to Dr Hong Yan, Department of Electrical Engineering, University of Sydney and Alan Davies, State Library of New South Wales.

ANNE-MARIE WILLIS

1   Guy Debord *Society of the Spectacle* Detroit, Black & Red 1983 p18.
2   Theodor Adorno & Max Horkheimer *The Dialectic of Enlightenment* New York, Herder & Herder 1972.
3   Jean Baudrillard *Simulacra and Simulations* New York, Semiotext(e) 1983 and *The Political Economy of the Sign* St Louis, Telos Press 1981.
4   Umberto Eco *Travels in Hyper-reality* San Diego, Harcourt Brace Jovanovich 1986.
5   Stuart Ewan *All Consuming Images: the Politics of Style in Contemporary Culture* New York, Basic Books 1988.
6   Marshall McLuhan & Quentin Fiore *Understanding Media, the Extension of Man* London, Sphere Books 1967.
7   Vance Packard *The Hidden Persuaders* London, Longmans 1957.
8   Fredric Jameson 'Foreword to Jean Francois Lyotard' *The Postmodern Condition: A Report on Knowledge* Manchester, Manchester University Press pviii 1984.
9   Nikon publicity brochure, Tokyo, not dated.
10 Canon publicity brochure, London, 1989. Canon's system is designed for playback through a television set or home video system. At this stage the pictures it produces can only be used with a computer if they are processed through a frame grabber.
11 Alan Sekula 'The Traffic in Photographs' in Benjamin HD Buchloh et al (eds) *Modernism and Modernity* Halifax, Press of the Nova Scotia College of Art and Design 1983 p122.
12 John Tagg 'Power and Photography' in *The Burden of Representation: essays on Photographies and Histories* Basingstoke, Macmillan 1988.
13 Quoted in Helmut & Alison Gernsheim *LJM Daguerre: The History of the Diorama and Daguerreotype* New York, Dover 1968 p95.
14 Publicity kit, Image Data Corporation, San Antonio, 1988.
15 *Computerworld Australia* v12 n18 3 November 1989 p9.

12
NEGOTIATING PRESENCE – PERFORMANCE AND NEW TECHNOLOGIES

ANDREW MURPHIE

The historical origins of performance, conceived of as a form and activity distinct from (narrative) theatre, are imprecise. But while its progenitors include various popular cultural, 'high' cultural and avant garde practices, it came to particular prominence in its own right during the Sixties and Seventies. It flourished during this period on the strength of its *presence*. It was *live*, separate from the re-productions of film and the static arts on one hand and from the imaginary narratives of theatre on the other. But suddenly, as artists and performers embraced advances in video production, computer sampling and the mechanics and electronics of high technology in general, the nature of performance itself was questioned. There was now confusion between claims that performance was both 'dead'[1] and active as never before.[2] Whether you agree with one side or another seems to depend on how you view technology in relation to the live qualities of performance. For example, in an interview published in 1984, performance artist Terry Fox said:

> *I think that the original impulse for performance was vital, and it's still – it's really important . . . But it is so bastardized . . . that now performance has become a cliché – every performance exactly the same; you know what to expect, you know it's going to be slides, and pre-recorded tape and so on . . . You can only do things within the limits of the technology and . . . to me that's a terrible restriction.*[3]

For Fox, technology interferes with the freedoms of real time, space and bodies in performance. On the other hand, Laurie Anderson completely embraces technology as a component of 'real life', even if any sense of real time, space and bodies is destroyed in the process. As she emphasises:

. . . technology affecting people's lives on a daily basis, this is what my work is really centred on. How does a person really cope in an electronic world. You turn on a TV and it doesn't work, and unless you're a technician or an engineer you probably can't fix it. You're living in a world that's extremely alienating.[4]

In the same interview she also says 'I love machines'. The world of technology may be alienating but for Anderson, it *is* the world. Other performance artists have taken this further. Stelarc for instance, suspended by steel hooks through his skin or working with his high-tech 'third hand', welcomes technology as a messianic force – the final supplement to humankind's ailing evolution.[5]

New communications and information technologies have radically affected various aspects of our perception of self, society and the universe. Technology has, for example, brought about significant changes in the way we perceive our own bodies, mapping these out with its own peculiar distance and detail. Through various processes of video-photography, scanning and imaging, we are increasingly coming to know our bodies as 'foreign objects' viewed from *outside*. Performance work has recognised and responded to this in various ways. In performances such as Elizabeth Chitty's *Demo Model* (1978) for example, where the performer scrutinizes her body in detail using video, this has been expressed in terms of anxiety. At the other extreme, works such as Stelarc's film of the interior of his body or his 'acoustical landscapes' of the same, have been marked by their ecstacy.

In another response, the body in many performances has become not so much anxious, or ecstatic, as *absent* – particularly as the 'site of truth' it became in much Sixties and Seventies performance. Over the last five years this has given performance work a particular focus, as it attempts to forget a body of knowledge based on the body-as-truth syndrome. At the same time, living as we do in the high speed information dispersal world of Jean Baudrillard's more general 'ecstasy of communication', it has also tried resuscitating a body which can resist the demon of information technology, a demon which some would say would turn the body into nothing more than another station in the mesh of communicative networks. In the early Eighties, Josette Féral perceived and advocated technology as a set of extra alienation effects which could return to the body the kind of presence that theatre had 'stolen' from it:

Performance rejects all illusion, in particular theatrical illusion originating in the repression of the body's "baser" elements . . . To this end it turns to the various media – telephoto lenses, still cameras, movie cameras, video screens, television – which are there like so many microscopes to magnify the infinitely small and focus the audience's attention on the limited physical spaces arbitrarily carved out by the performer's desire . . . the body is not cut up in order to negate it, but in order to bring it back to life in each of its parts, which have, each one, become an independent whole. This is Derrida's differance *made perceptible.*[6]

These comments are premised on the supposedly innate ability of technology to 'alienate' when used in performance work. This *may* have been the case in the late Seventies and early Eighties, but several factors have made technical alienation effects strangely familiar now. In some ways, what began at the start of the Eighties as an attempt to use technology to re-gain the body in performance has ended with the body's elision.

Total Theatre and Beyond

Whatever their effect on performance work, both computer and information technologies have offered theatre the realisation of one particular trajectory. They have created the best conditions yet for a Wagnerian 'total theatre'. Even the computerisation of lighting has, for instance, greatly increased the parameters of what can be done to enhance the fullness of the theatrical illusion. Nothing need now be left to chance. Most theatre companies have experimented with the latest video and computer technology in order to enhance the total effect of the theatrical illusion and its subsequent transformative power. Now, in opera, computer guided slide projections even allow opera-goers to read translations of the libretto, projected above the stage *as it is sung*.

Such uses of contemporary advanced technologies are of course, completely opposite to the use of technology as an alienation effect in early performances. It is as if there is an essential dichotomy in its use in theatre – you either use the extra elements and *speed* gained in a 'Wagnerian' way, such as in the recent work of Robert Wilson; or otherwise in a Brechtian way, such as in the work of Richard Foreman. However, with the exception of its use in concealed contexts such as computerised lighting changes, the use of high technology invariably tends to disrupt the narrative accumulation of fixed symbols and make 'theatre', as such, increasingly impossible. Many theatrical performances which strive for total theatre by using video, laser and computers to enhance a fixed theatrical narrative in symbolic structuring, cannot help but start to look a little awkward. Wilson in particular has understood this and largely abandons narrativity in his more recent work.

There is however another approach outside the dichotomy between Brechtian alienation or Wagnerian total theatre, both of which foreground the separation of elements as a theatrical means of reaching 'truth'. This approach is that which regards the performance of the new technologies *themselves* as events simply existing among other events. In John Cage's terms, they produce 'just another noise in the silence'. This is good for performance in that, while it does not valorise or demonise technology, it broadens the scope of what can be *considered* performance. In some senses, the *dethroning* of the body and direct human activity in performance by the use of technology can lead to performance conducted outside of either individualistic or humanist attitudes – performance which is not just an attempt to supplement the human will and harness technology to humanity's further 'progress'.

John Cage himself has continued to use new technologies without necessarily foregrounding or valorising them more than any other element in the 'silence'. In this sense technology ceases having to 'mean' anything, or even be the sainted deliverer of meaning, and is instead simply one component in the presentation of the present. In his recent *Europeras 1 & 2* for example, Cage has used technology so that

> . . . *spectators behold . . . an apparently random procession of stage elements ordered by a computer program (called 'IC' because it simulates the I Ching's divinatory method). Actors, technicians, and musicians are 'conducted' by this program, which cues people via video monitors set in front of the stage . . . The only true aleatory feature is IC's imperative, which ensures the order of events will be different every evening.* Europera's *program playfully points this up by providing twelve possible synopses for the opera.*[7]

This may seem little different to Cage's own direct manipulation of the I Ching but can be seen to be even less anthropocentric. A computer program becomes an element of organsation in the performance without becoming the dominant element – the structural centre of the performance

(IC's) is literally situated on the margin.

Such a use of technology in performance work has distinctly different qualities and associations from Jameson's notion of *pastiche*, in which a sense of history, place or unity is lost. In Cage's work, technology is not so much constructing a substitutive culture (or in Jameson's famous example, a hotel foyer) but playfully re-ordering culture to make its determinations more obvious. In fact, Mead Hunter claims that Cage's *Europeras I & II* is 'finally subversive in that it returns culture to people, as their property to slice up at will. Far from ending opera, Cage has given us a heightened awareness of its historicity'.[8]

When performance treats technology as another component, another noise in the silence, much of the debate about technology's significance becomes insignificant. Indeed what Cage's work shows is that it may only be in the context of play/performance that technologies divorced from their usual cultural efficiencies can be seen more clearly for what they are, for the way in which they structure experience. This is even more true of information and media technology than it ever was of literature or even body-based performance; since the former have a high speed of dispersal and a consequent ephemerality as objects or monuments. Cage's statements about his work have also demonstrated an awareness of possible forms of postmodern consciousness which involve 'a spacializing of the cognitive faculties'.[9] As David Hughes has emphasised, Cage's approach perceives the individual as making 'sense out of the multiplicity of messages, creating a private logic and narrative; being the perceptual and active centre of his/her world; selecting and combining by choice and instinct; and being open to all possible inputs . . .'[10] The beauty of this Cagean approach is that it abandons both the need to control the machine and/or feel overwhelmed by it. The dilemma his approach leaves behind is essentially one of 'protocols versus vanquishment'. It is the masculine nature of this scenario, with both positions representing displacements of ego uncertainty into social control, which has informed much of the use of new technologies in performance.[11]

Technoscapes and the Global Sample

Over the last decade there has been an increasing tendency for performance artists to appear at fashionable metropolitan dance parties. During the same period, the Barcelona troupe La Fura Dels Baus have toured the globe with their mixture of savage theatrical nihilism and macho meat-eater regression.

Both forms are environmental theatres on a large scale. Performance at such events is immediately assimilated because the environment itself is one of the performers. Yet in the context of the dance parties (and increasingly there are similar audiences for both), La Fura seems increasingly archaic and caricatured in its physical and macho intimidation.

At dance parties, the presence of technology controlling the performance guarantees its presentability as fashion. Everyone can participate in its repeatable culture because the technology ultimately stands outside any one person or group of people. It is a mathematical cathexis with a guarantee of safe patterning. Nothing is really 'happening', there is only the repetition of that which is the latest in fashion and the least localised.[12] The *samples* for this come from somewhere else. At the dance party all is postponement, a continual deferral of everything that has not been sampled into that space and time. Even the conflicting performances of the performance artists who respond to the newspaper advertisements and promotional handbills are just another piece of the décor – unlike La Fura's demand to be dealt with as *the* performers. Performance itself, its relation to bodies and their motion, has become a commodity.

I have dwelt on dance parties because they are emblematic of performance at present. They represent one of the prime sites at which desire is filtered and all other forms of performance seem increasingly aligned to the global grid which they represent. In attempting to characterise them, Andrzej Wirth's remarks on Victor Turner are singularly apposite, 'a new transcultural communicative synthesis . . . indeed took place', but 'without a visible contribution to global cultural understanding'.[13]

The proliferation of various elisions of cultural boundaries in diverse art forms partly results from information technologies themselves, and is partly the result, in the arts at least, of the way in which the advances in such information technologies have been discussed. When various European theorists declare that the new technologies have led to McLuhan's global village, Baudrillard's various ecstasies or Virilio's economies of speed; it seems that postmodernity is bigger than all of us. Performance is not only free to, but forced to, participate in global ecstasies and cultural borrowings with very low rates of return to the source cultures. As Johannes Birringer has emphasised:

> *This colonizing flow incorporates all art or cultural forms as long as they can be made to reinforce the consumption of the 'audio-visual space' . . . the topography of boundaries*

between native and foreign, dominant and marginal, is made to disappear into the audio-visual space of a 'global culture' modelled on a closed-circuit theory.[14]

Such tendencies are indeed visible in the work of groups such as Japan's 'Dumb Type', who consciously elide their cultural difference in the belief that the differences between Tokyo and other major cities of the world are rapidly disappearing. Other performers such as Sha Sha Higby arrive at this point from another angle. Her dance performances resemble nothing so much as an inter-cultural costume change which comes perilously close to a fashion display – borrowing appearances as if the differences between whole cultures and ethnicities were no longer significant, as if the differences no longer existed in any significant way.

Indeed, much of the debate in performance at the moment seems to centre around the political ambiguities of such borrowings, trying desperately – after the fact – to determine whether it might be possible to rewrite ethical considerations faster than artists can profit from colonising third world cultures and crossing sex and class divisions. The more we can observe advanced technologies and a metropolitan consciousness ruling our perception, the more technologically framed and determined ideas about cities will come to dominate whole cultures. As Birringer emphasises, such ideas would be mistaken, it 'is a scenography that also speaks of the failed replacement of History; the audio-visual space of mass media, however dominant, cannot quite sublimate the exclusionary boundaries of class and race . . .' For Birringer, the theatre, as opposed to the mass media, 'is more revealing in its limitations since it does not operate in a virtual space. It has always been closely connected to a historical space'.[15]

Reclamation and Re-inscription

Recent work with older technologies has been largely derived from the Futurists, who idolised machines for their visible speed and for their ability to catalyse culture into a permanent state of market expansion.[16] While the visual and audial *effects* of the new technologies are often spectacular, the technologies themselves are largely *in*visible. They offer no visual manifestation such as that which inspired the original Italian and Russian Futurists, yet they have still shown an ability to catalyse culture with a speed which would blind even Marinetti. This difference in visibility also effects performance. In many ways the purpose of performance no longer seems

Jill Scott performing Strange Attractor *in Sydney 1990 (reproduced by kind permission of* Follow Me Gentlemen *magazine)*

to be the valorisation of new technologies but rather their interrogation. Performance seems increasingly moved to educate its audiences back to a point where the new technologies become visible and accessible. In this way education about technology is inevitably going to destroy postmodern illusions about the lack of technology's limits, much as the sudden experience of World War One shattered a number of Futurist illusions.

In this educative and interrogative project Laurie Anderson has been a brilliant pioneer. The work of Jill Scott and Derek Kreckler has also moved in similar ways, building bridges between blind faith or abjection in the technoscape and reinstating the remnants of a memory of a human culture in contact with the body and landscape. Crucial to the work of these three artists and indeed the project in general, has been the relationship between video and the body. When video becomes the basis for the structure of the whole performance (or when the performance is recorded and played back as a 'performance video'), it is hard to see this project as 'performance' any longer. This is so, even though it may rely, as some recent French dance does, on the (cleverly edited) physicality of the performers. It may be 'Video Art' but the basis for its approach to bodies, objects and their interaction is not what we might call 'gravitational languages' but rather electronic languages, the signal and post production techniques.

Yet some of the best performers *have* moved into video production during the last decade – Jill Scott for example. When Scott was asked in an interview whether her shift to video work represented a renunciation of the physicality of performance, she replied

> *Not at all. I'm still doing it, but it's for the camera. It's entirely transferred. What I really used to hate was not having control. For a time I really liked the whole risk component. Then after a while, I proved all that, that I could take those risks. Now I'm much more interested in control – performance for the camera . . . The element of control can be played with in the pre-production level, not only in the post-production.*[17]

Video Art aside, there are many instances where video is neither the basis of the performance nor merely an accompaniment to it. Derek Kreckler's work in particular has integrated video, performance, and in the latest, *Interruptions*, audio-sampling. This work merits detailed attention as an example of the productive integration of various new technological elements with the live presence and force of performance and the performer.

As usual with Kreckler's work, *Interruptions* is deceptively simple in structure and ingredients.[18] The performance begins with a large screen in front of which a woman arrives to deliver a lecture, ostensibly on James Joyce's *Ulysses*. Her mouth is half open to begin when she is interrupted by a 'worker' who makes a lot of noise with bits of tangled wire and bolts in a tin bucket (already the framework of language is being defeated by noise). After several, increasingly furious attempts to stop the interference, the lecturer suddenly becomes distracted, a little as if in a dream but more as if doped up to the eyeballs. The lights dim, she stares into space and simultaneously, a sampled soundtrack begins and video images are projected onto a huge screen. Underneath the screen sit fifteen performers lit by a blank slide from a slide projector.

The video images at this stage consist of personal pronouns run so quickly after each other that attention is chiefly drawn to the font in which they appear. At the same time, the performers repeat an initially audible word in a seemingly arbitrary, but actually carefully constructed, crescendo. The word is 'everyone'. This continues for about five minutes until the crescendo suddenly cuts. The performers freeze and the video projects chopped vignettes from American TV shows. These are both deliberately *banal* and also absolutely appropriate to the performance situation – two TV hostesses talk about the "nice audience" and a humdrum looking male talks about beauty and mediocrity. The performers then suddenly turn to look at the 'dreamer' and begin their chant again, a chant which would almost be machine-like if it were not so arbitrary. Sampled music sounding a little like a carousel going three times its normal speed then comes in, with a sampled opera singer singing 'dream' over and over again. Amidst this organised cacophony, the last images on the screen are of a spinning globe and then static. The performers then go back to their seats, the 'worker' cleans up and finally the 'lecturer' leaves, embarrassed, often long after the audience has already applauded.

Derek Kreckler's
Interruptions
(1989, Sydney,
Performance Space)

The beauty of this piece was that all of the separate elements were acknowledged within their own structural parameters, and yet, far from dominating each other, they contributed to a kind of mutual deconstruction. One did not merely experience the skill of the performances, which included elements of naturalism and blatant *a-realism*, video manipulation, audio sampling and composition and so forth. The audience was forced into realising that each element not only performed its duty well but had that duty reduced in the process to its most basic elements.

The screen used in the performances for video projection was so huge that the spectator was forced to acknowledge the texture of the video image, its physical construction. The very process of acknowledging and positioning subjectivity (exemplified by the personal pronouns) became also a questioning of the relation of computer styled fonts to that subjectivity. Language broke down to one word but gained its force *as* it lost its meaning in the crescendo. This word, 'everyone', was not an insignificant one to be pared down to the force it carried in that situation. A lecture – the dissemination of knowledge – about the quintessential modernist text no less – finishes in white noise, visual static and an embarrassed 'realist' performer who has been staring into space for five minutes.

The whole performance of *Interruptions* is contextualised by the questioning of the relations between subjectivity and the media information technology that has enabled the performance to take place. And in the performance's original Australian context, the Americanness of the video quotes have a distinct cultural meaning. The piece does not just play with, but *reveals* the fractal nature of our media experience and the effect it has on our subjectivities and their fantasies. Yet in some ways, through the process of rehearsal, the performers were caught in the structures of repeatability that sampling and the other technologies demanded as a result of performing *with* them. The force and tension of the crescendo came from the subjugation of the performers to the edited constraints of the accompanying sights and sounds. The piece thereby ultimately returned to the very position it seemed to question.

The Finality of Narratives

When Lyotard proclaimed the end of the 'grand narratives' in *The Postmodern Condition*[19] he did not, of course, mean the end of *all* narratives. The narratives have not disappeared but rather changed. Their operative force has just found more efficient spaces through which to flow. They increasingly operate through the invisible efficiencies of technological interfaces and their careful regulation of subjectivities. Performance using technology has often dwelt on the absence of narrative, but the opposite, ie how narrative *works through* technology is as important. Similarly, it is important to demonstrate how that technology requires its own set of supportive mystifications and processes in order to channel human energies through narrative flows. Such concerns are strongly evident in Laurie Anderson's work. As Rose-Lee Goldberg has pointed out, Anderson has sought to demystify some of these new narrative flows through the use of the very same technology which they flow through:

> . . . United States *was a flattened landscape that the media evolution had left behind* . . . Oh Superman, *a song at the heart of the show, was an appeal for help against the manipulation of the controlling media culture; it was the cry of a generation exhausted by media artifice.*[20]

For Baudrillard and many others however, that cry is not one of anguish, but of ecstasy. An ecstasy of a technological world so pre-connected that it is without (individual) narratives. Within such a world view, it is of course impossible to chart any sort of course through the narratives of technological culture. The realist view that everything in the world is knowable (usually within set Marxist narratives) falls foul of its reliance on those narratives and taxonomies which no longer apply in the world technoscape. Both Baudrillard and the realists indulge in dangerous projections. In the former we are totally overwhelmed by 'connectivity' (we might call this the 'fear of the mother', with its attendant ecstasy); in the latter, the projection that we are not drowning but still waving the red flag in the technological ocean (the clinging to the phallus, or in the case of writers such as Howard Barker, *phallic abjection* – 'I've lost my flag'). Such approaches are of course at odds with much feminist politics and theory and as Jill Nolan has emphasised, 'feminist performance theorists have . . . chastised the commodified brands of postmodernist performance that devolve into an endless plurality of meaning; a chic, politically apathetic ennui; or a retrograde nostalgia for master narratives'.[21]

Both the postmodern anxiety about being overwhelmed by technology and the realist anxiety about not having the picture soon enough, are profoundly *intellectual* anxieties, often more relevant to the acquisition of academic knowledge than to the operation of knowledge in lived social relations. This is especially so when it comes to actual relations between knowledge and technology. Performance is perhaps the only significant mediation between the two, because it creates a redundancy of technology in a situation marginal to social functions. This is especially the case when technology's use in performance is compared to its enormous productive potential and seamless operations in other positions within the market. It is this very *redundancy*, as in the performances of Laurie Anderson or Japan's Dumb Type group which can make our social relations to technology apparent, and which, as in *Interruptions*, can help us define the way in which technology participates in the construction of our subjectivities. These performances also have the crucial function of showing us how things actually *work*.

The later stages of capitalism depend not just on technological efficiency, but also upon the narrative mystique of that efficiency. This has made the politics of performance the more complex, as it must avoid buying into the new narratives of technical mystique whilst pointing to the actual fractal function of narratives and technological flows. Without such precautions, performance will effectively function to support the market mentality of capitalism in much the same way as the Italian Futurists did.[22] Peter Nicholls has taken this parallel further, comparing the Postmodern perception of Western culture to the Futurist's 'destruction of syntax' in favour of an 'abstract grammar of functional mathematical signs'.[23] Taking Baudrillard's *America*[24] as his specific referent, he argues that the book's 'rather lame conclusion' that life, in America 'is cinema', signals an apocalyptic elision of culture and technology', a tendency which signals and precipitates the 'end of the speaking subject'.[25] Referring back to Baudrillard's earlier work *In the Shadow of The Silent Majorities*,[26] Nicholls argues that Baudrillard's contention that it is only possible to abolish contemporary systems by pushing them into 'hyper-logic' 'seems, finally, less a ground of possible negation than – like Futurism – a delirious surrender to forces which must always lie beyond control and understanding.[27] For Nicholls the salient point to be learnt from the comparison of these two spectacular theorisations of technological modernity is that their grand systems ultimately reveal themselves to be 'fantasies and not unspeakable necessities'.[28] This is the Postmodern delusion.

Puppets, Gods and Machines

Present theories about technology have left us with a reflection and no original. Baudrillard's simulacra, Jacques Lacan's language of broken eggs (which come from making an *hommelette*) or Heinrich von Kleist's bodies, which, in his story *On The Marionette Theater*, are drawn into their own reflection (consciousness) and become bodies without their original 'grace'[29] – all embody this quality. Theatre, packed to the brim with all the deferrals that mimetic consciousness can offer, has, since its departure from ritual into reflection, never really recovered that original grace. Yet, is this so of performance?

Just as it is easily forgotten that many of the theories about simulacra (and so on) were developed *in response to* aspects of classical philosophy and its constant acting out of mimetic deferral, it is similarly forgotten that the 'absence of presence' currently perceived in classical theatre is not the same 'presence' as that which manifests itself in performance. It increasingly appears that presence in performance lies outside the dichotomies which still exist in classical and postmodern thought. It is therefore performance which, avoiding the pitfalls of classical mimeticism, reactionary postmodernism and failed realism, and more importantly, avoiding reflection; may find some sense of grace within the bodies and actions involved. Chantal Pontbriand has characterised presence in performance work as 'an obvious presence, not a presence sought after or represented', a 'desire to discover . . . a here/

now which has no other referent except for itself'.[30] Accepting this characterisation, we can see that performance offers a way in which, even if only for a moment, the participants and event can come close to recovering the grace of innocents, puppets and gods in Kleist's story.

Such a perception can even lead us to a more radical perception. Perhaps, with its *a-conscious* puppet-like grace and its distinctive relation to reflective mimetic narratives, technology may also function in some wave *as* pure performance. Performances using technology do not have to conform to the predominantly nihilistic anti-classical scheme of current Eurocentric theory. They can, instead, operate outside of the forgotten equation of mimesis, as an antithesis to positivist faith. The puppet-master function of technology, its ordering and direction of human bodies, can be used to enact a liberation of both those bodies and the mimetic narrative split between body and consciousness. As long as it is not trying to represent mimetically, or on the other hand, splash around in the sea of simulacra; performance with technology could, in short, return us to grace. This would be a grace where 'clumsiness' is just another way to perform, not in itself the failure of mimetic representation or of human cultural evolution. Kreckler's *Interruptions*, by constantly drawing us into a present which has less and less meaning, in which the shadows of mimesis dissolve as the performative aspects of the piece become more and more productive; enacts a graceful puppetry which indulges itself in neither mimesis nor a simple parody of simulacra. Such performances are however, perhaps rarer than one would wish.

The body in performance is now challenged to an unprecedented extent by technology. It seems too often destined to have either the codings of information technology (or the beat of House music) forced upon it. As Philip Monk has emphasised, this tendency has profound effects and leads to the 'realisation of a coded body'. In work which uses video 'as part of the live performance space' this results in an effect where 'just as the artist's body and actions make that space, so the two, artist and video . . . reconfigure a body between them. A 'space' is 'composed' in performance through recording technologies and distributive networks'.[31] In the case of works such as Elizabeth Chitty's reknown *Demo Model*, this space has been used to speak of a body reduced and cut-up by technology and to mourn the body as unified truth – since as Rose-Lee Goldberg has written, we 'can only claim our bodies if we stop claiming that they give us truth'.[32]

In the end, while technology has real effects on real bodies, it is hard to avoid the notion that, in performance at least, technology sometimes enacts a dispersal of more abstract subjectivities divorced from those bodies. This may account for the 'live again and again' phenomenon in sampling and dance parties, where, according to Tony Mitchell 'the best dance music gives a recurring sense that however clumsy, we can, we have (but we can't, we haven't) achieved a state of grace.[33] A similar illusory perception may well be that which informs the current attitude to environmental theatre in the United States, where audiences seem 'interested in a novel experience, but without the participatory demands or political agendas that characterized much of the late '60s avant garde'.[34]

In both contemporary work and the style established in the Sixties, technology often provides *both* a bodily fantasy of grace and a kind of reactionary alienation effect that substitutes fetishism for 'real' grace. The body itself is repressed and regulated through a combination of 'reproducible aliveness' and the montage with which this is orchestrated. Thus, performance may be seen to embody an effect of making the body docile for its tasks in the technological age – unless, that is, the flows and codes through which the lived montage is made are brought into some kind of disorder.

1   See *Tension* n19 January 1990 p14, where in its round up of the decade's art trends, it claims that Jill Orr *is among the few to carry performance into the 80s.*

2   It is worth noting that journals such as *Performance* have flourished for most of the Eighties by happily incorporating work with new technologies alongside more 'traditional' work.

3   Quoted in Richard White 'An Interview with Terry Fox' in Gregory Battcock and Robert Nickas (eds) *The Art of Performance* New York, E P Dutton 1984 p213.

4   Cited by Rob La Frenais in 'An Interview with Laurie Anderson' in Battcock and Nickas *op cit* p264.

5   For another perspective on this see Paul Brown 'Metamedia and Cyberspace' in this volume.

6   Josette Féral 'Performance and Theatricality: The Subject Demystified' *Modern Drama* v25 n1 1982 pp171-2.

7   Mead Hunter 'Interculturalism and American Music' *Performing Arts Journal* 33/34 1989 p201.

8   *ibid.*

9   David Hughes 'Moving Forwards and Backwards in Time' *Performance* 50/51 1987 p25.

10   *ibid.*

11   Note for instance Luce Irigaray's remarks that 'The eyes of the seer are not open to the world or the other in a contemplation that seeks and respects their different horizons. Does he turn over the world as he turns his hand, his plaything, his creation? Could he possibly plumb the structure of the world, or encompass it? But what gesture, or quality of gesture could make him believe that he has encompassed the world?' Cited by Brigitte Carcenac de Torne 'On The Male Sex in Luce Irigaray's Theorising' *Art and Text* n20 1988 p105. In this sense, by thinking and moving faster than the human body, new technologies have, for the first time, created a world within which man is *obviously* 'other' to himself and his work. There is of course nothing new to this position for those who have always taken the position of 'other' and much less angst about the whole thing for them too.

12   Points raised by Ed Scheer in conversation with the author (1989).

13   Andrzej Wirth 'Interculturalism and Iconophilia in the New Theatre' *Performing Arts Journal* 33/34 1989 p185.

14   Johannes Birringer 'Invisible Cities/Transcultural Images' *Performing Arts Journal* 33/34 1989 p129.

15   *ibid* pp130-131.

16   See Peter Nicholls 'Futurism, gender and theories of postmodernity' in *Textual Practice* v3 n2 1989 p210.

17   Jill Scott, quoted in Rob La Frenais 'Jill Scott' *Performance* n42, 1986 p26.

18   *Interruptions* was first peformed in Sydney in 1989.

19   Jean-Francois Lyotard *The Postmodern Condition: A Report on Knowledge* Manchester University Press (UK) 1984.

20   Rose-Lee Goldberg *Performance Art* London, Thames and Hudson 1988 p190.

21   Jill Dolan 'In Defense of the Discourse: Materialist Feminism, Postmodernism, Poststructuralism . . . and Theory' *The Drama Review* v33 n3 p60.

22   As Peter Nicholls has pointed out. 'Futurism proposed a view

of capitalism whose extreme implications were to a large extent obscured by the dismissive (and non-political) interpretations of the Anglo-American avant-garde. For modernization, as it was hailed by Marinetti and his colleagues, amounted to more than a series of stunning technological innovations; it entailed the extension of the market'. Nicholls *op cit* p202.

23 *ibid* p217.
24 Jean Baudrillard *America* London, Verso 1988.
25 Peter Nicholls *op cit* p217.
26 Jean Baudrillard *In The Shadow of the Silent Majorities* New York, Semiotext(e) 1983.
27 Peter Nicholls *op cit* p217.
28 *ibid.*
29 See the passage for example where Kleist's protagonist relates that 'I went bathing with a young man whose constitution then displayed remarkable grace . . . It happened that just a short time before, in Paris, we had seen the 'youth drawing a splinter from his foot'; the statue is well known . . . A glance that he cast in a large mirror the moment he placed his foot on a stool to dry it off reminded him of it; he smiled and told me what a discovery he had made . . . I laughed and replied that he was probably seeing ghosts! He blushed, and raised his foot a second time to show me . . . the experiment failed. Confused, he raised his foot a third and fourth, maybe even ten times'. In vain! – (It was all downhill from here for the poor young, now graceless, man) Heinrich von Kleist *On The Marionette Theater* in Michel Feher (ed) *Fragments for a History of the Human Body: Part One* New York, Zone 1989 p418-9.
30 Chantal Pontbriand 'The eye finds no fixed point on which to rest . . .' *Modern Drama* v25 n1 p157.
31 Philip Monk *op cit* p164-5.
32 Rose-Lee Goldberg cited in Jill Dolan *op cit* p68.
33 Tony Mitchell 'Performance and the Postmodern in Pop Music' *Theatre Journal* v41 n3 p280.
34 Steve Nelson 'Redecorating the Fourth Wall: Environmental Theatre Today' *The Drama Review* v33 n3 p73.

13
METAMEDIA AND CYBERSPACE:
Advanced Computers and the Future of Art

PAUL BROWN

Donald Michie[1] has suggested that the problems of global pollution and population are too complex for humans to understand and solve, that our only hope is to develop artificial intelligence systems that can grasp the totality of the problem and so suggest viable paths of action. A dilemma here is that in order to create that technology we need a level of industrialisation that will, in the short term, increase pollution: by committing ourselves to this particular solution we also guarantee its need.

When any new material or technology is introduced it takes a while to mature – for its intrinsic nature to become apparent. By considering the future of information technology and its implications for the creative visual arts we can, perhaps, identify the unique features of this new meta-medium. This essay speculates on the development of the super-intelligent technology that is likely to evolve in the near future and, in particular, upon the implications of this technology for the creative visual arts. Not only are artists discovering a new meta-medium and, possibly a new role for art but, in my opinion, they should also become directly involved in developing this new technology.[2] Computer aided art in its purest form is not concerned with the production of artefact but instead with communication and interaction.

For over thirty years I have been an avid fan of science fiction and many readers will suspect that it is there, and not in science fact, that I have found my inspiration for what follows. I disagree, modern science and mathematics are, almost daily, demonstrating concepts and methods that are far more fantastic than those in fiction. The subject known as Chaos and the products of pure mathematics that belong to the astounding Mandelbrot Set are just the latest offerings to catch the public's fascination.

What Does Fast Mean?

A modern supercomputer can sustain about one thousand million instructions per second (or 1000 MIPS). These instructions could be, for example, simple integer sums – the addition of two whole numbers. If a human wished only to read this many numbers, and could read one each second, it would take them 32 years of full-time work, with no breaks for eating or sleeping, to complete the task. In making such a simplistic comparison, that one second of supercomputer time equates to 32 years of human time, we must retain perspective. The internal processing speed of the brain appears to be a good deal faster than that of the supercomputer, as we shall see below. And this comparison makes no allowance for human psychophysical processes like intuition, about which we still know very little. Nevertheless, a grand-master chess player can still beat powerful chessplaying computers by making inspired decisions during the complexities of the end-game.

Imagine that we have those 1000 million numbers before us. We know that most are in the range 0 to 100 but one, just one, is much larger, say 30,000. Our task is to find this renegade value as fast as possible. We can convert those numbers to colours, so there is a direct relationship between colour and value, then display them as pixels on a computer graphic display screen. If we use a resolution of 1000 rows of 1000 pixels each we can see 1,000,000 numbers simultaneously. 1000 screens are required for all the numbers so if we play these back at 25 frames per second we get to see all the numbers in just 40 seconds. The renegade number will be apparent on the first or second viewing and after a period of cueing we should be able to isolate the unique frame containing the number, then its row and column number will identify it absolutely. I suspect that we could find that rogue number in this way in about 5 or 10 minutes at the most.

It's worth commenting that in facilitating that perception we have traded speed against precision. We can find the rogue number quickly but we have no idea of its precise value. We only know that it is significantly different from its neighbours and, with well selected colour attributes (via a look-up-table) we should also be able to estimate the magnitude and the sign of that difference. Here's the power of computer visualisation at work. Scientists associated with projects at the National Centre for Supercomputer Applications in Illinois[3] have reported finding errors in their algorithms as a direct result of using visualisation-based analysis tools similar to the process outlined above.

The human brain has evolved as an elegant processing

system that is fashionably labelled *wetware* in contrast to the soft- and hardware of 'electronic brains'. Vision is one of its masterpieces. Lou Doctor[4] has suggested that we can increase the speed of modern supercomputers by a factor of 100 before we begin to tax the processing power of the human visual cortex.

During this last decade we can expect to see increases in processing speed that surpass even that factor. A researcher in Queensland[5] has outlined a reversable gate (so-called gates that implement logical functions like AND, OR and NOT are the fundamental building blocks of digital computer systems) that operates on quantum or sub-atomic levels. It could theoretically use single photons as bit information carriers, be very small and be able to steal energy from its environment in the form of spare heat. As such it may be considered potentially non-polluting. However, as I have expressed elsewhere[6] the pollutant generated by a computing device is a function of the quality and quantity of the information it is processing and eventually outputs into the environment.

Researchers at IBM have taken these sub-atomic concepts further and produced a practical communication device that operates on quantum levels and uses the uncertainty principle to ensure security.[7] What is particularly interesting about this system is that it is the first practical computational device to exceed the capabilities of the Turing Machine, a theoretical model (based on classical rather than quantum mechanics) proposed in 1936 by the English visionary mathematician Alan Turing. This machine reads an infinite sequence of binary symbols (1 and 0, mark and space, etc . . .). It can carry out four operations as it reads: advance one unit; retreat one unit; make a mark and; erase a mark (this last operation has since been proved to be unnecessary). The machine can execute any program that can be expressed in binary form. All digital computers with the exception of the IBM system (above) and other research machines are, and always have been, the formal equivalent of a Turing Machine.

Another route for the computer of the future is the bio-chip. I have spoken with one researcher who referred to Drexler's work at MIT[8] and who speculates that we should be able to produce supercomputer systems that will be the size of large organic molecules by the year 2010. Like modern pharmaceuticals they will be capable of being targeted for specific psychophysical sites and functions. Once introduced into the body they will be capable of tackling illness; restoring immune deficiencies and attacking damage like carcinogenic tumors. They will be able to act as an adjunct to memory and, perhaps most exciting of all, they could conceivably aid with DNA replication. The implication here is that such systems may be able to stop, and perhaps even reverse the ageing process.

Parallel processing, where several interlinked processors work together on the same problem is now a viable technology. Massive parallelism and in particular the attempts to emulate human wetware by the use of neural networks shows great promise. In the human brain there are a very large number of neurons (about 1,000,000,000,000 to 10,000,000,000,000) and each of these is connected via input dendrites and output axons. Axons link to dendrites, via synaptic 'gates', to anywhere between a few tens to several hundred thousand other neurons which are all simultaneously active. Human (and animal) brains can learn to do complex tasks without being pre-programmed for this specific activity. A neural net computer will not be programmed to solve specific problems (as are current computers) but will have strategies for tackling problems. It's hoped that they will be able to learn how to solve complex problems and maybe even problems (like ecological issues) that appear to be too complex for human understanding. The value of even simple systems is well demonstrated by the Neural Net demonstration program running on the Next Computer (an innovative personal computer system designed by the person who was responsible for the Apple Macintosh – Stephen Jobs) which shows a seal learning to balance a stick on its nose by trial and error. There are many other interesting and exciting examples of the new worlds being opened up by modern information processing not least the concept of the universe itself as a virtually infinite computational process.[9] Within research and industry the rate of change of change itself is increasing and even hardened professionals are expressing surprise and occasional concern at the pace.

Although with parallel computing, neural networks, quantum and bio-chips, the measurement of performance in MIPS is less indicative, there seems to be general expectancy that sometime during this Last Decade we will achieve 1,000,000 MIPS – the ability to process one million million numbers per second.[10] Using my earlier metaphor, a human would need 32,000 years to merely scan that many numbers. 32,000 years ago humans were hunter gatherers. The foundations of the kind of social order that led to civilisation would not appear for over 20,000 years. The earliest evidence of human settlement in Australia comes from this period as do the elegant paintings of hunting scenes on the cave walls at Lascaux in the South of France. Bearing in mind my reservations above it's nevertheless remarkable that we could soon have an information technology that will have the potential of condensing these phenomenal human time scales into just one second.

If we now apply computer graphics visualisation to this vast quantity of numbers – animating one million numbers per frame – we require 40,000 seconds, 666 minutes (a portent here that would amuse Mary Shelley[11]) or 12 hours. It's a long movie but still a big improvement on 32,000 years. Nevertheless, visualisation is here being pushed to its limits and it is important that we improve human-computer communication in order to handle the ultra-high bandwidths that will be associated with the coming generations of supercomputers.

Computers can now communicate with each other, and quite often do so, quite independently of their human users. An important development that has taken place during the Eighties has been more and more sophisticated long-distance interprocessor communication. A key to the development of Fourth Generation Computing and the success of personal computers were the networks that link them together and now cover the planet and extend into space like a fine global system of nerves. Although high-speed nets link inter-departmental and occasionally inter-institutional sites, the major national and international data highways are painfully slow. Steps are being taken to ameliorate this bottleneck by using more efficient and sometimes novel data compression methods[12] and higher bandwidth optical transmission technology.

Networks open a system up to attack from without and have also brought problems – as anyone who has had to upload reams of junk electronic mail via a slow telephone connection in order to extract an important message will know to their cost. But the real villains are the diseases that have infected the globalNet. As far back as 1975, science fiction author John Brunner suggested a data processing construct that would travel along networks changing or destroying their node contents. Brunner called it a *Worm*.[13] The first real worms, together with their streetwise cousins the viruses appeared in the Eighties. They have caused, and indeed are still causing, major damage. The concept of computer security has been modified and what is virtually a new technology has evolved – information system immunology.

The personal computer on your desk is not a closed system. Connected to a modem it becomes one processing node in a metasystem – the globalNet – that includes just about every other computer in use anywhere that humans have been, or sent their remotes. Currently it's unlikely that this metasystem has any concept of itself. Developments in artificial intelligence, neural networks (indeed I believe that we can think of this globalNet as a potential neural network in its own right) and in particular the refined analysis of human cognitive activity are likely to trigger self perception in such a system. Spencer-Brown[14] infers that any system that goes beyond a certain complexity has to develop self perception in order to be able to resolve the space/time paradox. A system that has no awareness of self, for example, is unlikely to discover the Uncertainty Principle.

Gateway to the Brain

Epileptics suffer violent and seemingly chaotic electrical brainstorms. Outwardly they lose control of their body and suffer distressing and often damaging muscular fits. One treatment for this condition involves severing the corpus callosum. Whatever its efficacy, studies of patients who have had this treatment have given insight into aspects of brain functioning. In particular, it is relatively easy to induce sensory paradox using material that to a 'normal' person would appear trivial. This is particularly the case when material mixes visual information handled by the right lobe of the brain with literary material which is processed by the left. This is because the corpus callosum is the highway that allows the two lobes of the brain to communicate with each other. Studies of others who have suffered brain damage has confirmed that, under normal operation, specific parts of the brain are dedicated to particular functions. Nevertheless it has been demonstrated that if one part of the brain is damaged another area can often learn to do the work associated with the lost tissue.

Over the last two years I have been involved in helping physicists at the Swinburne Centre for Applied Neurosciences[15] to develop low cost visualisation tools. One of their experimental rigs uses a modified bicycle helmet to hold 64 electrodes in place on the scalp. Electrical activity is sampled several hundred times each second at each of these sites and stored in digital form. Postprocessing reveals detail and demonstrates dynamic links between brain structure and cognitive processing. It would appear that humans have evolved a twin processor. Each is capable of maintaining a basic level of independent functionality. However, under normal circumstances each is dedicated to particular functions and, communicating with each other along the corpus callosum, a very high level of activity can be maintained. The corpus callosum is like a bus structure that allows rapid and high-bandwidth exchange between the two processors. It may well be that all high-level brain activity finds itself commuting along this route. If we wish to bypass the sensory inputs (touch, sight, smell, taste, vision and esp) to establish high-

An early premonition of super-intelligences – Stanley Kubrick's film of Arthur C. Clarke's 2001

bandwidth and direct communication with the brain it would appear that the corpus callosum, rich in interbrain information traffic, may provide an excellent gateway.

Current theory suggests that we first monitor the electro-chemical activity across the corpus callosum and have an artificial intelligence (AI), probably in the form of a neural network, try and figure out what's going on. Once it thinks it does it will be allowed to send some signals back. We will have begun to build a direct link between brain and computer. Not too long after this I would expect to see the first artificial super-intelligences (SIs) emerging.

It has been suggested that we should have computing systems with the physical capacity of the human brain within fifteen years. Connect something like that up to the corpus callosum and it shouldn't be too long before we see a true artificial cognitive system emerging. Its links to globalNet will give it a source of information and knowledge that will reinforce an ultra-fast learning curve. Very soon after it has evolved, machine intelligence will eclipse human facilities and the new SIs will begin to inhabit the Net. A growing number of researchers are suggesting that by facilitating this process we are, in fact, fulfilling the dictates of our own DNA and creating a more rugged intelligence that will become our evolutionary successor.

Graphics, the mainstay of current computer-human-interface (CHI) development, may seem redundant once direct communication is developed. I doubt it and suspect that visualisation will still provide a semiologically rich gateway, possibly via direct stimulation of the visual cortex. From about the age of six, when the child learns metric vision – the ability to estimate measure by just looking – sight begins to dominate other senses in the learning and communication process. The potential here – of directly controlling and manipulating vision, of creating virtual spaces (whole new and coherent universes of interest) – is one of the most exciting challenges the artist has ever faced.

Art and Beyond

The implications for humanity of a self-aware superintelligent globalNet are mindboggling as are the implications for the visual arts. Most artists to date have used computers as tools, using pre-packaged software that emulates traditional techniques for artefact production like painting, drawing, photo-retouching and so forth. Oil paint is a simple thing and its lack of intelligence makes it easy to simulate. Despite their limitations these graphic arts systems have proved of value:

they are non-toxic or significantly less toxic than traditional media; they can significantly enhance productivity and, despite the often strong signature of the particular system in use, they have proved the viability of this new meta-medium to handle a diversity of styles and methods, ranging from the formal and often geometrical languages of structuralism to the free association of surrealism and abstract expressionism.

A few artists have pioneered new ground and are helping to define the unique attributes of this information transaction based meta-medium. Two immediate potentials seem to offer themselves. The first is involved with establishing an interaction or intercourse between a human and an AI. The second is interaction between two, or more, humans mediated by an AI. Several artists including the Melbourne-based Simon Veitch have begun to investigate the former. Others, most notably Myron Kruger, have pioneered the latter.

Veitch is an artist who has developed an interactive system he calls 3-Dis. Using two or more small monochrome video cameras, volumes of space as small as a few cubic centimetres or as large as a whole room can be identified and tagged. Up to 96 of these volumes can be monitored simultaneously. When the contents of a volume change, this can be converted by the computer into a command that can trigger any number of events like, for example, the control of a MIDI channel on a sound synthesiser or a remote video surveillance recorder (pointing, for example, at a number of safety deposit boxes in a large vault and automatically recording images of everyone who touches those particular boxes). The essential simplicity of the concept belies its application and usefulness. Although there are similarities with the work of Canadian artist David Rokeby[16] there are subtle and essential differences, not least the ability to independently track the behaviour of a large number of people or events simultaneously. Applications in the arts have brought the system to a wider audience via performances where groups of dancers create their own soundtracks as they moved; and via installations where fountains followed visitors about as they strolled around gardens at the 1988 Brisbane World Expo. Now the security people are getting interested and promise Veitch a new source of support.

Kruger's installation at SIGGRAPH 85 in San Francisco[17] used a single monochrome camera and clever edge-detection software to allow individuals and groups to interact with images of themselves that were projected onto a facing wall. The projection also included computer generated artefacts like little green gremlins and b-spline curves that participants could interact with. What was particularly notable about this exhibit was the way it encouraged people to play together.

On several occasions I discovered salespeople in suits interacting with the most unlikely partners – students in sawn-off jeans amongst them – in a completely uninhibited, joyful and humorous way. Encounter group therapists have been trying to create this degree of relaxed and intimate behaviour for decades and yet here a relatively modest computer program acted as a catalyst for close spontaneous human interaction. Nevertheless, four years later at SIGGRAPH 89, critics and gallery curators on the panel 'Computer Art – an Oxymoron'[18] still felt confident to reiterate their belief that computer art is cold, intimidating and heartless.

Those speakers, like many in the art mainstream, were expressing their problems in getting a suitable handle on this kind of work. Their complaints mainly concern the lack of tangibility of the artwork – that it can't be framed, revered or monetarised. Computer art is not concerned with the production of artefact. By contrast it is exactly the inverse of those attributes the mainstream miss that defines this area's uniqueness and potential. Computer art is based upon an information-transaction meta-medium and, like Dada and many of the works of the Art Language and other conceptual groups, is essentially, an ephemeral and virtual artform concerned with communication and interaction.

It is my opinion that practitioners shouldn't waste their time trying to convince the arts mainstream of the value of their work. Our involvement in alternative events like the now ten-year-old SIGGRAPH Art Show, Ars Electronica, the biennial International Symposium on Electronic Art and other events, constitute the evolution of an international and interdisciplinary *Salon des Refusés*. Putting energy into consolidating this movement is infinitely more valuable than wasting time trying to convert the high-priests and culture-vultures of the establishment who, in any case, are mortified by the threat to their quasi-religious and usurious value systems that this new and egalitarian artform endorses. They will come over in the end never fear; just as soon as they find out how to get an edge. Look at what they did to the Dadaist's dream of undermining the academy – the establishment now drinks champagne from Duchamp's Urinal.

Twenty First Century Alchemists

If today's artists can achieve so much with the limited computer technology that's currently available we can look forward to a classical/constructive Renaissance as they contribute to the development of the brain interface and a fully interactive globalNet with its resident SIs. The 300 year stranglehold of Romanticism; the view of the artist as alienated outsider, preoccupied with their own obsessions, that has culminated in the petulant absurdities of post-modernism can be brushed aside and the artist can once more look forward to a central role as contributor and initiator. By entering globalNet, creative artists will bring knowledge of a host of human experiences to the system, the expression of both intellect and emotion and, not least, the value of the celebration of existence. Most often the aims of artists are benevolent – a quality they will do well to pass on to the new intelligence. They also will bring the streetwise consciousness – an ability to survive, both within and from, whatever is at hand.

Many express concern regarding an all pervasive superintelligence and, in particular, about close linked machine-human symbiosis. If we consider human freedom to be nothing more than a measure of the inadequacy of our governing institutions then such response to authority can be seen as a natural and reasonably healthy human reaction. Nevertheless I am concerned that the majority of critics of these issues are women. The Australian artist Stelarc, who has pioneered symbiotic technology in his performances, has suggested that this is because such issues threaten the concept of maternity – self replicating machine intelligences and human symbions won't need mothers. Whilst several women have agreed with this prognosis many, in particular those representing the feminist viewpoint, strongly disagree. The gender bias in the forces developing this technology is a major cause for concern and requires attention. A vision of the controlling technology of the 21st century containing an inherent gender biased perspective is as unhealthy as it is undesirable.

A tightly coupled human-computer symbiosis should lead to a close creative collaboration between human and machine. Eventually it's likely that we will see pure machine art – the product of what is essentially an alien intelligence – for the first time in human history. The potentials offered by interaction with these artificial and, once they pursue an independent evolutionary path, alien intelligences will open up exciting new potentials for the creative artist. Already two young Australian artists take their inspiration from the area.

The CyberDada events of Troy Innocent and Dale Nasons are an anarchistic, acid-house mix of free-form sound, scratch video, analogue and digital screen displays, slides and live performance. Their equipment looks like it was built with a sledgehammer – a sound deck that features a raw and mangled cassette transport linked (functionally?) to a caseless Apple II – all hooked together with recycled wires and bits of dead circuit board. Although both are young and their work still immature, it has attracted the attention of the alternative arts network and the two are likely to get financial support to complete a videographic version of their Cyberdada Manifesto along with facility support from leading professional digital video studios like The Video Paint Brush Company. Their work bears similarities with the British group Stakker and other artists associated with the acid-house genre.

These artists are amongst the first generation of kids who have had computers around for most of their lives and who are not, in the least, phased by either their existence or potential. Although both are used to microprocessors, until recently they had little opportunity to learn about the more mainstream activities in computer science, graphics and CHI and have been surprised to discover that many of the concepts that excite them are actually being developed 'for real' by scientists and engineers. Their main source of inspiration has been science fiction and, in particular, the work of the cyberpunk writers[19]

William Gibson is author of the canonical texts of cyberpunk – the CyberSpace trilogy: *Neuromancer; Count Zero* and *Mona Lisa Overdrive*. Cyberspace is the virtual space within the matrix – the globalNet – reached by jacking in via a socket or a 'trode net'. When Gibson wrote *Neuromancer* (on a manual typewriter) he was unaware that NASA and others were working on the real thing. He's also concerned about the attention his work has brought him from the technical world: 'it never occurred to me that it would be possible for anyone to read these books and ignore the levels of irony'.[20]

As many sci-fi authors realised, cyber or virtual space has been around since the first digital computing machine. If we consider a computer to be a collection of individual storage units or 'bits' then the total number of states those bits can represent is 2 raised to the power of the count of bits. Even with a fairly dinky computer this state potential is very large – a 1Mb PC gives 2 to the power of 8,388,608; a number that is inconceivably vast but nonetheless trivial compared to the potential states of the human brain. Many of these states will be chaotic, though some, probably only a small proportion (but still a large remainder of the vast total) will be stable and contain meaning. When we add the PC to the globalNet the number of states becomes so big that its count dwarfs even the count of all the sub-atomic particles in the known universe and, significantly, the total states of the human brain. We can consider this total as the current potential of cyberspace.

Virtual space, by comparison, is the current availability of cyberspace. Using the teletypes and low-level languages of the Fifties, virtual space was small and limited to a few specialists. With the advent of graphic communications in the early Sixties, virtual space grew and, significantly became available to the non-specialist. The enhanced graphic tools of the Fourth Generation opened up new spaces like spreadsheets, relational databases and hypermedia. Now a new generation of behavioural interaction tools allow the user to seemingly physically interact with a virtual or computational construct and the terminology has gained a revitalised and popular meaning. By wearing a headset containing twin video screens (parallax vision for depth measurement is as important here as it is in the 'real' world) and a device that communicates position and orientation to the computer, a human can now physically inhabit a coherent and recognisable virtual reality. A walk through non-existent buildings, which in virtual space can be photorealistically presented, is a typical architectural example. The control of robots in distant situations like space factories or dangerous ones like atomic reactor cores are promising industrial applications. The potential of creating a coherent and consuming artificial reality – live representational or abstract movies that you can interact with and live within – is exciting many artists.

Brave New Worlds To Go

The goals of science don't seem to have changed much in millennia. The Chinese Taoist alchemists of the Han Dynasty sought the elixir of youth over 2000 years ago. They and their colleagues down the ages have also attempted the creation of life from inanimate matter. Now with biotechnology and quantum communications there seems to be some reasonable expectation that we may be getting close. (Yet another claim that alchemists of all ages have made – particularly to their patrons.) Whilst some, taking Mary Shelley's lead, are concerned about the religious, moral and ethical implications of such speculation, others rejoice in the fact that we may at last be able to create an intelligence that is capable of understanding the fragilities of the tenuous ecosystem of planet Earth and may be able to help us remedy our past errors. The tax inspectors and defence experts are already involved with developing this technology. As I have suggested elsewhere[21] this could well lead to paranoid superintelligences – a hideous prospect. My interest in getting artists involved in the process of developing these new intelligences is because they will bring a whole set of values, particularly those that should complement the militaristic and personal surveillance aspects that authorities are likely to want (and quite reasonably expect since they require these tools to help them manage and govern). By involving artists (and I use the label in its widest possible sense) and other creatives, I believe that we may be able to help ensure that the new technology is balanced and potentially benevolent. Many questions must wait to be answered. By plugging into globalNet will humans bring requisite self-awareness to the system or instead will we need to create an autonomous self-awareness? Will the Net be dependent on, or independent of, its human creators?

Such questions aside, the potential for the creative arts is promising. We may, at last, have broken the stranglehold of the gilded frame and bypassed the parasitic high-priests and culture vultures to establish an egalitarian art of, for, and by the people. Not the constrained and hierarchical social realism of totalitarianism but a hetrachical and streetwise cyber-grafitti, an art from the grassroots of democracy that, like urban spraycan walls, will impinge upon and possibly integrate all our diverse consciousnesses.

Notes

1 Donald Michie and Rory Johnson *The Creative Computer* London, Viking 1984.
2 Paul Brown 'Art at the Computer Human Interface' *Artlink* v9 n4 Summer 1989 pp64-65.
3 Mathew Arrott and Stephen Fangmeier speaking at SIGGRAPH 88 pointed out that their simulation of the interaction of the solar wind with the ionosphere of Venus showed peculiar visual artefacts that they later identified as errors in calculation. They speculated that without visualisation such errors could have been overlooked.
4 Lou Doctor (President of Raster Technologies) speaking on the videotape *Visualisation: State of the Art, (ACM/SIGGRAPH Video Review* v30, New York 1988).
5 'Reversable computers take no energy to run' (*New Scientist* 10 June 1989 p14) A report on the work of GJ Milburn at the University of Queensland.
6 Paul Brown 'Art and the Information Revolution' *Leonardo* Supplemental Issue, Computer Art in Context – the *SIGGRAPH 89 Art Show Catalogue* pp63-65. The International Society for Art Science and Technology, Oxford, Pergamon, 1989.
7 'Quantum communication thwarts eavesdroppers' *New Scientist*

9 December 1989 n1694 p13. A report on the work of Charles Bennett and John Smolin at IBM's Thomas J Watson Research Lab.

8   K Eric Drexler *Engines of Creation* New York, Anchor-Doubleday 1986.

9   Heinz R Pagels *The Dreams of Reason* New York, Simon & Schuster 1988.

10   'Data Parallel Computers From MasPar Top Out At 30,000 Mips And 1,250 Mflops' *Klein Newsletter* v11 n23 p3 8 December 1989. MasPar offers this 16,384 processor system for just US$25 per Mip.

11   Mary Shelly *Frankenstein*. This 19th century author was one of many commentators who have been critical of humankind's efforts to create life. The current debate over the scientific use of human embryos demonstrates many similar concerns. As yet the critics have not directed their attention to the issues raised by digital simulation.

12   Michael Barnsley, the author of *Fractals Everywhere* (Academic Press, 1988) has developed one of the more novel data compression methods. A raster graphics image is scanned to extract its fractal initiators which are then transmitted. The receiver then reconstructs the image. Barnsley claims that an image can be reduced to less than 1% of the normal storage, ie it can be transmitted at least 100 times faster.

13   John Brunner *The Shockwave Rider* London, J M Dent & Sons, 1975. Brunner, along with the more poetic sci-fi author Samuel Delany has been a major influence on the development of the streetwise, cyberpunk style (see 20 – below).

14   G Spencer-Brown *The Laws of Form* London, George Allen and Unwin 1969.

15   SCAN – the Swinburne Centre for Applied Neurosciences, PO Box 218, Hawthorn, Australia 3122. Director Dr Richard Silberstein and his colleagues are currently preparing to publish their initial results on monitoring cognative activity. The speculative conclusions that I draw above have been inspired by their scientific rigour but owe a generous debt to my interest in sci-fi.

16   David Rokeby is featured in *ACM/SIGGRAPH 88 Art Show: Catalog of Interactive Installations and Videotape*, also see 'Experimental Computer Art' in *ACM/SIGGRAPH 89 Course Notes* n7, both published New York, ACM/SIGGRAPH.

17   Myron Kruger is featured in the previous reference (see 16 above). A pioneer artist of virtual spaces, his book *Artificial Reality* (Reading [USA], Addison Wesley, 1983) introduced this term and is, unfortunately, long out of print.

18   'Computer Art – an Oxymoron – Views from the Mainstream', a panel at ACM/SIGGRAPH 89 (unpublished).

19   Bruce Sterling (ed) *Mirrorshades – the cyberpunk anthology* London, Paladin/Grafton 1988, is a good introduction to the work of the Cyberpunk sci-fi authors by one of their members. Essential reading includes the 'Cyberspace' trilogy by William Gibson – *Neuromancer* (1984) *Count Zero* (1986) and *Mona Lisa Overdrive* (1988) (all London, Gollancz); Rudy Ruckers *Wetware* London, Avon 1988; and Greg Bears *Blood Music* New York, Arbor House 1985.

20   William Gibson, cited by Richard Guilliatt in 'SF and the tales of a new romancer' *Melbourne Sunday Herald* 17 December 1989.

21   See footnote 2 above.

Philip Hayward lectures in Media and Theatre Studies at Macquarie University, Sydney. He has contributed to various journals and edited a previous anthology entitled *Picture This: Media Representations of Visual Art and Artists* (also published by John Libbey in association with the Arts Council of Great Britain).

Marga Bijvoet is a curator and critic. She was formerly director of Time Based Arts (Amsterdam) and is currently working at the Stedlijk Museum.

Andy Darley is a part-time lecturer in Animation at West Surrey College of Art and Design and at the London College of Printing. He is currently undertaking PhD research at Brunel University on the history of computers and animation.

Rebecca Coyle is a part-time lecturer in Sound and Radio at the University of Technology, Sydney, and a freelance radio producer. She was formerly editor of the British radio magazine *Relay* and a columnist for the London magazine *City Limits*.

Philip Brophy lectures at the Philip Institute in Melbourne and is also a prolific writer, filmmaker and musician. His contribution to the volume is taken from a work-in-progress entitled *SONIC CINEMA: Technology, Textuality and Aural Narratology in the Cinema*.

George Barber is a video maker whose best known videos include *Yes Frank No Smoke, Absence of Satan, Taxi Driver II* and *The Venetian Ghost*.

Jeremy Welsh is a video maker, critic and lecturer currently based in Trondheim, Norway. His best known videos include *Reflections, Echoes* and *IOD*. He has also written for periodicals such as *Mediamatic* and *Independent Media*.

Tony Fry lectures in Design and Art History at the Power Institute of Fine Arts in Sydney and is associate director of the Sydney University Key Centre for Design Quality. He has also taught in Britain and the USA and is author of *Design History Australia* and *Old Visions of Modern Worlds*.

Alan Durant is Professor of English at Goldsmith's College, London University. He is author of *Conditions of Music* and has contributed to various journals.

Anne-Marie Willis lectures in Art and Photographic History at the University of New South Wales College of Fine Art and is author of a critical history of Australian photography entitled *Picturing Australia*.

Andrew Murphie is a performance artist and freelance lecturer currently based in Sydney. He has previously written for the performance periodical *Spectator Burns*.

Paul Brown is creative director of the Advanced Computer Graphics Centre at the Royal Melbourne Institute of Technology and was formerly head of the Centre for Advanced Studies in Computer Aided Art and Design at Middlesex Polytechnic. He has contributed to a number of international publications including *Leonardo*.

Other Titles Available from John Libbey

ACAMEDIA RESEARCH MONOGRAPHS

Satellite Television in Western Europe
Richard Collins
Hardback ISBN 0 86196 203 6

Beyond the Berne Convention
Copyright, Broadcasting and the Single European Market
Vincent Porter
Hardback ISBN 0 86196 267 2

The Media Dilemma: Freedom and Choice or Concentrated Power?
Gareth Locksley
Hardback ISBN 0 86196 230 3

Nuclear Reactions: A Study in Public Issue Television
John Corner, Kay Richardson and Natalie Fenton
Hardback ISBN 0 86196 251 6

Transnationalization of Television in Western Europe
Preben Sepstrup
Hardback ISBN 0 86196 280 X

BBC ANNUAL REVIEWS

Annual Review of BBC Broadcasting Research: No XV - 1989
Peter Menneer (ed)
Paperback ISBN 0 86196 209 5

Annual Review of BBC Broadcasting Research: No XVI - 1990
Peter Menneer (ed)
Paperback ISBN 0 86196 265 6

Published in association with
UNESCO

Video World-wide: An International Study
Manuel Alvarado
Paperback ISBN 0 86196 143 9

Other Titles Available from John Libbey

BROADCASTING STANDARDS COUNCIL MONOGRAPHS

A Measure of Uncertainty: The Effects of the Mass Media
Guy Cumberbatch and Dennis Howitt
Foreword by Lord Rees-Mogg
Hardback ISBN 0 86196 231 1

Violence in Television Fiction: Public Opinion and Broadcasting Standards
David Docherty
Paperback ISBN 0 86196 284 2

BROADCASTING RESEARCH UNIT MONOGRAPHS

Quality in Television
Richard Hoggart (ed)
Paperback ISBN 0 86196 237 0

Keeping Faith? Channel Four and its Audience
David Docherty, David E. Morrison and Michael Tracey
Paperback ISBN 0 86196 158 7

Invisible Citizens: British Public Opinion and the Future of Broadcasting
David E. Morrison
Paperback ISBN 0 86196 111 0

Published in association with
THE ARTS COUNCIL of GREAT BRITAIN

Picture This: Media Representations of Visual Art and Artists
Philip Hayward (ed)
Paperback ISBN 0 86196 126 9

Culture, Technology and Creativity
Philip Hayward (ed)
Paperback ISBN 0 86196 266 4

Other Titles Available from John Libbey

IBA TELEVISION RESEARCH MONOGRAPHS

Teachers and Television
Josephine Langham
Hardback ISBN 0 86196 264 8

Godwatching: Viewers, Religion and Television
Michael Svennevig, Ian Haldane, Sharon Spiers and Barrie Gunter
Hardback ISBN 0 86196 198 6 Paperback ISBN 0 86196 199 4

Violence on Television: What the Viewers Think
Barrie Gunter and Mallory Wober
Hardback ISBN 0 86196 171 4 Paperback ISBN 0 86196 172 2

Home Video and the Changing Nature of Television Audience
Mark Levy and Barrie Gunter
Hardback ISBN 0 86196 175 7 Paperback ISBN 0 86196 188 9

Patterns of Teletext Use in the UK
Bradley S. Greenberg and Carolyn A. Lin
Hardback ISBN 0 86196 174 9 Paperback ISBN 0 86196 187 0

Attitudes to Broadcasting Over the Years
Barrie Gunter and Michael Svennevig
Hardback ISBN 0 86196 173 0 Paperback ISBN 0 86196 184 6

Television and Sex Role Stereotyping
Barrie Gunter
Hardback ISBN 0 86196 095 5 Paperback ISBN 0 86196 098 X

Television and the Fear of Crime
Barrie Gunter
Hardback ISBN 0 86196 118 8 Paperback ISBN 0 86196 119 6

Behind and in Front of the Screen - Television's Involvement with Family Life
Barrie Gunter and Michael Svennevig
Hardback ISBN 0 86196 123 4 Paperback ISBN 0 86196 124 2